Raillery and Rage

Raillery and Rage

A Study of Eighteenth Century Satire

DAVID NOKES

Senior Lecturer in English
King's College, London

St. Martin's Press
New York

First published in the United States of America in 1987.

Printed in Great Britain.

ISBN 0-312-00958-5

Library of Congress Cataloging-in-Publication Data

Nokes, David.
  Raillery and rage.

  Bibliography: p.
  Includes index.
    1. Satire, English—History and criticism.
2. English literature—18th century—History and criticism.
I. Title.
PR935.N64   1987   827'.5'09   87-9487
ISBN 0-312-00958-5

For Bevis, Gerald, John, Ray, Robin and Vijay
of the Class of 1969

'I am always writing bad prose, or worse verses,
either of rage or raillery, whereof some few
escape to give offence, or mirth, and the rest
are burnt.'
(Jonathan Swift, 21 March 1730)

Hence Satire rose, that just the medium hit,
And heals with Morals what it hurts with Wit.

(Pope: *The First Epistle of the
Second Book of Horace Imitated*, 1736)

Contents

Preface

The intentions behind this book are unashamedly utilitarian. It is designed to enhance the understanding, and consequently the enjoyment, by modern readers of eighteenth-century satire. Many of those who read it will be students, perhaps encountering for the first time the teasing paradoxes and allusive parodies of the genre. Others, I trust, will be general readers, stimulated by curiosity to investigate the masterpieces of a still much misunderstood literary period. Both groups, unaided, are likely to find their appreciation of eighteenth-century satire hampered by the copious allusions to classical literature and contemporary politics which crowd its pages. Without in any way attempting to simplify satiric texts, I have endeavoured to suggest certain general strategies for evaluating the significance of allusions which may, I hope, assist the modern reader to approach the frequent references to Tibbald or C----r, to 'Bays' or 'a Great Man' with greater confidence and pleasure. I have not attempted to offer any new theory or definition of Augustan satire; nor have I sought to erect any rigid taxonomic boundaries between satire and such associated literary devices as parody, irony, mock-heroic and burlesque. Instead, by describing the range of theoretical justifications formulated by the satirists themselves, I have tried to demonstrate the practical synergy of rhetorical techniques which contributes to the creative vitality of the satires of the period.

As part of my critical method in this book I have sometimes drawn analogies between eighteenth-century and twentieth-century works. My aim in doing so is not merely to identify parallel themes—an exercise which may often seem both modish and tendentious—but rather to analyse certain underlying similarities of literary technique. The rhetorical devices of neo-classical satire may seem less esoteric or

remote when translated into the terms of a modern mass culture
which produces such works as *Private Eye* and *Spitting Image*. In the
first two chapters of the book, I outline the general themes,
assumptions and techniques of eighteenth-century satire. In the four
chapters which follow I develop and illustrate these points through
the detailed analysis of works by Pope, Gay, Fielding and Swift.

It will be evident that, in my selection of texts by these authors, I
have not always chosen to discuss their most famous or familiar
satires. For example, there is no full-length analysis of *The Rape of the
Lock* or of *Gulliver's Travels,* although both works are treated
extensively in my general discussions of satiric themes and styles.
Such omissions are deliberate since I wish to challenge the tendency
to view eighteenth-century satire as a narrow and predictable genre
composed of a familiar canon of a few classic texts. Professor Ian
Jack's excellent book *Augustan Satire, Intention and Idiom in
English Poetry 1660-1750* (1952), which concentrates on a restricted
selection of key texts from Butler's *Hudibras* to Johnson's *The Vanity
of Human Wishes,* offers a useful outline for the verse satires of the
period. In some ways the present book might be regarded as a
successor to Professor Jack's study, but in offering a new approach to
the subject I have also wanted to redefine its territory. Not only do I
treat prose satires as well as verse satires, operas, novels, poems,
pamphlets and a tragi-comi-pastoral farce, I also examine both minor
and major satires, introducing some unfamiliar titles and unregarded
themes. I have tried not to let the reputation of some satiric works
determine the shape and form of the book and if in consequence the
contents are less predictable than anticipated, that too is part of my
purpose.

Certain of the satiric texts produced during this period—I am
thinking in particular of *The Rape of the Lock* and *Gulliver's
Travels*—have acquired a kind of classic or paradigmatic status. In the
innumerable critical commentaries on these works their very
familiarity has turned them into convenient battlegrounds for
contending theories, or test-beds for new critical methodologies. *The
Rape of the Lock* has recently been studied by several critics wishing
to offer ideological redefinitions of our understanding of Pope's verse
specifically and of Augustan culture generally. Laura Brown's analysis
of the poem in *Alexander Pope* (1985) presents it as a celebration of
the consumer fetishism of an emerging imperialist culture. Both Ellen
Pollak in her book *The Poetics of Sexual Myth* (1985) and Brean
Hammond in his *Pope* (1986) offer feminist readings of the poem.

Pollak argues that while Belinda appears to be the subject of the poem, she is in fact marginalised in the text as a figure of phallocentric myth (p.79). Hammond, less harshly, sees the poem as a satire on 'the exaggerations of sexually stereotypical forms of behaviour' (p.171).

Readings such as these perform a valuable, indeed a vital, function in re-examining our literary preconceptions and cultural axioms. Yet there is a concomitant danger that the texts which are consistently singled out for such analyses become divorced from their cultural and historical context, transformed instead into the darlings of examinations syllabuses, case-book studies and methodological seminars. By refusing to grant these works their customary status as isolated masterpieces, I have attempted to emphasise the generic continuities of eighteenth-century satire rather than treating it as a sequence of greatest hits. In this way I trust that my principle of selectivity and my aim of comprehensiveness will complement rather than contradict each other.

It is my opening contention in this book that 'the literature . . . of the entire century from the Restoration of Charles II to the accession of George III is dominated by satire'. That being the case, any attempt to provide comprehensive coverage through a blow-by-blow analysis of all the most celebrated satires would have resulted in a work of encyclopedic proportions, starting with Dryden and Rochester and concluding with Charles Churchill, Johnson and Sterne. In place of this I have endeavoured to offer some new perspectives on satiric themes and to examine a number of contextual issues.

In making my selection of texts and themes for detailed discussion I have attempted to adhere to a central Augustan principle of literary composition, *concordia discors;* that is, I have examined two or more contrasting elements in an author's works in order to suggest some underlying unities. In my treatment of Pope I examine *The Dunciad* as a comic palimpsest of ancient heroes and modern hacks. But I also discuss Pope's more sober and sententious style of satire in the *Moral Essays* and the *Imitations of Horace,* where he combines the idealism of a moral philosopher with the censoriousness of a one-man tribunal. Gay's *Beggar's Opera* is sometimes regarded as a heavyweight work of social criticism, but my study of the opera is preceded by an analysis of his genial mock-pastoral *The Shepherd's Week,* which would seem to place him firmly in the lightweight division. Both works are linked by their ironic reversals of pastoral themes and conventions. However, my own analysis concentrates on Gay's language and suggests a level of verbal sophistication not often

associated with his writing. In my chapter on Fielding I have avoided
a straightforward *seriatim* study of the satiric fictions: *Shamela,
Jonathan Wild, Joseph Andrews* and *Tom Jones.* Instead, I have
chosen to look at two specific ingredients which help to produce the
unique satiric tone of his fiction: the language and imagery of
violence, and the language and imagery of food. The section on the
language of food opens out into a general discussion of satiric
treatments of this subject in the century. In my study of Swift I have
concentrated on the apparent discrepancy between the
authoritarianism of his personal pronouncements and the anarchy of
his satiric wit. Here again, by choosing a less familiar text, *The
Directions to Servants,* I have attempted to examine Swift's
ambiguous attitudes, part master, part servant. In many ways the
paradoxes revealed in this work duplicate the alternating charge
produced by the opposition of Houyhnhnms and Yahoos in
Gulliver's Travels. But I hope, by opening up this bypass to Swift's
main satiric preoccupations, to relieve some of the critical congestion
surrounding his most famous work.

I should like to offer here my grateful acknowledgement for the
encouragement, inspiration and assistance which I have received
from the following people in the writing of this book: Andrew
Carpenter, and the organisers of the Inaugural Conference of the
Eighteenth Century Ireland Society; Nigel Wood, and the organisers
of the John Gay Tercentenary Conference at Durham, 1985; Janet
Barron, Tom Deveson, Hanif Kureishi, David Perry and Pat Rogers.

David Nokes
London, 1986

CHAPTER ONE
Satire and Society

I

Satyre. Girding, biting, snarling, scourging, jerking, lashing, smarting, sharp, tart, rough, invective, censorious, currish, snappish, captious, barking, brawling, carping, fanged, sharp-tooth'd, quipping, jeering, flouting, sullen, rigid, impartial, whipping, thorny, pricking, stinging, sharp-fang'd, injurious, reproachful, libellous, harsh, rough-hewne, odious, opprobrious, contumelious, defaming, calumnious.   (Poole)[1]

The literature of the early eighteenth century, indeed the literature of the entire century from the Restoration of Charles II to the accession of George III., is dominated by satire. It would be difficult to find another comparable period of modern literary history whose tone was so firmly established by a single dominant genre. This is not to deny that a vast amount of the literature of the period was non-satirical. The early decades of the eighteenth century, after all, witnessed the rise of the novel and the development of periodical journalism. Following the lapsing of the Licensing Act in 1695 there was an outpouring of, if not literary, at least printed artefacts of every conceivable shape, size, style, tone and genre to suit all tastes and pockets. Secret histories, travellers' tales, criminal lives, spiritual autobiographies, cautionary tales, fabulous adventures, sober lectures, sermons, pastorals, panegyrics and polemics all rolled off the press. It was a period, writes Martin Scriblerus (alias Pope) in the Introduction to *The Dunciad Variorum*, when 'paper became so cheap and printers so numerous that a deluge of authors cover'd the land'. With the new computerised resources of the *Eighteenth Century Short Title Catalogue* available to him, the modern scholar can, at the touch of a button, call up a visual display of the rich diversity of the literature of this period. It may well be that a careful sifting of the previously uncatalogued works which have now been rediscovered will lead to some of the traditional assumptions about the homogeneity of 'Augustan' culture, based upon a selective reading of a few elite texts, being challenged. Yet we may be confident that no amount of new discoveries of obscure chap-books or children's tales will alter our perception that the dominant tone of the literary world was set by the satirists. 'If the moderns have excelled the ancients in any species of writing,' wrote Joseph Warton in 1756, 'it seems to be in satire'.[2] In terms of voice, register, theme and style, satire set the fashion.

This book is devoted to interpreting the main themes and techniques of eighteenth-century satire, with the hope of assisting modern readers to understand and appreciate the often allusive and ambiguous strategies of such works as *Gulliver's Travels* and *The Dunciad*. Yet perhaps we should begin by tackling another question too often ignored by critical accounts of these works, but often enough raised (or implied) by modern students who find their path to appreciation barricaded by mounds of allusion, and their enjoyment hampered by the burden of annotation they are required to carry with them. Why should one read 250-year-old satires at all? What *literary* pleasure or edification are to be gained from works whose primary purpose may often appear to have been the excoriation of some topical vice, or the exposure of some ephemeral vanity? For satire is pre-eminently a social genre. Unlike the novel which is an autonomous entity, creating and sustaining its own fictional world, satire always has its object and validation in external reality. Satire must always have an object to satirise and hence exists in a direct critical relationship with the society which produces it. As a genre it is teleological rather than ontological, finding its own full meaning only in relation to meanings outside itself. In a sense, though, this distinction between satire and the novel may be more apparent than real, since all fictional works necessarily have some implicit relationship with the worlds which they imitate. Nor is it self-evident, for example, that a reader totally unfamiliar with eighteenth-century society would find the novel *Moll Flanders* more immediately accessible than the satire *Gulliver's Travels*. Even in the more specific matter of identifying allusions, the satiric *Beggar's Opera* presents fewer problems to the untutored reader than such non-satiric works as *Paradise Lost* or *Ulysses*. Yet, if satire is understood as a rhetorical form with a remedial purpose (however ambiguously that purpose may be expressed), such as the exposure of scandal, the censure of hypocrisy, the punishment of vice or even the removal of ministers, should it not be judged at least as much in terms of its efficacy in achieving these aims as in terms of its literary sophistication? One might draw an analogy here with advertising. Is the good advertisement the one that is beautifully filmed, expensively designed, witty, subtle and original, that picks up all the artistic prizes? Or is the good advertisement the one that sells soap, however crude or unsubtle its appeal?

Not only is the satire of this period predominantly social; it is also, to an unprecedented degree, political. At no other time has the relationship between literature and politics been so close, even incestuous. Addison, Steele, Swift, Defoe and Fielding all wrote political propaganda. Defoe and Prior were employed in Robert Harley's secret service while Swift acted as his unofficial press officer. Even those not directly engaged in promoting a party line were largely dependent upon political patronage, usually in the form of a government sinecure. Congreve was in charge of licensing hackney carriages; Steele was commissioner for stamps; Gay had a minor diplomatic post; Addison was Secretary of State. Only Pope, whose Catholicism disqualified him from holding government office, was excluded from such patronge. Typically, he made a virtue of this necessity, loudly proclaiming his independence of party allegiances: 'Tories call me whig, and whigs a tory'.[3] Yet even he, before achieving this enviable position of financial independence on the strength of his hugely lucrative translations of Homer, had written poems, such as *Windsor Forest*, containing clear political signals. And his later poems, too, though loftily disclaiming any partisan affiliations, are permeated with political preoccupations.

But why should modern readers, approaching these authors' works as literature, rather than as historical documents, be concerned by such ephemeral considerations as the alleged political short-comings of Marlborough, Walpole or George II? The conventional response to this question tends rather to evade than answer it by evoking the concept of transcendence. The imagination of the great satirist, it is argued, transforms the quotidian elements of its subject matter into permanent symbols of human folly and corruption. Thus one recent writer on Pope, confronted by the awkward preponderance of real names of real people in his satires, assures us that 'so vividly is a context and a situation created' that there is 'no real need of a more particular knowledge of their names and reputations . . . Pope has transcended the originals, so that what began as a caricature ends as a satiric portrait of a human type.'[4] According to this view, the essence of the satirist's art is a kind of metaphorical inflation which raises specific political targets to a level of general moral concern. It is a form of literary alchemy, turning local heroes and forgotten villains into universal types and icons.

Obviously, imaginative transformations of this kind are an important ingredient in the satiric power of such portraits, but the notion that the original subjects can be conveniently ignored runs the risk of reducing them all to a level of moral banality. Much of the wit of these satires resides in the appropriateness—or otherwise—of the match between specific targets and their travesties. The characteristic devices of satire—parody, caricature, *reductio ad absurdum*—all rely upon some recognition of both the similarities and the differences between the original and its satiric imitation. Moreover, mock-heroic satire of the kind which flourished in the eighteenth century, requires us to make two separate but related kinds of recognition. When we encounter a figure such as Tibbald in Pope's *Dunciad* we are asked to recall to mind not only the real-life Lewis Theobald but also Virgil's Aeneas (and sometimes Milton's Satan too). Only if we make both identifications and register the pantomime-like incongruity between the two, will we understand Pope's view of the yawning gap that separates modern pretenders to taste from their classical forebears. Behind Pope's Atticus portrait lies not only the contemporary figure of Joseph Addison but also the classical model, Titus Pomponius Atticus; behind Fielding's Jonathan Wild lies both the real-life criminal of that name and the long line of 'Great Men' stretching from Alexander the Great to Walpole. In all these cases we are required to view the satiric object through a perspective device that is the literary equivalent of a pair of 3-D spectacles. Between the red lens of contemporary politics and culture, and the green lens of the classical tradition, a kind of stereoscopic vision is produced that gives an ironic depth-of-field to the satire.

Yet this is not to urge an impossible counsel of perfection. Readers of Pope and Swift, Fielding and Gay are not required to arm themselves with an encyclopedic knowledge of Greek myths, Roman history and eighteenth-century court and social life before they can have any hope of responding to their satires. Nor should modern students exaggerate their own incapacity for comprehending the allusions in *Gulliver's Travels* and *The Dunciad* by contrast with some supposed omniscience among the eighteenth-century readership for whom they were written. Swift himself drew ironic attention to the ephemeral and esoteric nature of much topical satire in *A Tale of a Tub,* where he writes, 'Such a jest there is that will not pass out of Covent Garden; and such a one that is nowhere intelligible but at Hyde Park Corner.' More seriously, writing from Ireland in 1728, Swift urged Pope to include 'very large' notes with his *Dunciad:*

> for I have long observed that twenty miles from London nobody understands hints, initial letters or town-facts and passages; and in a few years not even those who live in London. I would have the names of those scribblers printed indexically at the beginning or end of the poem, with an account of their works, for the reader to refer to. I would have all the parodies (as they are called) referred to the authors they imitate.[5]

Similarly, in his *Author's Farce* Fielding presents a picture of a Grub Street sweat shop where the publisher Bookweight presides over a production line of toiling hacks who interlard their formulaic pamphlets, odes and panegyrics with a random decoration of Greek mottoes and Latin tags in a spirit of cheerful ignorance, confident that not one in a hundred of their readers will take the trouble to translate them. What is required is less a detailed knowledge of the policies of Robert Walpole, the philology of *The Aeneid* or the career of Colley Cibber, than a facility for detecting intertextual resonances. Modern readers need to regain a skill for recognising those places in a text where, behind the single note printed on the page, the echo of a chord or descant can be heard. These, to pursue the musical analogy, represent the key signatures of satiric works, the harmonic home-base where past and present, classical and contemporary are sounded together, throwing any dissonance into prominence. The recognition of such chords or counterpoints is, naturally, a particular kind of literary skill which, like other literary and artistic skills, takes time and practice to perfect. Eighteenth-century mock-heroic satires, like Petrarchan sonnets or Handelian operas, follow certain conventions and do not reveal their full meaning at a first or even a second reading. But with patience and attention the skill can become a habit, and the full subtlety of these works can be enjoyed. The important point is that the difficulty posed by these satires is less a matter of knowledge than of technique. What is required is not a dogged determination to study the minutiae of the lives of the denizens of Grub Street, but an ability to read with an alert ear for those tell-tale echoes of parody which indicate a false bottom to a line that may drop us down to the bathos of Ward or Curll.

Yet how can one possibly tell if a line is parodic without knowing the source of the parody? The answer is, because the satirists tell us so. In *Tom Jones*, Chapter 8 of the fourth book is entitled 'A Battle sung in the Homerican style, and which none but the Classical Reader can taste'. Here is an extract:

> But now Fortune, fearing she had acted out of character, and had inclined too long to the same side, especially as it was the right side, hastily turned about: for now Goody Brown, whom Zekiel Brown caresses in his arms; nor he alone, but half the parish besides; so famous was she in the fields of Venus, nor indeed less in those of Mars. The trophies of both these, her husband always bore about on his head and face; for if ever human head did by its horns display the amorous glories of a wife, Zekiel's did; nor did his well-scratched face less denote her talents (or rather talons) of a different kind.
> No longer bore this Amazon the shameful flight of her party. She stopt short, and calling aloud to all who fled, spoke as follows: 'Ye Somersetshire men, or rather ye Somersetshire women, are ye not ashamed, thus to fly from a single woman; but if no other will oppose her, I myself and Joan Top here will have the honour of the victory.' Having thus said, she flew at Molly Seagrim, and easily wrenched the thigh bone from her hand, at the same time clawing off her cap from her head. Then laying hold of the hair of Molly, with her left hand, she attacked her so furiously in the face with the right, that the blood soon began to trickle from her nose.

This is a typical piece of mock-deference on the part of that consummate literary showman, the narrator of *Tom Jones*. He flatters us by allowing us to see ourselves as 'classical readers', while making sure that the parodic tone of the chapter is easily accessible to those whose acquaintance with Homer may be entirely vicarious. The main effect of this passage is a kind of slap-stick farce, and the contrast between epic vocabulary and domestic disputes offers an obvious kind of bathetic comedy. Fielding's burlesque tragedy *Tom Thumb* contains similar examples of self-evident literary parody. The giant princess Huncamunca falls desperately in love with the lilliputian Tom Thumb, and expresses her passion thus: 'O Tom Thumb, Tom Thumb, wherefore art thou Tom Thumb?'[6] One might reasonably expect any audience, then or now, to pick up the comic echo of *Romeo and Juliet*, but the *cognoscenti* might realise that Fielding is not actually seeking to parody Shakespeare's line but rather the anthologised appeal of Juliet's speech which had already had several witless imitations. In satiric terms Fielding's real target is Otway's tragedy *Marius*, containing the line, 'Oh Marius, Marius, wherefore art thou Marius . . . ?'

At another climactic moment in *Tom Thumb* we witness a dispute between Grizzle and Noodle, two rival suitors for the princess's affections:

> Grizzle: I will not hear one word but Huncamunca.
> Noodle: By this time she is married to Tom Thumb.
> Grizzle: My Huncamunca?
> Noodle: Your Huncamunca? Tom Thumb's Huncamunca, every-
> man's Huncamunca![7]

An audience does not need to know the source of any parody here to feel a rich comic sense of burlesque. The style proclaims as much. The princess's name is gross, physical and vaguely suggestive: the form of the exchange has a kind of set-piece patter, like the 'I say, I say' routine of a stand-up comedian. Actually, the satiric target is once again the verbal stereotypes offered by heroic adaptations of Shakespeare's plays; in this case, the specific source is Dryden's *All for Love*:

> Antony: What woman was it whom you heard and saw
> So playful with my friend? Not Cleopatra?
> Ventidius: Ev'n she, my lord.
> Antony: My Cleopatra?
> Ventidius: Your Cleopatra,
> Dollabella's Cleopatra, everyman's Cleopatra.

It is sometimes argued that as modern schools have increasingly moved away from teaching the classics, or even the Bible, so modern readers will be cut off from understanding and appreciating these neo-classical and mock-heroic works which draw upon such sources. Yet the decline in the numbers of those compulsorily required to construe their way through Caesar or Tacitus has led to no corresponding decline of interest in eighteenth-century satire. On the contrary, there is now a far wider sympathy for the satiric writings of Pope and Swift than was ever the case in the Victorian age when classical and biblical instruction formed the core of the public school curriculum. This is hardly surprising, since an appreciation of these satires depends less upon an identification of allusions than upon a discrimination of tone. It was Thackeray's failure to distinguish and respond to Swift's ironic tone that led him to denounce *Gulliver's Travels* as 'shameful, obscene, unmanly', and to describe Swift himself in terms of horror: 'What had this man done? What secret fever was boiling in him that he should see all the world bloodshot?'[8] Matthew Arnold, dismissing Dryden and Pope as 'not classics of our poetry' but merely 'classics of our prose' offered a definition of poetry that is exclusively sublime. It must be of 'high seriousness' and must express 'poetic largeness, freedom, insight, benignity'. Arnold writes in the Romantic tradition of Wordsworth, who declared:

> Poetry is the breath and finer spirit of all knowledge; it is the impassioned expression which is in the countenance of all science . . . Poetry is the first and last of all knowledge—it is as immortal as the heart of man. [The poet] is the rock of defence for human nature; an upholder and preserver, carrying everywhere with him relationships and love.[9]

With such elevated notions of the role and duties of the poet, it is hardly surprising that critics like Arnold found the eighteenth-century satirists trivial, facetious, prosaic and pessimistic. However, our own unheroic age has lost that Victorian confidence in absolute moral standards, imperial destiny, heroic ideals, progress and high seriousness. 'At Dachau, Yeats and Rilke died', wrote Donald Davie.[10] Post-war British literature, as represented by poets like Larkin, novelists like Braine, Burgess, Amis, playwrights like Osborne and Pinter, has been predominantly anti-heroic, wry, self-deprecating, ironic. It has also been characterised by a revival of interest in satire of all kinds. Indeed, one might detect several affinities between contemporary cultural attitudes—particularly since the 1960s—and those of the Augustan satirists. The somewhat self-conscious satire 'boom' of the 1960s—which produced such diverse phenomena as *Beyond the Fringe* (theatre), *Private Eye* and *Oz* (magazines) and *That Was The Week That Was* (television) and whose metropolitan in-jokey style frequently invoked models from Swift and Hogarth—has passed. But it has left behind a fondness for pastiche, an instinct for parody and a pervasive ironic tone in much of contemporary culture, demonstrated, for example, in the plays of Tom Stoppard and the *Monty Python's Flying Circus* television show.

A play like Stoppard's *Travesties* is constructed out of interlocking patterns of allusions, not only to the works and reputations of Joyce, Lenin and the Dadaists, but also to Shakespeare, Oscar Wilde, T.S.

Eliot and Gilbert and Sullivan. These allusions are, as the title indicates, burlesqued and travestied in a series of cultural juxtapositions that echo Swift's comic confrontation of the giants of ancient and modern learning in *The Battle of the Books*. Naturally, it is particularly pleasing to a literate audience to identify the interwoven lines from *Ulysses, The Importance of Being Earnest* and Lenin's *What Is to Be Done* that culminate in the librarian's striptease on top of her desk. But the parodic effect of the play does not depend upon us recognising every single allusion, but rather upon our general sense of the surreal incongruity generated by confrontation of philosophies and styles. Similarly, in *Rosencrantz and Guildenstern*, there is a pleasure to be gained from noting the skill with which Stoppard's lines dovetail with Shakespeare's, but the play's success relies upon a more general sense of mock-heroic displacement, as these attendant lords elbow Prince Hamlet from his familiar place in the centre of the stage.

The secret of such parodic allusions resides in giving the audience enough of the original to establish a tone and standard of cultural expectations. Thus one needs to have a general sense of the status and reputation of James Joyce to appreciate the fantastic travesty of his initial appearance wearing a waistcoat embroidered with enormous shamrocks, doing a soft-shoe shuffle and singing absurd limericks:

> Top o' the morning! James Joyce!
> I hope you'll allow me to voice
> my regrets in advance
> for coming on the off-chance,
> b'jasus I hadn't much choice![11]

'This Joyce is obviously an Irish nonsense' the direction notes, and the scene that follows is written entirely in limericks, with Tzara holding forth on surrealism and Joyce trying to scrounge money. The effect is beautifully comic, and presents a more enduring image of literary surrealism than any of Tzara's theories. However, those familiar with Ellmann's biography of Joyce will recognise the richness of authentic detail and scholarly allusion woven into this comic vignette.

In the same way, one doesn't need to have read Proust to appreciate the humour of the *Monty Python* sketch which featured a 'Summarising Proust' competition; or to relish the absurdity of their 'semaphore version' of *Wuthering Heights*. The satire in these allusions is based on an expectation that these classic literary names hold for us. We don't expect the differences between ancient Greek philosophy and nineteenth-century German philosophy to be presented as a football match that degenerates into absurd and appalling scenes of soccer violence; but this is one *Monty Python* sketch that has a direct equivalent in Swift's *Battle of the Books*. Such parodies satirise the *forms* in which our culture is codified and packaged; each form with its own rules and conventions. *Monty Python* constantly satirised the forms of communication, more especially the forms adopted by the media that rapidly become clichés: TV interview, TV discussion, outside broadcast, TV phone-in, soap opera, party political broadcast, quiz show, and so on. But this also extended into the 'set-pieces' of everyday life: the complaining customer who returns with his dead parrot; the returning holidaymaker with his fantastic monologue picked out with a recurrent motif of Watney's Red Barrel; the nervous young couple intimidated by the mysteries of a continental menu. Ridicule is directed at the attitudes people adopt in familiar situations, and at the self-stereotyping tendencies in all of us that lead life to imitate art. The mock-heroic satire of the Augustans presents us with the same techniques. There is a meticulous eye for the discrepancies between form and content, and a continuous parodic awareness of the absurdities of heroic postures when adopted by contemporary dunces.

Thus Pope begins his Epistle 'To Augustus' in his series of ironic *Imitations of Horace,* with this bold mock-encomium:

> While You, great Patron of Mankind, sustain
> The balanc'd World, and open all the Main;
> Your Country, chief, in Arms abroad defend,
> At home, with Morals, Arts and Laws amend.
>
> (ll. 1-4)[12]

The fact that George II also bore the Christian name Augustus made the satiric contrast with Horace's praise for his patron and emperor all the more piquant. Each commendation here is in fact a barely concealed insult. The Hanoverian monarch's government had indeed made 'open all the Main', but for Spanish privateers, not English merchantmen; while George's contempt for the arts was well known. In the words of his vice-chamberlain, he

> used often to brag of the contempt he had for books and letters; to say how much he hated all that stuff from his infancy; and that he remembered when he was a child he did not hate reading and

learning merely as other children do upon account of the confinement, but because he despised it and felt as if he was doing something mean and below him.[13]

But the most telling, yet simplest piece of satiric deflation in this description is the phrase 'in Arms abroad', which refers not, as implied, to military prowess but rather to the arms of George's new Hanoverian mistress, Amelie Sophie Marianne von Walmoden. She was soon afterwards imported to England for his entertainment, as Maynard Mack observes, 'like the Westphalian ham he also favoured'.[14] It is a deft ironic touch which in one word transforms the pose of classical hero into the exposure of a boor and lecher.

II

The post-war revival of interest in eighteenth-century satire has given rise to an abundance of critical and scholarly studies which may be conveniently divided into two main camps or tendencies. The first camp contains the decipherers, literary sleuths whose main aim is to pinpoint borrowings, elucidate allusions and uncover cryptic political codes. Decipherers tend to concentrate on enigmatic details, such as the game of cards in the *Rape of the Lock* or Gulliver's urinating in the Queen of Lilliput's apartment, carefully decoding them to reveal specific political messages. Decipherers are also particularly keen to interpret the hidden significance of textual revisions. The alteration of the colours of the ribbons awarded to the courtiers of Lilliput for their agility on the high-wire, or Pope's substitution of Cibber for Tibbald as arch-dunce of *The Dunciad* are discussed with the same kind of fascinations that Kremlinologists apply to Stalin's elimination of the early Bolsheviks from photographs and documents of the Russian Revolution.

The findings of such decipherers have added enormously to our understanding of key eighteenth-century texts. To take the example of Pope: Reuben Brower's book *Alexander Pope: The Poetry of Allusion* offered detailed documentation of the extent and significance of Pope's borrowings, confiming the general sense that there is hardly a line in Pope which does not include one, and often two, antithetical or complementary allusions.[15] Aubrey Williams' study, *Pope's Dunciad*, illustrates the ways in which Pope's poem not only draws upon Dryden's translation of *The Aeneid*, but also how its structure and topography follow closely the patterns of such popular processions as the Lord Mayor's Show or the progress of convicted criminals from Newgate to Tyburn. Howard Erskine-Hill's *The Social Milieu of Alexander Pope* documents the depth of social and political detail that lies behind the teasing clues presented in Pope's satiric portraits. And this list could be lengthened to include a great many other invaluable studies by Maynard Mack, Earl Wasserman and others.[16]

Yet there comes a point at which the discovery of yet more borrowings from Ovid or Manilius, Dryden or Dorset, may cease to illuminate and begin to obscure our appreciation of Pope's poetry. Literary criticism should not be confused with literary antiquarianism, nor should we allow our attention to be too long distracted from those larger qualities of the imagination which lead us to read Pope in the first place, rather than Ambrose Philips or Richard Blackmore. 'Allusions are dumb witnesses until they are cross-examined', writes Irvin Ehrenpreis in *Literary Meaning and Augustan Values*,[17] arguing that the insistence of some modern scholars on finding echoes of Virgil and traces of Cowley throughout Pope's writing may confuse rather than enrich our understanding of his poetry. 'Allusion as such may decorate, handsomely; it cannot deepen.' The obsession with parallel-hunting by some decipherers may lead to a kind of myopia; straining too hard to peer through our magnifying glasses at some decorative detail or accidental stain, we may miss the broad outline altogether.

In a recent study of *Gulliver's Travels* John Traugott objects strongly to the decipherers' tendency to see the work as a secret history or allegory. 'We become a species of the cryptographers of Laputa', he argues, if we insist on deducing allegorical messages and political signals from the book's doll's house imagery.[18] The imaginative and, indeed, the satiric power of the book resides not in the reductive analogies it applies to the disputes between Whigs and Tories, High and Low Church, but rather in the way it evokes childlike fantasies of power, vulnerability and caprice. 'The pervasive imagery is that of childhood play', he writes, seeing Gulliver's 'bath-tub wars', the Lilliputian doll's house, and the general fascination with the movements of bowel and bladder as symptoms of an innocent world we have lost. Viewed from this perspective, Traugott argues, we can 'take pleasure in the images of childlike dolls' play throughout the first two voyages without scurrying off to our moral bunkers.'

Arguments like these place Traugott in the opposite camp, among those who might be called synthesisers rather than decipherers. Synthesisers are more interested in general theories than in local details.

They study broad imaginative concepts, pervasive metaphors and rhetorical structures for indications of underlying assumptions and pre-occupations. In particular, satire has attracted the attentions of Freudian critics who see its characteristic strategies and devices as manifestations of an identifiable range of neuroses. Thus Karpman, in an article entitled 'Neurotic Traits of Jonathan Swift', writes: 'It is submitted on the basis of such a study of *Gulliver's Travels* that Swift was a neurotic who exhibited psychosexual infantilism, with a particular showing of coprophilia, associated with misogyny, misanthropy, mysophilia and mysophobia.'[19] Norman O. Brown, anxious to rescue Swift from both the clinical witlessness of the psychoanalysts and the moral outrage of some critics, redirects our attention to Swift's 'excremental vision' not as a symptom of madness but as a diagnosis of civilisation's discontents. 'If we are willing to listen to Swift we will find startling anticipations of Freudian theorems about anality, about sublimation, and about the universal neurosis of mankind.'[20] Michel Foucault's observations on the paradoxical obsession of the Enlightenment with building remedial prisons has been adopted by other synthesisers as an analogy for satire's ambiguous role, part judge, part anarchist. In his essay 'Tis Only Infinite Below', Claude Rawson borrows Foucault's terms as part of his approach to Swift's satiric uses of madness:

> Eighteenth century discussions examined by Foucault are frequently informed by more or less internalized versions of this paradox: the madman imprisoned by the liberty of hallucination; the sane quotidian pressures of life, the rhythm of the seasons and the discipline of work, conversely constraining madness, 'Freeing man from his freedom'; the concept of cure as a restoration of liberty by means of these constraints upon the other and fatal liberty.[21]

Whereas nineteenth-century critics were often content to portray Pope and Swift as at best misanthropic, at worst mad, modern synthesisers see their misanthropic postures as both the symptoms of, and specific for, a more general malaise. Thus Rawson writes of

> the peculiarly personal testiness which enters into Swift's uses of the satiric commonplace of the world's unmendability. ... The rhetorical posture of a noble, protesting madness is allowed to curdle into a pathological absurdity, in which the distinction between the vicious and the virtuous folly becomes horribly and insultingly blurred, and in which rhetorical madness (of both kinds, vicious and virtuous) becomes medical—perhaps incurable.[22]

More generally, there is an enduring fascination with the paradox that the so-called 'Age of Reason' should have produced so many haunting evocations of madness. Satire, certainly in the works of Pope, seems like an increasingly muddy filter through which the despairing satirist attempts to sift *is* into *ought*, and to force the irrational world of experience into the ordered perspective of hope. Reading these satires leaves one with the distinct impression that humankind cannot bear very much rationality. The Great Anarch whose hand lets down the curtain of Universal Darkness, and the Yahoos who discharge their excrement on Gulliver's head, are both figures from that nightmare world which Goya represented under the title 'The Sleep of Reason Breeds Monsters'.

Even those critics who have acquitted these satirists of the charge of madness, have often felt constrained to comment on a general tone of gloom or pessimism in their works. Joseph Warton was among the first to complain of the excessive gloom of Pope's satires:

> Our country is represented as totally ruined, and overwhelmed with dissipation, depravity and corruption. Yet this very country, so emasculated and debased by every species of folly and wickedness, in about twenty years afterwards, carried its triumphs over all its enemies, through all the quarters of the world, and astonished the most distant nations with a display of uncommon efforts, abilities, and virtues.[23]

Samuel Johnson, too, took exception to the gloating pessimism and selfrighteousness of the Scriblerian group:

> From the letters that pass between [Swift] and Pope it might be inferred that they, with Arbuthnot and Gay, had engrossed all the understanding and virtue of mankind, that their merits filled the world; or that there was no hope of more. They shew the age involved in darkness, and shade the picture with sullen emulation.[24]

In a famous essay on this topic Louis Bredvold writes, 'that a dark, almost impervious gloom enveloped them is undeniable', but goes on to distinguish some silver linings in the clouds: 'Even the darkest page of Swift leaves us with this feeling of soundness at the core, with a firm conviction of our moral competence and responsibility. It is the expression of a bitter but not a sick mind, and has the invigorating power of a call to action.'[25] One familiar explanation for the apparent gloom of these satirists is that they were Tories, and hence condemned to political impotence and frequent threats of prosecution after the death of Queen Anne. This is part of Orwell's argument in his essay on Swift entitled 'Politics versus Literature': 'When Swift utters one of his characteristic diatribes against the rich and powerful, one must . . . write off something for the fact that he himself belonged to the less successful party and was personally disappointed. The "outs" for obvious reasons are always more radical than the "ins".'[26]

Yet we must beware of a tautology here. A number of recent decipherers have examined the precise political sympathies of the major satirists, and their findings should lead us to use the generic label 'Tory satirists' with some caution. Pope, Swift and Gay all began their careers as Whigs, and at least one recent scholar has argued that Swift remained faithful to 'Old Whig' principles throughout his life.[27] In a sense, one might argue that the satirists became, or associated with, Tories, *because* they were outsiders, rather than the other way round.

Between the Freudian and the political interpretations of these satires are a range of explanations based on biographical, or pseudo-biographical, theories. Pope suffered not only the civil disabilities associated with his religion but also severe physical disabilities. As Bredvold writes, 'much has been made of the impairing influence on Swift and Pope of their "crazy constitutions", as if their satire were a phase of their medical history.'[28] Swift was a posthumous child who never ceased to lament his misfortune at being 'dropped' (i.e. born) in Ireland. He regarded it as a punitive exile to be sent back there in 1713: 'I reckon no man thoroughly miserable unless he be condemned to live in Ireland.' For the last thirty years of his life he suffered acute bouts of deafness and dizziness which became steadily more severe and made him irritable and morose. For much of his life Pope was unable to dress himself, or rise from his bed without aid. Neither man enjoyed a happy sexual relationship. Both kept careful, obsessive lists of the humiliations, disappointments and betrayals they encountered, and Swift himself declared that disappointment was the key to his character: 'I remember when I was a little boy, I felt a great fish at the end of my line which I drew up almost on the ground. But it dropped in and the disappointment vexeth me to this very day and I believe it was the type of all my future disappointments.'[29]

In this way satire may sometimes be seen as a form of revenge; a consolation for personal as well as political impotence, and a distillation of long-nursed anger. Certainly, Swift would appear to offer evidence for such an interpretation. Writing to Lord Bathurst in 1730 he described his only diversions during his sixteen years of 'exile' in Ireland as

'studying as well as preaching revenge, malice, envy and hatred and all
uncharitableness'.[30] Yet one should also recall that, at precisely the
same time, Swift was composing a teasingly oblique self-portrait in his
Verses on the Death of Dr Swift, in which he insists:

> Yet, malice never was his aim
> He lashed the vice but spared the name.

'Inconsistencies', as Imlac remarks in *Rasselas*, 'cannot both be right,
but, imputed to man, they may both be true.'[31] Part of the challenge of
Swift's satires resides in the perpetual contradictions, inconsistencies
and paradoxes which they present. The object of such satires is not that
we should be able to deduce what Swift 'really' thought, but rather that
we should be schooled in the delusive arts of rhetoric and the
ambivalent impulses of human nature. Those who content themselves
too easily with any one of the self-portraits conveniently but
deceptively offered throughout Swift's writings, as either a champion
of liberty or a misanthropic monster, have failed the essential test of his
satire. Swift's irony warns us that all such lapidary formulations, when
applied to so contradictory a thing as a human being, are illusory, even
when—perhaps especially when—they come from the author's own
mouth.

By now it should be evident that it would be foolish, and indeed
impossible, to attempt to prescribe any single approach to eighteenth-
century satire. As a tentative guideline, however, I would suggest that
modern readers should devote enough attention to the specific details
of these satires to enable them to grasp the subtlety of their general
conclusions. But such attention to detail should be literary rather than
political or antiquarian, enabling the reader to understand how the
satire works. Naturally, our final judgements on the works of Pope,
Swift, Fielding and Gay will be based not on their attitudes to Newton
or Walpole but on such larger issues as their humanity, the quality of
their imaginations, their verbal skills and moral values. But we will only
find the answers to these larger questions by applying ourselves to the
often allusive and paradoxical details of their art.

III

In his Introduction to a recent collection of essays on satire, Claude
Rawson writes:

Satire is a conservative art and the example of Augustan England suggests that it flourishes most in an order-minded culture, perhaps at moments when order is felt to be slipping: hence the peculiar desperation of Swift and at times of Pope, even as they assert values confidently believed in. The opposition to it in the eighteenth century came from 'liberalizing' or 'progressive' sources, and the great art of revolutionary aspirations at the end of the century is not in the main satiric.[32]

There is an important paradox here which takes us to the heart of satire's peculiar fascination. At first sight it might appear that satirists who, either implicitly or explicitly, seek to expose corruption and punish vice should be considered as radicals, even revolutionaries. Certainly, there is abundant historical evidence, from the time of Aristophanes to the present day, to confirm that authoritarian regimes have always feared the subversive powers of satires and lampoons, and have banned them and burned them and imprisoned their authors. Yet on closer investigation there is reason to suggest that satire tends to be an instrument not for change but for grumbling acquiescence. By allowing anger and indignation to vent themselves in laughter, rather than build into action, satire may be a substitute for, not a summons to, revolution.

For satire is a two-toned genre, being both sweet and sour, a weapon and a toy. As a weapon it exists to inflict the pain of public ridicule and humiliation of those whose vices it exposes. The pages of Pope and Swift are filled with references to whips, lashes, scourges and purges.

Yet simultaneously, as a literary or aesthetic object, satire exists to amuse and entertain us; to tickle us with its wit, stimulate us with its daring, divert us with its parodies and delight us with its art. By seeking the endorsement of laughter, satire draws the sting of its own attack choosing instead to deflate the pretensions of those it pillories. It also relies implicitly upon some assumed consensus of values or moral expectations by which its victims are to be judged. In much eighteenth-century satire these values and expectations are made explicit in the form of the 'Augustan parallel' as contemporary society is held up for judgement against the standards of a range of idealised classical models. Those models in their turn stand as convenient symbols for the order of nature itself. When in his *Essay on Criticism* Pope writes of Virgil's discovery that 'Nature and Homer were, he found, the same',[33] he makes clear the identification between the natural and the cultural orders that informs all his poetry. Classical models, both in literature and

politics, are viewed less with an eye for scrupulous historical accuracy
than as symbols of those organising principles and universal values
which, to the classical mind, were embodied in the concept of nature.
Commenting ironically upon a divergence from these principles and
values when, following an affray in *Tom Jones*, the good lieutenant
seems more concerned to apprehend the aggressor, Northerton, than
to rescue the victim, Tom, Fielding's narrator writes:

> It surprizes us, and so, perhaps, it may the reader, that the lieutenant,
> a worthy and good man, should have applied his chief care, rather
> to secure the offender, than to preserve the life of the wounded
> person. We mention this observation, not with any view of
> pretending to account for so odd a behaviour, but lest some critic
> should hereafter plume himself on discovering it. We would have
> those gentlemen know we can see what is odd in characters as well
> as themselves, but it is our business to relate facts as they are; which
> when we have done, it is the part of the learned and sagacious reader
> to consult that original Book of Nature, whence every passage in our
> work is transcribed, tho' we quote not always the particular page for
> its authority.   (VII.xii)

Even where the appeal to nature and the classical tradition is less
explicit, the use of comedy itself involves the assumption of certain
shared normative values. Comedy depends upon the perception of
incongruity, and thus upon some pre-existing notion of harmony. By
laughing we align ourselves with the order of the universe, however
uncomfortable or implausible that order may seem. In Beckett's *Happy
Days* Winnie comments, observing an emmet pass: 'How can one
better magnify the Almighty than by sniggering with him at his little
jokes, particularly the poorer ones?' It is the element of comedy in satire
which makes it safe, turning it from a weapon into a toy. Its anger,
however serious, is contained within a form whose ultimate target is the
anguished earnestness of the reforming satirist himself. Satire, as
described by Swift's Hack in *A Tale of a Tub*, is 'but a ball bandied to and
fro, and every man carries a racket about him to strike it from himself
among the rest of the company'. Those whose genuine wish is to change
society, eliminate vice, purge away corruption and establish the tyranny
of virtue, are not satirists but idealists whose literary style is
characteristically evangelical and humourless. The Levellers, Ranters
and Diggers were utopians of this kind, who wrote in an enthusiastic
and millennialist style, full of spiritual exhortations. Revolutionary
writings, such as *The Communist Manifesto* or *Mein Kampf* are hardly

remarkable for their wit. Indeed, a significant characteristic of revolutionary prose, both in the seventeenth and twentieth centuries, has been its preoccupation with forging a new purified vocabulary and grammar, purged of the accumulated assumptions inherent in the language of a corrupt society. One of the revolutionary's first targets must always be language itself, cutting off at source the currency of established ideas and replacing them with his own ideal notions. The satirist, on the other hand, trades and revels in the rich accumulations of imaginative resources stored in the language of the past to confront the utopian schemes of the Aeolists, or the Newspeak of Oceania. In the Appendix to *1984*, entitled 'The Principles of Newspeak', Orwell explains how this new revolutionary language was designed to purge away traditional thoughts and expressions.

> The purpose of Newspeak was not only to provide a medium of expression for the world-view and mental habits proper to the devotees of Ingsoc, but to make all other modes of thought impossible. It was intended that when Newspeak had been adopted once and for all and Oldspeak forgotten, a heretical thought—that is, a thought diverging from the principles of Ingsoc—should be literally unthinkable, at least so far as thought is dependent on words. . . . Newspeak was designed not to extend but to diminish the range of thought, and this purpose was indirectly assisted by cutting the choice of words down to a minimum.

This is the ultimate triumph of totalitarianism, the control of thought not through the external force of repression but through the centralised command of language itself. It is in reaction against such tendencies that satirists, both Augustan and modern, have exploited the ironic ambiguities, puns and paradoxes inherent in the rich associations of a traditional language, as if to demonstrate a proof, through etymology, of the organic links between mind and body, success and failure, utopia and a pratfall. To take just one example, Pope and the other Scriblerian satirists make great play with the ironic puns contained in the words 'profundity' and 'gravity'. Tracing the word 'profound' back to its Greek original, '*bathos*', they contrive to prove that the self-conscious seriousness or profundity of much modern literature is synonymous with a ludicrous lowness. Tibbald/Cibber is presented as one who has studied deeply The Art of Sinking in Poetry: 'Sinking from thought to thought, a vast profound!' (I. 118). A scientific dimension is added to the basic structural pun when the word 'gravity' is substituted for 'profundity'. By thus alluding to the dicoveries of Newton, the guru of modern thinkers, Pope offers further proof that the whole weight of modern thought has been in a downwards direction:

> None need a guide, by sure Attraction led,
> And strong impulsive gravity of Head. (IV. 75-6) [34]

The natural tendency of such profound heads is, as both Greek etymology and Newtonian physics agree, downwards. 'Attraction' here suggests both the superficial novelty of much contemporary culture and the magnetic force of the Earth's field. 'Led' carries a punning suggestion of its homonym 'lead', adding further weight to the natural descent. And 'impulsive' neatly combines a sense of wanton irresponsibility with an irresistible force of nature. In this way Pope manages throughout *The Dunciad* to imply that the genius of language is on his side as he seeks to demonstrate that the most profound achievements of modern art and science are bathetic descents into the depths which reduce human beings to mud-larks or leaden automata.

If the language that satirists employ tends to assume certain consensus values, this may also be true of the literary forms and devices which they use, in particular irony. There has been a good deal of scholarly debate in recent years concerning the presence or absence of irony in the writings of Swift and Defoe. In the course of this debate some have insisted on the inherent conservatism and elitism of irony as a literary device. Thus Professor J.T. Boulton, dismissing the idea that Defoe was an accomplished ironist, writes:

> To write ironically with success a writer needs to be alert to two audiences: those who will recognise the ironic intention and enjoy the joke, and those who are the object of the satire and are deceived by it. This implies that the ironist has ranged himself with those of his readers who share his superior values, intelligence and literary sensibility; together they look down on the benighted mob. This vantage point Defoe did not share. His Dissenting background engaged his sympathies with those who, on the political and social planes, were struggling to assert their rights, rather than with those whose struggle was to maintain an inherited position and traditional privileges. [35]

Maximillian Novak, on the other hand, reminding us of Defoe's varied and colourful career as, among other things, a political spy, double-agent, crime-writer and propagandist, argues that Defoe loved the deception and disguises of literary irony. According to Novak, 'the image of simple, honest Daniel Defoe, a plain dealer and stylist—an image which he frequently tried to palm off on his disbelieving contemporaries [and which Boulton has attempted to revive]—should be replaced by that of Defoe the ironist.'[36] On the whole, I'm inclined to agree with Novak. As one reads through the letters which Defoe, acting as a political spy, sent back to the Secretary of State, Robert Harley, one finds him exulting in the power and virtuosity of his role-play. In one letter he boasts, 'I act the old part of Cardinal Richelieu. I have my spies and my pensioners in every place, and I confess tis the easiest thing in the world to hire people here to betray their friends.' In another letter he describes his own disguises, and his method of talking 'to everybody in their own way'.

> To the merchants I am about to settle here in trade, building ships &c. With the lawyers I want to purchase a house and land. . . . With the Glasgow mutineers I am to be a fish merchant, with the Aberdeen men a woollen and with the Perth and western men a linen manufacturer, and still . . . I am all to everyone that I may gain some.[37]

Elsewhere he defends the use of political lies, drawing a distinction between 'the design of false speaking' and a public-spirited 'dissimulation', which shows more evidence of rhetorical skill than Dissenting morality. 'This hypocrisy is a virtue', he concludes.[38] Throughout his advice to Robert Harley, Defoe betrays no lack of political or verbal sophistication. On the contrary, he frequently manifests a thoroughly elitist delight in controlling and manipulating an audience's responses— sharing in the privilege of power, and enhancing his own authority through the dissemination of disinformation which actually seeks to widen the gulf between insiders and outsiders which it purports to bridge. What is interesting to examine, however, is the relationship in the works of such writers as Swift and Defoe, between the ironic elitism of the insider and the satiric indignation of the outsider. Kierkegaard has argued that the true end of irony lies not in any utilitarian purpose but in the private satisfaction and delight of the ironist.[39] As we shall see, such a definition holds no less true for Defoe than for Swift. In both, the secret delight of the hoaxer, enjoying an elaborate private joke at the expense of his audience, mingles with the indignation of the social reformer, seeking to carry that audience with him. Often the precise tone of an individual satiric work is best gauged by examining the relationship between these private and public motivations.

IV

In the course of this book I shall consider works published throughout
the century from the Restoration of Charles II to the accession of
George III, though the main focus will concentrate on the early
decades of the eighteenth century. In the second half of that century
satire ceased to be the dominant literary genre, gradually eclipsed by the
growing interest in sentimental, gothic and romantic writings. Certainly,
satires continued to be composed and published. Sterne's *Tristram
Shandy* contains many satiric elements, often modelled on Rabelais and
Swift; Charles Churchill's *The Rosciad* sought to emulate the mock-
epics of Dryden and Pope; Sheridan's plays represented a bowdlerised
revival of at least the style if not the substance of Restoration comedy;
Gillray and Cruickshank developed and professionalised the art of
political caricature, turning it into something more recognisable today.
Even into the next century, Peacock's novels and Byron's satiric poetry
kept alive something of the spirit of Augustan wit. But the fact remains
that by 1760 the pre-eminence of satire—which had reached its apogee
in the late 1720s with the triumphal apperances in succeeding years of
Gulliver's Travels, The Dunciad and *The Beggar's Opera*—was over.
Why did it happen? Did the accession of the Tory monarch George III
put an end to the gloom of the Tory satirists? Did the development of
spas, the example of Dr Cheyne's dietary regimen or the new fashion for
opium prove efficacious against the spleen? Did the benighted and
malignant species of dunces, Aeolists, virtuosi, projectors, Great Men
and Yahoos suddenly disappear from the face of the earth?

The most plausible explanation for the sudden demise of satire is that
it was killed off not by sentiment but by the novel. P.K.Elkin writes, 'It
is the eighteenth-century novel, more than any other literary form, that
reflects the century's changing attitude to satire.' The novel, he argues,
shows 'a developing interest in the personality of the wrong-doer,
which runs counter to the satirist's natural bent':

> Characteristically the satirist is concerned with the actions of wrong-
> doers and the effects of those actions on other people and society.
> The satirist sees a man for what he does; or, to put the matter another
> way, the satirist equates what a man does with what he is. . . . It
> follows then, that a writer who is interested in what a man is rather
> than in what he does, in his responses to life, and who explores a
> character's personality and environment in order to understand and
> explain why he thinks and feels and acts as he does, will not produce

satire. Increasingly in eighteenth century literature the centre of interest shifted from the consequences of characters' actions to the workings, often the obscure workings, of their personalities.[40]

Characters in satires, whether imitated from classical models, or drawn from contemporary politics, are essentially types, bearing a significance which is more a matter of expression than psychology. They belong to a literature, and a society, whose values can be interpreted through a variety of codes and cultural symbols. Here again one might anticipate a difficulty for the modern reader. On the face of it, modern democratic societies would appear less conventional, rule-bound and hierarchical, more diverse and flexible than Hanoverian society, and hence less amenable to comic stereotyping. In some ways this is true. Certainly there is little in democratic Western societies to rival the rigid protocol and byzantine rituals that denote precedence and rank at the funeral of a Soviet leader or at a march past in Red Square. It is when we observe the complex codes and signals implied by positions, timings, formulaic sentences and salutes in a totalitarian society, that we gain a certain insight into the formal rituals and conventions celebrated in classical and neo-classical literature. Yet in Britain too, politics has become increasingly a matter of slogans and images. The length of a standing ovation at a party conference or the clothes worn by a party leader at a Remembrance Day ceremony become political issues in their own right.

In fact, late-twentieth-century society has developed its own complex and extensive stereotypes and conventions. Some of the more obvious barriers of class and sex may have been dismantled: the Received Pronunciation of BBC English has given way to an acceptable diversity of regional accents; there is less emphasis on the old school tie; certain traditional society rituals, like the presentation of debutantes at court, have been abolished. But our conventions have been altered, not abolished, and our dominant conventions now are all codified and embodied in the mass media. We live in a world in which there is scarcely an object or experience of our daily lives which has not been modified for us by its presentation in a TV programme or advertisement. Every day we instinctively respond to a range of separate and distinct cultural genres whose codes and conventions make the Aristotelian unities seem as simple and permissive as a child's comic. We accept, without noticing, the strict formulas and conventions of the sit-com, the quiz show, the soap opera or police drama. In a police drama, for example, there will be the ritual inclusion of certain staple

ingredients of the genre, such as the car chase and shoot-out; there will
be the formulaic arrangement of characters, carefully paired off, nice
and nasty, rich and not-so-rich, married and single, black and white,
young and old, idealistic and cynical, male and female; there will be a
synthetic interrelation of two or more plot lines, timed to produce
suspense hooks in time for commercial breaks; there will be an
identifiable 'grammar' of camera angles and scenes, the juxtaposition
of long-shots with close-ups, action-shots with reflective moments. And
all this is without taking into account the external social or political
requirements which may be imposed upon such a show; such as the
numbers of blacks or women in the cast; the amount of violence for a
young audience; the amount of 'strong' language before a certain time
in the evening; the political 'balance' of the script. A television police
drama observes so many rules and conventions that it makes even the
most rigidly correct of neo-classical dramas, such as Corneille's *Horace*
or Addison's *Cato* appear almost irresponsibly formless. Yet most
modern readers persist in the notion that eighteenth-century literature
is intolerably reined-in and rule-bound, while believing that
contemporary culture is, within the laws of libel, free of regulations and
controls. In fact, the rules and expectations which differentiate the style
of a police drama, for example, from that of a quiz show, are easily
comparable with those which separated lyric from epic, or comedy
from tragedy, according to neo-classical theory. And, just as eighteenth-
century satirists gained many of their most successful effects from
assaulting their readers' expectations with a mock-heroic ragout of high
and low styles, so there is no more familiar comic device now than the
deliberate confusion of television stereotypes. Popular parodies, such
as spoof advertisements, comedians adopting the style of newsreaders,
or soap operas turned into Grand Guignol, rely upon our recognition
of absurd generic contradictions, just as if the front page of *The Times*
were to be printed using the style and vocabulary of *The Sun*.

Ever since the emergence of the mass media, their awesome
persuasive powers to mould attitudes and manipulate ideas have been
recognised, and it is no coincidence that the totalitarian regimes of
Hitler and Stalin were created simultaneously with the development of
radio and cinema as instruments of mass indoctrination. In this sense
the twentieth century has been called the Age of Propaganda. For as
long as the mass media have existed there have been anxieties about
their powers to 'brainwash' an audience with seductive or terrifying
images and thus pervert and frustrate the proper democratic processes
of reasoned argument and debate. Increasingly, politics is conducted as

a series of media events and, at all levels, from demonstrations to hijackings, the most important element is the presence of the cameras, which can turn a local protest into a national or international incident. Diplomacy, speeches, summits have all become photo-opportunities in which the settings—Williamsburg, Geneva or the Great Wall of China—are merely scenic backdrops for the global theatre of politics. The emergence of an actor as President of the United States is the logical outcome of a system in which Nixon allegedly lost the presidency in 1960 because of his five o'clock shadow. Modern politics has realised the central metaphor of Pope's *Dunciad* in which the masquerades of the actor-manager Cibber mimic the powers and authority of monarchy.

Such a process of imaginative stereotyping need not be explicitly 'political' to be regarded as propaganda since American values, for example, are as effectively promoted by the world-wide appetite for *Dallas*, Levi jeans and Coca Cola as by the Voice of America or the CIA. Goebbels himself, high priest of propaganda, argued that his own techniques were merely a refinement of tendencies inherent in the mass media themselves. 'Even *The Times*', he wrote, 'the most democratic paper in the world, makes propaganda in that it deliberately gives prominence to certain facts, emphasizes the importance of others by writing leaders or commentaries about them, and only handles others marginally or not at all.'[41]

Propaganda and advertising are the direct obverse of satire, like convex and concave images presented by the distorting mirror of art. Advertising, as a form of mass rhetoric, attempts to mould social attitudes by promoting particular ideas and desires through the use of idealised stereotypes (young, happy, healthy, etc.). Satire seizes upon and reverses those selfsame stereotypes for its own subversive purposes. The deliberate simplifications and imaginative formulas produced by advertising and propaganda naturally supply the satirists with the forms and terms of their own ironic reversals. Indeed, the two forms, advertising and satire, instinctively feed off each other's caricatures, just as in the eighteenth century, the forms of epic and panegyric hyperbole provided irresistible models for mock-heroic parodies and lampoons.

For, bombarded as we are by the conformist stereotypes of Hollywood and Madison Avenue, we are not merely passive consumers of their two-dimensional smaller-than-life images. On the contrary, our perception that all forms of art, literature and information carry within them implicit elements of propaganda, has made us increasingly distrustful of all claims to objectivity. We see civilisation as a process of

cultural assimilation and imperialism, and 'objectivity' itself as the
apotheosis of certain liberal assumptions. We are no longer confident
in the use of a language of moral absolutes, nor in such ideological
certainties of our nineteenth-century forebears as the notion of
progress. Even medicine, for long the last outpost of the Enlightenment
ideal of conquering ignorance and disease, is now often seen as a form
of high-tech, drug-obsessed Western fetishism. Unconvinced of the
possibility of arriving at truths or facts, we concentrate on 'points-of-
view' and 'unreliable narrators'. Philosophy retreats to hermeneutics
and semantics; history becomes historiography—that is, not what really
happened, but what some particular people, representing their own
particular attitudes, *say* happened, from their own limited selection of
evidence. We study forms rather than content, and cultural codes rather
than moral values. Language itself, we now recognise, is not a
transparent or impartial medium for intellectual discourse and artistic
expression but a complex system of relations which imply and
perpetuate certain distinct cultural assumptions. It is not simply in the
use of such words as 'terrorist' rather than 'freedom-fighter', or 'napkin'
rather than 'serviette' that social and political attitudes are indicated.
The syntax and grammar of language represent the organisation of
significant traditional values and, for example, feminist literary critics
have pointed to a range of male assumptions which permeate 'standard'
English.

Even when we may not endorse the linguistic interpretations offered
by feminist and structuralist critics, our consciousness of language as
a *form* has been sharpened by their investigations.[42] They have
transformed our view of it as an objective medium into a recognition
of its function as an ideological system. Coincidentally, they have also
enriched both the vocabulary and subject-matter of satire, for satire
deals essentially in forms. The rash of 'Person-chester' jokes that greeted
feminist objections to the traditional use of such masculine terms as
chair*man* or spokes*man* is merely the most obvious example of this
process.

In the eighteenth century, as Ian Watt has observed, no one could use
the term 'a great man' without irony. The phrase had become so
devalued in sycophantic panegyrics and servile dedications that it could
not longer be used without compromising both the donor and the
dedicatee. In *Jonathan Wild* Fielding deliberately parades the word
'*Greatness*' like one of Brecht's placards; 'Great' and 'Greatness' appear
in twenty of the fifty-six chapter headings, for example, 'Containing
many surprising adventures, which our hero, with *Great Greatness*

achieved'. Fielding's aim, throughout this novel and elsewhere in his writings, is to equate greatness with criminality, and 'Great Men', such as statesmen and politicians, with petty villains and cheats. In his *Covent Garden Journal* Fielding provided a 'Modern Glossary' of the 'real' meanings of a number of abstract terms familiarly used in polite society, whose awkward moral implications had been softened into acceptable social euphemisms. 'Honour' is now merely the polite term for 'duelling'; 'learning' is equated with 'pedantry'. A 'patriot' is glossed as 'a candidate for a place at court', and 'politics' as 'the art of getting such a place'. 'Honour' and 'honourable', like 'great' and 'greatness', were terms frequently exploited by eighteenth-century satirists, who objected to this hijacking of a moral vocabulary for purposes of political decoration, as in the title 'Right Honourable' bestowed on Privy Councillors. In *The Art of Sinking in Poetry*, the Scriblerian satirists observed ironically that 'Every Man is honourable who is so by Law, Custom or Title.' The satirists in effect seek to rescue the abstract, moral signification of such terms as 'honour' and 'greatness' from the reductive political perversions of those who wish to appropriate them for their own purposes. To this end they replace one set of stereotypes with another, turning a euphemism into a caricature. In our own period one might suggest that terms such as 'democratic' in politics, or 'natural' in advertising have undergone a similar process of devaluation which now makes them potentially self-parodic. Satires which are directed against the propagandist use of such terms depend for their success upon the assumption that there is a residual shared consensus concerning the 'real' meaning of such words. Here again we may note a further confirmation of the inherent conservatism of satire as a form.

Satire, one might argue, involves the subversion of an image or statement through the evocation of a standard of values drawn from outside. There is an implicit appeal to a normative judgement which is different from the ostensible values presented on the surface of the work or text. Yet, as we become increasingly sceptical of the objectivity of literary texts, and correspondingly more adept in detecting sub-textual ironies and contradictions, we may begin to sense parody where none was intended. In this sense the satirical content of a work may be entirely independent of the 'intentions' of the author, and may be produced simply by a contradiction between our own values and assumptions as readers and the words on the page. Titles, in particular, can easily become self-parodic. When in *Gulliver's Travels* we are informed that the Emperor of Lilliput has, among his many resplendent titles, the appellations 'Terror of the Universe' and 'Monarch of all

Monarchs', we can be sure that Swift 'intends' to satirise the absurd
pretensions of such vain-glorious titles. Yet the designation of the Holy
Roman Empire, which as historians have noted was neither Holy nor
Roman nor an Empire, was an entirely unintentional piece of irony.
Similarly today, many may find the titles of several totalitarian
dictatorships as 'Democratic Republics' an unconscious example of
political self-parody.

I'd like to examine two literary passages to illustrate this point. The
first comes from Richardson's *Pamela*:

> And so when I had dined, up stairs I went, and locked myself up in
> my little room. There I trick'd myself up in my new garb, and put on
> my round-eared ordinary cap, but with a green knot, my home-spun
> gown and petticoat, and plain leather shoes, but yet they are what
> they call Spanish leather; and my ordinary hose, ordinary I mean to
> what I have been lately used to, though I should think good yarn may
> do very well for every day, when I come home. A plain muslin tucker
> I put on, and my black silk necklace, instead of the French necklace
> my lady gave me; and put the ear-rings out of my ears. When I was
> quite equipped, I took my straw hat in my hand, with its two blue
> strings, and looked in the glass, as proud as anything. To say truth,
> I never liked myself so well in my life.
>
> O the pleasure of descending with ease, innocence and
> resignation!—Indeed there is nothing like it! An humble mind, I
> plainly see, cannot meet with any very shocking disappointment, let
> Fortune's wheel turn round as it will.[43]

In later editions Richardson replaced Pamela's frolicsome verbal
phrase 'I trick'd myself up' with the more neutral term 'I dressed myself'.
Yet this does little to remove the deeply ambiguous tone of this whole
passage. Pamela's gesture of humility in reassuming her simple peasant
clothes is accompanied by a disconcerting display of fashion-
consciousness. It is evident that she is not only more at ease but also
more attractive in these simple and natural clothes than in the heavy
velvets and costly robes formerly belonging to Mr B.'s mother. Fielding
himself could not improve upon the ambiguous moral complacency of
Pamela's gloating declaration, 'O the *pleasure* of descending with ease,
innocence and resignation!' It is the coy self-satisfaction at combining
moral superiority with social humility which triggers a suspicion of
irony here. Pamela's effortless glide from admiring herself in the glass
'as proud as anything' to boasting of her 'humble mind' seems to
contradict Richardson's apparent desire to present her as an exemplary

moral paragon. Modern readers, even less inclined than Fielding to accept such moral abstractions as innocence, humility and virtue at their face value, inevitably detect a taint of hypocrisy in Pamela's convenient combination of deference and independence, humility and pride. They are likely to find more ingenuity than ingenuousness in her behaviour, and to see the book as rewarding virtuosity rather than virtue. As Mark Kinkead-Weekes writes, 'To a modern reader, disposed at any rate to resent overt moralising, the colloquial speech will seem natural, hence sincere, and the moralising an insincere rationalisation.'[44] It is the discrepancy between these two registers that produces a satiric effect.

One might compare this with a passage from a modern romantic novel:

She looked round, willing him to speak, and caught a strange, brooding look in his eyes. Her heart began to pound and she felt stifled, trapped. An enormous roll of thunder rumbled and reverberated all around, echoing through the valleys and booming over the mountaintops.

The room grew dark, the distant hills were lost entirely in the rainmist, while the nearer mountains became black and menacing. Streaks of lightning sliced jaggedly through the air and ran to earth; giant flashes lit up the violent scene, then darkness came again.

Tamsin felt Sarne beside her and as she shivered—with his nearness, but he thought it was fear of the storm—his arm lifted and came to rest across her shoulders. Rain rammed down on the roofs, beating on the green branches, pitting the surface of the swimming pool with its force. It ran down the road, emptying the streets. The thunder rolled, the lightning, in its fury, struck and struck again against the mountains.

He turned her abruptly and she saw that he had thrown aside his jacket. There was a storm in his eyes, his face, the tight lips. Seconds before they came together, she knew it would happen. The elements unleashed outside had released within him potent, primitive forces. His body was hard like the side of a mountain and the emotions aroused by their physical contact were like the lightning flashes searing the blackness beyond the windows and dazzling into momentary blindness the watching eyes.

Sarne kissed her, his lips exploring, possessive—and experimental, as if testing her response, her willingness to yield. The reserve he had shown before and which had until now prevailed in the kisses he had given her had been cast aside and she fought for breath as though she had been climbing a mountain.[45]

The stereotypical nature of the language here, linking the storm outside
to the emotional turbulence within the characters, will be obvious to the
least analytical of readers. Even the names, Tamsin and Sarne, are chosen
to reinforce the conventional gender roles presented in such popular
romances. Taken out of context, the melodramatic repetitions of all
those violent adjectives and verbs push the clichés of atmospheric
writing to the brink of self-parody. Lightning 'sliced jaggedly through
the air', the rain 'rammed down on the roofs' even Sarne's body was
'hard like the side of a mountain'. The fortissimo mood here, a crude
hotch-potch of D.H. Lawrence and the Brontës, is designed to signal one
of the novel's climatic moments. Yet the formulaic nature of the writing,
unrelieved by any subtlety or individuality of character, is like switching
on a sound-effects machine. The vocabulary, timing, situation and tone
are all perfect examples of genre writing. Indeed, it would be difficult
to see how a satirist, who might wish to parody the clichés of romance
writing, could improve upon such a passage, since all the exaggerations
of potential self-caricature are already present. Yet clearly the
'intentions' behind this passage from *Passionate Involvement* were not
ironic. It was written to create a mood of escapist fantasy, not for careful
satiric scrutiny. But, were one to remove it from its proper context, and
publish this passage unaltered in *Private Eye*, it would cry out as a piece
of brilliant parody, catching all the clichés and idioms of the genre.
Satire, that is, may often result from our own expectations and attitudes,
as much as from any definably satirical mode of expression. Any
conventional style, taken out of context, may appear ridiculous; the
solemnities of a funeral, the stylised expressions of grand opera, the
rituals of religion or sport may all provide excellent opportunities for
parody. Thus, for example, the patriotic recruiting songs of 1914, even
without the verbal emendations popularised by the soldiers in the
trenches, became not rousing anthems but bitterly ironic accusations
in *O What a Lovely War*.

    This does not mean, however, that satire is irremediably shallow or
gimmicky, merely trivialising the conventions of great art by drawing
moustaches on the Mona Lisa. Of course, there is always a kind of ham
comedy to be gained by sending-up the histrionics of King Lear in the
storm, or Hamlet's soliloquies. But in such cases it is the anthology
quality of the pieces which triggers off the parody; familiarity has
turned them into set-pieces for a kind of virtuoso display, rather than
elements in great poetic drama. Where the imaginative or intellectual
vitality of a passage still survives intact, parody can have little effect and
merely reveals itself as trivial and meretricious. The beauty of satire is

its deadly accuracy in detecting when a style or attitude, in either art or politics, has ossified into a formula or mannerism. It is a debunker of false images, heroic stereotypes, moralising postures and pious gestures, where the rhetoric is not sustained by any living content. It sniffs out propaganda, rhetorical exaggeration and metaphors that have degenerated into clichés. Wherever a discrepancy exists between expression and imagination, manners and morality, words and deeds, there is an opportunity for satire.

CHAPTER TWO

Themes and Forms of Augustan Satire

The Augustan Myth

The term 'Augustan' as applied to the literature of the century following the Restoration of Charles 11 has come in for a good deal of fairly well-deserved criticism in recent years. The prevalence of the term in such titles as the 'Augustan world', the 'Augustan milieu' or 'Augustan satire' has come to be little more than a form of convenient shorthand, like the similar terms 'metaphysical' and 'romantic'; and like them, has often been used with little specific or scholarly discrimination. In protest at the vagueness and slipperiness of the term, Donald Greene has even declared that the period in question was more Augustinian than Augustan, and that we might with equal logic and greater euphony refer to its literature as Mesapotamian.[1] Howard Weinbrot has reminded us of the important anti-Augustan elements in the literature of the period, and Maximilian Novak has suggested that 'perhaps the Brutan Age would be a more accurate appellation, since the appeal to English liberty might call on both the Brutus who invented Roman liberty and the Brutus who was the last to defend it.'[2] Yet before this term is finally deconstructed into oblivion, it might be useful to remind ourselves of the general significance of its use, the diversity of its applications and the relationship with Roman models which it implied. For, as Howard Erskine-Hill has demonstrated, the invocation of the 'Augustan parallel' by writers of the seventeenth and eighteenth centuries did not automatically indicate an endorsement of the supposed values of imperial Rome.[3] What it did provide, however, was a universally recognisable system of analogies, a thesaurus of precedents, to be used as yardsticks for measuring the achievements of contemporary society. The well-known episodes of Roman history acquired a quasi-mythic status which allowed them to be used as a kind of literary code or sub-text, providing instant parallels with, and commentaries upon, the state of English politics, literature and society.

Dryden was among the first to make systematic use of this Roman parallel, as, in Novak's words, he 'consciously attempted to develop an Augustan myth'.[4] His poem *Astraea Redux,* modelled in part on Virgil's fourth eclogue, compares the return of Charles II to England with Octavian's victory over Mark Antony at Actium, and goes on to prophesy a new golden age of peace, prosperity and imperial greatness:

> Oh Happy Age! Oh times like those alone
> By Fate reserved for great Augustus Throne!
> When the joint growth of Arms and Arts foreshow
> The world a Monarch, and that Monarch you!
>
> (ll. 320-3)

Johnson, in his life of Dryden, confirms that in style as well as subject-matter Dryden both embodied and expressed an Augustan classicism. 'What was said of Rome, adorned by Augustus, may be applied by an easy metaphor to English poetry embellish'd by Dryden; *later itiam invenit, marmoream reliquit,* he found it brick and he left it marble.'[5]

However, by asserting the Augustan parallel, writers were not simply establishing a fashion for more decorous verse, but were implying a view of society and an interpretation of the relationship between ruler and ruled. The age of Augustus was portrayed as an era of order and stability at home, expansion and enrichment abroad, replacing a period when republican liberties had degenerated into anarchy and civil war. Under the beneficent rule of Augustus, and through the enlightened support of such patrons as Maecenas, the arts of Virgil and Horace were fostered to spread Roman civilisation throughout the world. Roman institution, Roman law, Roman literature and architecture consolidated the best achievements of the classical tradition, enshrining them at the centre of an empire which brought enlightenment to the regions it conquered. The Augustan model offered an heroic ideal for later ages to imitate, and there were many Englishmen in the late seventeenth and early eighteenth centuries who seized upon the opportunities provided after the Restoration to do so. The Great Fire of London, which destroyed the heart of the old medieval city, cleared the way for the noble classical edifices of Wren, Hawksmoor and Gibbs. And although Wren's ambitious geometrical plans for a wholesale redevelopment of the city with broad avenues, classical monuments and piazzas, were not adopted, they demonstrate the same kind of grandiose imperial design for a new capital city that one finds in the later town plans of Napoleon and Hitler. Even such a resolutely non-Augustan figure as Daniel Defoe caught the infectious imperial enthusiasm, and in 1728 published a pamphlet entitled *Augusta Triumphans,* containing a number of schemes designed 'to make London the most flourishing city in the universe'. In literature the reformed, polished and regularised iambic couplets, known appropriately as 'heroic', were the new dignified, stately and public form chosen to express the odes, epics and panegyrics of an imperial age. Poetic diction too was marmorealised to make it more noble and formal, while 'low' terms, the indicators of crude, barbaric or 'gothic' sentiments, were excluded.

An important consideration in the minds of those Augustans who sought to purify and dignify the literary language of the age was the desire to give permanence to their work. The promiscuity of printing presses, the ephemerality of slang and jargon seemed to threaten the life and intelligibility of the artefacts of this new Augustan age. Whereas the ancients, according to Pope, wrote in languages which became universal and everlasting, 'ours are extremely limited both in extent and duration. A mighty foundation for our pride! When the utmost we can hope is but to be read in one island, and to be thrown aside at the end of one age.'[6] It is noticeable how often the imagery of stonework, or Roman memorial tablets and triumphal arches, recurs in this context. The desire for permanence is inseparable from the classical instincts underlying the urge for empire-building which tend naturally to think in terms of thousand-year dynasties. Swift had the same kind of monumental stabilty in mind when he published his *Proposals for Ascertaining the English Tongue:*

> How then shall any man, who hath a genius for history equal to the best of the ancients, be able to undertake such a work with spirit and cheerfulness, when he considers that he will be read with pleasure but a very few years, and in an age or two will be hardly understood without an interpreter. This is like employing an excellent statuary to work on mouldring stone.[7]

Ironically, it was the printing presses themselves, spewing out their abundance of pulp literature which were, coincidentally, establishing fixed norms of orthography and punctuation which have ensured that the language of Augustan literature has indeed lasted better than that of any previous generation. Their informal rules, motivated by market forces rather than classical models, resulted in a linguistic standardisation far more effective than any of the imposed doctrines of literary theory which sought to ensure verisimilitude by presenting only noble and dignified simulacra of human behaviour. This same irony can be found in many related forms. The Augustan Age did indeed create an era of stability, but based not on classical ideals so much as upon commercial institutions. J.H. Plumb has called the period between 1685 and 1725 an age of political stability, during which time many of the institutions which ushered in the modern world, from the Bank of England and political parties to hospitals and prisons, were established. If one looks through the list of projects outlined on the title page of Defoe's *Augusta Triumphans*, one can gain a clear view of the kind of optimistic, utilitarian enterprise that went hand in hand with the new heroic tendency:

> Augusta Triumphans: Or, The Way to Make London the most flourishing City in the Universe. First, by establishing an University where Gentlemen may have an Academical Education under the Eye of their Friends. II To prevent Murder &c by an Hospital for Foundlings. III By suppressing pretended Mad-houses, where many of the fair Sex are unjustly confin'd, while their Husbands keep Mistresses, &c, and many Widows are lock,d up for the Sake of their Jointure. IV To save our Youth from Destruction, by cleaning the Streets of impudent Strumpets, suppressing Gaming-Tables and Sunday Debauches. V To avoid the expensive Importation of Foreign Musicians, by forming an Academy of our own. VI To save our lower Class of People from utter Ruin, and to render them useful, by preventing the immoderate Use of Geneva, with a frank Explosion of many other common Abuses, and incontestable Rules for Amendment. Concluding with an effectual Method to prevent Street Robberies, and a Letter to Coll. Robinson on account of the Orphan's Tax.[8]

Broadly one might distinguish three kinds of reponse to the development of an Augustan or imperial ethic. First there was the attitude exemplified by Defoe, for whom the 'Augustan' tag is merely a kind of prestigious label, but whose real interest is in capitalist enterprise and utilitarian projects. The other two views might best be expressed in terms of the titles which their exponents adopted in the scholarly debates of the time, that is, the Ancients and the Moderns.

Both Ancients and Moderns acknowledged a debt to classical learning, but differed widely in reckoning its value. The Moderns, while conceding the useful pioneering work achieved by the classical philosophers in opening up the avenues of enlightenment, held to a notion of progress which saw all human learning as a process of steady accumulation and advancement. In their view, modern science, and by analogy modern culture in all forms, had surpassed the achievements of the Ancient Greeks. The two most frequently cited examples of the alleged superiority of modern learning came in the field of science. Copernicus's discovery of the heliocentric universe, and Harvey's discovery of the circulation of the blood were both given as examples of modern science outstripping and contradicting the axioms and rules of classical philosophy, proving that, great as they might be, the Ancients were not infallible, and that Hippocrates and Aristotle could, like Homer, nod. Indeed, the rapid succession of 'discoveries' in the natural sciences, culminating with Newton's *Principia* in 1687 led some of the more enthusiastic moderns to foresee a time, in the not too distant future, when all the mysteries of the universe would be revealed. William Wootton, satirised by Swift in *A Tale of a Tub,* was cheer leader for the moderns. In his *Reflections upon Ancient and Modern Learning* (1705) he proclaimed his faith in the intellectual progress of his own age, especially in the natural sciences, a field in which he believed knowledge would very soon be total: 'If this humour lasts much longer, and learned men do not divert their thoughts to speculations of another kind, the next age will not find very much work of this kind to do.'[9]

Just as Newtonian physics and Lockean epistemology might be deemed to have outstripped the ancient philosophers, so, it was implied, might Marlborough's victories eclipse those of Caesar, and Wren's edifices surpass the architectural monuments of Greece and Rome. For the moderns the new Augustan Age was an heroic era of progress and achievement to outshine all that had gone before it.

By contrast, the Ancients took the view that the Greek philosophers of classical antiquity had achieved a peak of human wisdom and enlightenment. Compared with the magisterial clarity and authority of their works, the vaunted discoveries and theories of the moderns appeared as the petty cavils of pigmy minds. Swift's patron, Sir William Temple, was the main champion of the Ancient cause. In his essay *Of Ancient and Modern Learning* he challenged the whole of modern thought:

But what are the sciences wherein we pretend to excel? I know of
no new philosophers, that have made entries upon that noble stage
for fifteen hundred years past . . .

There is nothing new in Astronomy, to vie with the ancients,
unless it be the Copernican system; nor in Physic, unless Harvey's
circulation of the blood. But whether either of these be modern
discoveries, or derived from old fountains, is disputed: nay, it is so
too, whether they are true or no; for though reason may seem to
favour them more than the contrary opinions, yet sense can very
hardly allow them; and, to satisfy mankind, both these must
concur. But if they are true, yet these two great discoveries have
made no change in the conclusions of Astronomy, nor in the
practice to Physic; and so have been of little use to the world,
though perhaps of much honour to the authors. [10]

It is worth noting here that Temple uses three contradictory
arguments in his attempt to refute these modern discoveries. First, he
argues that they are probably not modern at all but 'derived from old
fountains'. Second, he suggests that if they *are* modern, they are
probably not true. Finally, he declares that even if they are modern
and true, they are 'of little *use* to the world' and may consequently be
regarded as mere examples of personal vanity. There is an element of
polite desperation in the eclecticism of these arguments which
suggests a deep-rooted prejudice rather than calm philosophical
judgements.

Thereafter defenders of the Ancient cause more often sought to
parody their Modern antagonists than to confront them with outright
denials. Through satire they adopted a form of guerilla tactics, sniping
from cover rather than engaging in a full frontal assault. Swift's *Tale of
a Tub,* for example, ostensibly supports Temple and the Ancients; yet
its spiralling ironies and teasing paradoxes mock Temple's own
complacent assertions as well as the meretricious vanity of the
moderns.

Temple had justified and dignified his own retirement from the
world of active politics in favour of a life of gardening and meditation
by citing the example of Horace: 'It was no mean strain of his
philosophy, to refuse being secretary to Augustus, when so great an
emperor so much desired it.' [11] Increasingly in the Hanoverian period,
those who remained in the ancient camp also adopted the role and
imagery of Horatian retirement. They saw themselves as custodians
of the true classical traditions and values in opposition to the false

imperial classicism of the state. Detached from corrupting pressures of state ideology, their balanced and measured classical works sought to expose the designs of those who perverted and misapplied classical imagery as a way of legitimising their own grandiose ambitions. A classical tradition of order, moderation, dignity and self-knowledge was invoked to attack a modern Rome of vanity, pomp, ceremony and slavery. This distinction between true and false classicism can be seen in many guises. In literature Bentley and Theobald, Eusden and Cibber are the false classicists. In politics these places are filled by Marlborough, Walpole and George II. Hence it is that an age which proclaimed its belief in heroic literature and epic ideals became famous for mock-heroics and mock-epics as writers were increasingly fascinated by the discrepancies between the classical model and the modern copy, the heroic form and the puny content.

Another important aspect of the Augustan parallel was that it introduced a range of values, concepts and institutions which were primarily social. Rome, even under the emperors, was, like Athens, a city-state with a mixed constitution, and the use of Roman models served to dignify and legitimise not only new national institutions, like the Bank of England, but attitudes to the state based upon social assumptions. Where previously the twin foundations of authority and reverence had been the monarchy and religion, now a third set of institutions—the apparatus of the bourgeois state—emerged, with their accompanying imagery and ideology. Examining the works of earlier writers one observes that allusions to authority, whether in the forms of emblems, conceits, allegories or parallels, derive predominantly from one of these two traditional sources, the Church or the Court. Writers were either engaged in or dependent upon some form of courtly entertainment, or else were concerned with giving imaginative form to their religious sentiments. But in the post-Hobbesian world of the eighteenth century, the state demanded recognition as a source of authority quite distinct from either Church or Crown, though it might from time to time identify its interests with either. And the dress of Roman times was conveniently at hand to serve as a decent cover for this naked transfer of power. Moreover, throughout the seventeenth century both the Church and the monarchy had become so involved in civil wars that the imagery associated with them was too controversial to serve as a source of unity and imperial revival. It is an essential implication of the compromise enshrined in the Revolution Settlement of 1688 that political differences should be institutionalised and debated between political parties rather than fought out between opposing armies. There was a clear desire to move away from the polarised extremes that had become associated with the issues of kingship and religion, and towards classical ideals of moderation, tolerance and, of course, reason.

The eighteenth century, then, was a period which looked more towards social and civic models of behaviour than to the Court or Church for guidance. Bernard Mandeville's sneering description of Addison as 'a parson in a tie-wig' was at least accurate in this respect. The rational piety of Addison's Saturday sermons in *The Spectator,* interspersed as they were between articles on fashion or education, witty reflections on the cries of London or sage remarks on the pleasures of the imagination, exactly indicate the shift from treating religion as a solemn duty, to presenting it as the proper fulfilment of a civilised life. 'I shall endeavour to enliven morality with wit, and to temper wit with morality', he declared. It would be an over-simplification to present eighteenth-century literature as merely an extension of the clubs and coffee houses which suddenly sprang up in London to cater for this new emphasis on a social culture. Yet if we take *The Spectator,* which according to Addison's own reckoning had achieved a circulation of 3,000 copies (and a readership of 60,000 'disciples') by its tenth number, as one important indicator of literary tastes, we can see how the new public institutions of social and commercial life came to assume a central cultural significance. In *Spectator* No.69 Addison declared:

> There is no place in the town which I so much love to frequent as the Royal Exchange. It gives me a secret satisfaction, and, in some measure, gratifies my vanity, as I am an Englishman, to see so rich an Assembly of country-men and foreigners consulting together upon the private business of mankind, and making this metropolis a kind of emporium for the whole earth.[12]

Unlike Donne, whose sense of intimate theatre can make 'one little room, an every where', or Wordsworth, whose spirit and imagination soar at the prospect of a field of golden daffodils, Addison's imagination is fired by seeing the Stock Exchange at work. For him this vision of thriving business activity is a symbol of the positive and harmonious benefits of civilisation. Trade becomes a metaphor for mutual understanding, and the material fruits of commerce are the solid rewards for the virtues of tolerance and restraint.

In the third issue of *The Spectator* we find an elaborate allegorical vision. The subject however is not some ancient saint or classical deity, nor even Queen Anne, but the Bank of England:

> Methoughts I returned to the Great Hall, where I had been the morning before, but to my surprize, instead of the company that I left there, I saw towards the upper end of the hall, a beautiful virgin, seated on a throne of gold. Her name (as they told me) was Public Credit. The walls, instead of being adorned with pictures and maps, were hung with many acts of parliament written in golden letters. At the upper end of the hall was the Magna Charta, with an Act of Uniformity on the right hand and the Act of Toleration on the left. At the lower end of the hall was the Act of Settlement, which was placed full in the eye of the virgin that sat upon the throne.[13]

In this carefully staged 'vision' Addison writes as the high priest of established Whiggism, and this tableau seeks to canonise the Whig myth of historical progress, from Magna Carta, to the Bank of England. This tendency, found elsewhere in Whig panegyrics, to celebrate and apotheosise public credit as a classical deity, helps to explain Pope's mock-heroic eulogies of this fickle goddess in his *Epistle to Bathurst*. Even where we find political disagreements, however, this practice of using the social arena as the most natural metaphor for moral preoccupations remains a constant feature of eighteenth-century literature. From Pope's picture of Queen Anne taking tea at Hampton Court to Goldsmith's lament for the departed joys of his Deserted Village, the concern is for social harmony and values expressed through a formalised imagery of social behaviour.

The ficticious 'Spectator Club' from which Addison's periodical claims to emanate, typifies the era's new ethos of clubbability. Among its members are Sir Andrew Freeport, a Whig merchant, and Sir Roger de Coverley, a Tory squire. Fifty years earlier these two men might have taken up arms against each other in the civil war. Now they are content to argue out their differences over a dish of coffee or a glass of port in the congenial surroundings of a London club. Later in the century Johnson remarked that nothing had been contrived by men 'by which so much happiness is produced as by a good tavern or inn.'[14] This observation, and his praise of 'the supreme felicity of a tavern chair' were not intended as recommendations of the pleasures of alcoholism, but as recognition of the conviviality produced by those places specifically created and ordained for fellowship,

conversation and wit. In the Introduction to *Tom Jones,* the narrator
of the novel presents himself to the reader as the keeper of just such a
friendly hostelry:

> An author ought to consider himself, not as a gentleman who gives
> a private or eleemosynary treat, but rather as one who keeps a
> public ordinary, at which all persons are welcome for their money
> . . . Men who pay for what they eat, will insist in gratifying their
> palates, however nice and even whimsical these may prove; and if
> every thing is not agreeable to their taste, will challenge a right to
> censure, to abuse, and to d-n their dinner without control. To
> prevent therefore giving offence to their customers by any such
> disappointment, it hath been usual, with the honest and well-
> meaning host, to provide a bill of fare, which all persons may
> peruse at their first entrance into the house; and, having thence
> acquainted themselves with the entertainment which they may
> expect, may either stay and regale with what is provided for them,
> or may depart to some other ordinary better accommodated to
> their taste.(I.i)

The character of Fielding's narrator is urbane, witty, sophisticated,
the most charming of companions, a superb conversationalist, well-
informed but no pedant, conveying a sense of authority yet wearing
his learning lightly and imparting it with self-mocking nonchalance.
The culture of Augustan writers such as Pope and Addison, Fielding
and Johnson draws its sustenance from the social life which it
describes. It is a celebration of those values of good fellowship,
conversation, civilisation and humanity which society, at its best,
exists to foster. Even Defoe, whose lack of patrician credentials might
be thought to have excluded him from the ethos of the gentleman's
club, has his ex-solitary Robinson Crusoe describe the joys of
conversation in his *Serious Reflections:*

> Conversation is the brightest and most beautiful part of life; 'tis an
> emblem of the enjoyment of a future state, for suitable society is a
> heavenly life; 'tis that part of life by which mankind are not only
> distinguished from the inanimate world, but by which they are
> distinguished from one another.[15]

Our interest in *The Tatler* and *The Spectator* nowadays may be
more a matter of polite historical curiosity rather than of real literary
concern. Yet the impulse behind these periodicals is important to an

understanding of more general cultural preoccupations. They gave
voice to a strong desire to purge away all the residual barbarities
which deformed social life and which seemed to lend credibility to
the polemics of those who regarded all social gatherings as
incitements to vice. They sought to demonstrate the congruity of
morals and manners; to show humanity at its most perfect not in
church but in society; to transform the education of a gentleman from
the privilege of a courtier to the right of all reasonable beings.
Twentieth-century readers, encountering seemingly endless outcries
against Italian opera, protracted debates about the morality of
masquerades, or lurid accounts of the unwary rake's progress from
prosperity to beggary *via* the London vices of gaming and
debauchery, may find something exaggerated, even comical, about
these issues. Could it really have mattered so much what one wore,
whether one swore, whether one went to Italian operas? In fact, it did
matter precisely because writers like Addison, Pope, Steele and
Fielding were anxious to insist that social entertainments, such as the
theatre, could be both moral *and* entertaining, witty *and* exemplary.
In the satires of the period familiar landmarks of London topography,
Drury Lane and Change Alley, Smithfield and Covent Garden,
Newgate and Bedlam, take on the significance of mythological realms
or classical monuments. A character's moral progress can be charted,
street by street, as the social map of London is transformed into a
mock-epic battleground.

The Smithfield Muses

Eighteenth-century satire relies upon the invocation of social values
and public responsibilities as the basis for its censure. It is concerned
less with the redemption of individual sinners than with the
regulation of general standards of conduct. In *Joseph Andrews*
Fielding's narrator declares, 'once for all, I describe not men but
manners; not an individual but a species.' However this focus is less
restrictive than might at first appear. For just as literature, as described
in Pope's *Essay on Criticism,* represents a microcosm of creation, so
society may be viewed as a formalised theatre for the drama of human
relationships. The rules by which literature is fashioned and judged
offer an aesthetic corollary for the wider laws of natural order and
moral choice; in the same way, the vocabulary of manners, etiquette
and social conduct, like the vocabulary of classical myth, may in

some ways be regarded as convenient structural metaphors for more enduring moral preoccupations. A mixed metaphor, like a pompous building, a venal judge or an ill-mannered beau, are all public exhibitions of a kind of deformation that offends against the order— moral as much as material—of the universe.

I should like to illustrate, from just one area of Pope's satire, the full register, nuances and subtlety of reference which may be contained in this Augustan style of social judgement. In particular, I wish to demonstrate how classical models can both lend authority to a social role and simultaneously provide the imaginative source for a surreal subversion of that role. In the second book of *The Dunciad* the goddess Dulness proclaims a festival of 'high heroic games' to celebrate the coronation of her King Dunce, Great Tibbald, (Lewis Theobald, or in the 1743 version, Great Cibber, Colley Cibber). Here, as throughout *The Dunciad*, we are dealing with a number of interdependent levels of allusion. The central action of the poem, the removal of the empire of Dulness from its traditional capital in the City of London to a new, grander location in Westminster, is modelled on the action of *The Aeneid,* in which the Trojan hero Aeneas flees one vanquished empire in order to found a new and grander empire at Rome. Pope makes his general indebtedness to Virgil's epic explicit in his opening couplet, with its precise echo of Virgil's *Arma virumque cano:*

> Books and the Man I sing, the first who brings
> The Smithfield Muses to the Ear of Kings.

The reference to the 'Smithfield Muses' is explained by Pope in one of the plentiful notes which provide a constant bantering commentary on the poem itself, offering a satiric blend of mock-censure and ironic commendations:

> Smithfield is the place where Bartholomew Fair was kept, whose Shews, Machines and Dramatical Entertainments, formerly only agreeable to the Taste of the Rabble, were, by the Hero of this poem (i.e. Theobald) and other of equal Genius, brought to the Theatres of Covent-Garden, Lincoln's-Inn-Fields, and the Hay-Market, to be the reigning Pleasures of the Court and Town.

Antithetical oppositions between the East End and West End of the capital, the City and the Court, can be found in much of the literature of the previous century, and particularly in Restoration comedies. The City is traditionally presented as dour, puritanical, Whiggish, money-obsessed, vulgar; the Court is stylish, witty, polite with tendencies towards foppishness and lechery. Pope goes beyond these traditional stereotypes and concentrates instead on the artefacts, rituals and public exhibitions of the two cultures to suggest certain affinities of taste and appetite more potent than these traditional distinctions. Some years ago Aubrey Williams demonstrated that the westward progress of the Dunces through London from the Guildhall in the East to St Mary-le-Strand and Drury Lane in the West, is closely modelled on the annual route of the Lord Mayor of London to take his oath of office.[16] As the highest City authority, the Lord Mayor personifies the values of the City, and his procession thus represents a significant ceremonial metaphor for a confrontation between the commercial middle-class values of the City and the aristocratic territories of Westminster. More recently other scholars have suggested that this structual contiguity may have been used by Pope to veil an even more notable processional pageant. For when the first brief version of *The Dunciad* appeared in 1728, by far the most important recent ceremony, providing a direct analogy with the enthronement of the King Dunce Tibbald, would have been the coronation of George II in 1727. In the third couplet of the poem we read:

> Say from what cause, in vain decry'd and curst,
> Still Dunce the second reigns like Dunce the first.

In his note to these lines Pope typically muddies the waters of interpretation by pointing out the borrowing from Dryden's verses *To Mr Congreve:* 'And *Tom* the Second reigns like *Tom* the first'. But as Pat Rogers writes, 'It is hard to believe that the prime thrust of the allusion is not to the Georges, who bore the precise ordinal numbers in their title which the reference demands.'[17] Even the note to the Dryden source is rather an amplification than a deflection of the central political point here, for as Erskine-Hill has argued: 'those who noticed the clear echo of a line from Dryden's *Epistle To Mr Congreve* would know that Pope was linking his poem with a fundamental cultural and political attack, by the earlier poet, upon the Revolution Settlement.'[18] Viewed in this light, the implied attack on George II is less upon him as an individual than upon a succession of whiggish monarchs stretching back past Dunce (or George) the First, to the original 'foreign master' William III. Even the word 'cause' ('Say from what cause . . . ') may be significant, since the Whigs were often associated with the 'Good Old Cause' of Republicanism.

So while the fairground side-shows and Smithfield entertainments which traditionally accompanied the Lord Mayor's procession provide one source for the antics of Pope's Dunces, the coronation itself offered not only a deeper political theme but also some further examples of pompous anarchy. For coronations in the seventeenth and eighteenth centuries were not the dignified media events which they have become in our more formal and image-conscious age. In the course of the actual coronation procession in 1727, for example, the Duchess of Marlborough took a drum from a drummer and sat on it. According to an eye-witness, 'the crowd laughed and shouted at seeing the wife of the great and celebrated Duke of Marlborough, more than seventy years of age, seated on a drum in her robes of state.' The official feast also offered a magnificent opportunity for ingenious freeloaders, like the French exile M.César de Saussure who found a gallery seat above the formal banquet.

When we saw they had finished eating, we let down a small rope which, to tell the truth, we made up by knotting our garters together. . . . The peers beneath were kind enough to attach a napkin filled with food to our rope, which we then handed up, and in this way got plenty of good things to eat and drink. The napkin took several journerys up and down, and we are not the only people who had this idea, for from all the galleries round the same sight could be seen.[19]

At the end of the banquet the doors were thrown open and the crowd rushed in. The Duchess of Marlborough observed them 'take possession of the remains of the feast. . . . The pillage was most diverting; people threw themselves with extraordinary avidity on everything the hall contained; blows were given and returned, and I cannot give you any idea of the noise and confusion that reigned. In less than half an hour everything had disappeared, even the boards of which the table and seats had been made.' In *The Beggar's Opera*. written shortly afterwards, Peachum and Lockitt agree that their 'Coronation account' was highly profitable; that is, their inventory of goods stolen during the coronation is 'of so intricate a nature' and consists of such a 'great variety of articles' that 'it was worth to our people, in fees of different kinds, above ten instalments'. Costumes worn at the ceremony added a further touch of absurd theatricality, or farce. According to Lady Mary Wortley Montagu, the Duchess of Montrose had 'dozens of black snakes playing around her face', and Lady Portland was decked out as 'an Egyptian mummy embroider'd over with hieroglyphics'. The anarchic comedy and bizarre details of this regal ceremony lend the whole occasion an air of tawdry show-biz spectacle. It was this quality of accident-prone amateur theatricals that Pope seized on in *The Dunciad*.

Another ritualised westward progress through London that may have contributed to the scheme of *The Dunciad* was the regular transportation of convicted criminals from Newgate Prison, near Smithfield, in the East, to Tyburn (where Marble Arch now stands) in the West. Hanging days, or 'hanging matches' as they were termed, were always an occasion for mass popular entertainment. All along the route of the hanging procession crowds gathered, street hawkers sold ballads and 'dying speeches', and there were the usual fairground stalls and side-shows. Hundreds of people, or sometimes, when a star performer like Jonathan Wild or Jack Sheppard was to make his last appearance, thousands of people followed the procession or jostled for a vantage point around the gallows. These hanging matches, with their large popular following, their frequent brawls and disturbances, provided a kind of street theatre that offered a low-life parallel with the coronations or mayoral processions. Enthroned in the cart, the convicted felon took a last leave of his public, offering a few well-chosen words before the ritual sacrifice on the scaffold.

Finally, a more elevated source for the westward journey in *The Dunciad* should be noted. There was, in the seventeenth and eighteenth centuries, a widespread acceptance of the notion of the *translatio studii,* that is, a belief in the steady progress westward of the seat of learning. Sir John Denham celebrated this theme in his poem 'The Progress of Learning', but its clearest exposition is to be found in Temple's *Essay upon Ancient and Modern Learning:*

Science and Arts have run their circles, and had their periods in the several Parts of the World. They are generally agreed to have held their course from East to West, to have begun in Chaldaea and Aegypt, to have been transported from thence to Greece, from Greece to Rome, to have sunk there, and after many ages to have revived from those ashes, and to have sprung up again, both in Italy and other more Western provinces of Europe.[20]

The *translatio studii* theme provided a comforting authority for those who looked on London as the new Rome or Troynovant, and who eagerly anticipated the emergence of a British empire which would rival and even surpass the glorious domains of Greece and Rome. However, in the pisgah-sight of the approaching empire of Dulness which the Dunce-King is permitted in Book III of *The Dunciad*, Pope offers a negative version of the *translatio studii,* as he pictures a steadily advancing shadow of ignorance and apathy darkening the globe:

> And see! my son, the hour is on its way,
> That lifts our Goddess to imperial sway:
> This fav'rite Isle, long sever'd from her reign
> Dove-like, she gathers to her wings again.

Throughout *The Dunciad* these various versions of the 'progress' theme, intellectual, Virgilian, regal, mayoral and criminal are interwoven to provide both the structures and the metaphorical resonances of the poem. Nor have we by any means exhausted the allusive riches of this multi-layered work. Milton's *Paradise Lost* ranks second only to *The Aeneid* as a literary source for some of the poem's most significant ironic effects. Homer too contributes a number of epic models, while the influence of Shakespeare and Shakespeareana is so all-pervasive that one scholar has described the poem as 'a Shakespearean document pure and simple.'[21]

But we already have more than enough material to begin an examination of the games of the Dunces to see how Pope blends the iconography of heroic ceremony with satiric images of fairground sideshows, popular antics and political lampoons.

The third of the gymnastic contests included among the heroic games in Book V of *The Aeneid* is a boxing match. The corresponding trial in Book II of *The Dunciad* is a urinating competition, to see which of the Dunces can piss highest. In Virgil the first prize is a bull; the second prize a helmet and sword (*Aeneid* V.482ff.) In *The Dunciad*, correspondingly, the first prize is Eliza Haywood, the novelist, described in bovine terms as a 'Juno of majestic size/with cow-like udders, and with ox-like eyes.'; the second prize, a chamber pot.

> See in the circle next, Eliza plac'd;
> Two babes of love close clinging to her waste;
> Fair as before her works she stands confess'd,
> In flow'rs and pearls by bounteous Kirkall dress'd.

The Goddess then: 'who best can send on high
The salient spout, far-streaming to the sky';
His be yon Juno of majestic size,
With cow-like-udders, and with ox-like eyes.
This China-Jordan, let the chief o'ercome
Replenish, not ingloriously, at home.

(ll.149-158)

In his note to these lines Pope looks past his main source in *The Aeneid* to Virgil's source in Homer in order to prove that far from disparaging Mrs Haywood by this bovine analogy, he was actually paying her a considerable honour:

> In the games of Homer *Iliad* 23.262-51 there are set together as prizes, a lady and a kettle; as in this place Mrs *Haywood* and a Jordan. But there the preference in value is given to the kettle, at which Madame *Dacier* is justly displeas'd. Mrs *H* here is treated with distinction, and acknowledged to be the more valuable of the two.[22]

In one sense Pope's description of Eliza Haywood with her 'two babes of love' seems merely a malicious piece of gossip; yet her pose also suggests a parody-Madonna with holy family. Likewise the recollections of her resplendent portrait in the frontispiece to her *Works* 'in flowers and pearls' suggests an opulence of wealth and nature appropriate to a mock-Juno. Eliza Haywood then serves the dual function of presiding deity and chief prize at this particular contest. Her physical endowments make her an appropriate judge of the contestants' prowess, just as her literary output, 'who in libellous Memoirs and novels reveal[s] the faults and misfortunes of both sexes, to the ruin or disturbance of public fame or private happiness', makes her the perfect prize for a competition between two Grub Street publishers:

Chetwood and Curll accept the glorious strife,
(Tho' one his son dissuades, and one his wife).
This on his manly confidence relies,
That on his vigour and superior size.
First Chetwood lean'd against his letter'd post;
It rose, and labour'd to a curve at most:
So Jove's bright bow displays its watry round,
(Sure sign, that no spectator shall be drown'd).
A second effort brought but new disgrace,
For straining more, it flies in his own face;

Thus the small jett which hasty hands unlock,
Spirts in the gard'ner's eyes who turns the cock.
Not so from shameless Curll: Impetuous spread
The stream, and smoking, flourish'd o'er his head.
So, (fam'd like thee for turbulence and horns,)
Eridanus his humble fountain scorns,
Thro' half the heav'ns he pours th'exalted urn;
His rapid waters in their passage burn.

(ll 159-176)

Nowhere is better illustrated not only Pope's close parallelism with Dryden's translation of *The Aeneid,* but also the comic-reductive effect of that parodic imitation. This is the Dryden/Virgil description of the two heroic gauntlet fighters:

One on his youth and pliant limbs relies:
One on his sinews and his giant size

(V.570-1)

Here is Pope's genital emendation.

This on his manly confidence relies,
That on his vigour and superior size.

The same mock-heroic blending of the sublime and the ridiculous is maintained throughout the description. Allusions to the poetry of Homer (Juno's bright bow), Virgil and Denham (the river Eridanus) are brought down to earth by the comic image of a garden hose as the unfortunate Chetwood pisses in his own face. Curll's more successful performance is annotated by a lengthy note parodying the pedantic editorial manner of Theobald or Bentley. According to this note, a manuscript variant offers the reading 'his rapid waters in their passage *glow*' instead of 'burn'. Despite the undoubted elegance of the word glow, and Pope's own fondness for it in *The Iliad,* the note assures us 'that *burn* is the proper word to convey an idea of what was said to be Mr Curll's condition at that time.' In other words, it implies that Curll has a venereal infection. The note continues with typical irony: 'But from that very reason I infer the direct contrary. For surely every lover of our author will conclude that he had more humanity than to insult a man on such a misfortune or calamity, which could never befal him purely by his *own fault,* but from an unhappy communication with another.'

Thus a number of sniping personal attacks are included in these lines which are not, however, significant in themselves but serve as part of a satiric texture which constantly debases heroic images and pretensions, reducing them to a comic level of schoolyard posturing, sexual misadventure and locker-room braggadocio. Just as Grub Street publishers like Curll and Chetwood vie with each other in debasing literary culture, so literary allusions and metaphors are correspondingly debased when describing their activities. The gap between their salacious pamphlets and 'real' literature is as wide as that between an Olympian trial and a schoolboy prank. The comic collision of these two worlds of allusion demonstrates how the formal strictures of satire can generate their own mythopoeic forces.

Snarling or Smiling

With their neo-classical love of codification, eighteenth-century writers were keen to distinguish between a variety of different forms and styles, all of which might now be lumped together promiscuously under the one generic heading—satire. One source of distinction was the disputed etymology of the word itself: 'Anything sharp or severe is called a satyr', stated Cocker's *English Dictionary* (1704), thus perpetuating the traditional derivation from *satyrus,* 'an hairy monster, like a horned man with goats feet . . . [hence] *satyre,* a kind of sharp and invective poem.' It was the essence of satire, as defined by this etymology, to be harsh, rough and biting; 'a tarte and carpyng kynd of verse'. But increasingly in the Augustan period literary theorists including Dryden were inclined to trace the origins of the term back not to *satyrus,* but to *satura,* as in the phrase *satura lanx,* a full dish. This etymological question was not merely a matter of pedantry, since it affected the attitude one took to the essential nature, and spelling, of satire itself. Satyre, as derived from *satyrus,* was essentially harsh: 'girding, biting, snarling, scourging, jerking, lashing, smarting, sharp, tart, rough . . .' (Poole).[23] Whereas satire, derived from *satura,* should be varied, a tasty dish to suit all palates, a sophisticated confection of sweet and sour: 'that *olla* or hotchpotch which is properly a satire'[24](Dryden). This latter form of satire was a much more civilised and social genre altogether; less violent, more pleasing. Similarly, nice distinctions were drawn, though perhaps more in theory than in practice, between several further antithetical pairs of definitions: rallery versus railing; smiling satire versus snarling satire; Horatian satire versus Juvenalian satire. In many cases these definitions overlapped. Thus Dryden used the distinction between rallery and railing to distinguish between the Horatian and Juvenalian styles: 'Juvenal has railed more wittily than Horace has rallied. Horace means to make his readers laugh, but he is not sure of his experiment. Juvenal always intends to move your indignation, and he always brings about his purpose.'[25] The same two classical authors were conventionally used to illustrate the distinctions between smiling and snarling satire. Thus Joseph Trapp wrote, 'Satire in *general,* is a poem design'd to reprove the Vices and Follies of Mankind: It is twofold: either the *jocose,* as that of *Horace;* or the *serious,* like that of *Juvenal.* . . . The one is pleasant and facetious: the other angry and austere: the one smiles; the other storms.'[26] According to an older English tradition, favoured by such Jacobean dramatists as Marston, Hall, Rowlands and Goddard, 'smiling satire' was a contradiction in terms: 'in soothe, 'tis not my liste/To make thee laugh, for I'm a satyrist'[27] (Goddard). The Jacobean satirist was a malcontent, determined to scourge the vices and corruptions of society. Pope, on the other hand, recognised a wide range of satiric styles from a gentle ridicule to a savage lampoon. The ambiguous pleasure of a gentle satire he described perfectly when he said of his own *Rape of the Lock,* ''Tis a sort of writing very like tickling'.[28] Swift, perhaps surprisingly, claimed to share this preference for subtle humour over savage indignation: 'Humour is certainly the best ingredient towards that kind of satire, which is most useful, and gives the least offence; which instead of lashing, laughs men out of their follies, and vices, and is the character which gives Horace the preference over Juvenal.'[29]

At this point clearly the usefulness of such prescriptive categories begins to break down, since both of these last two satirists could also use and defend a very different kind of satire. 'When you think of the world, give it one lash the more, at my request', declared Swift in a more typical mood; and for Pope in his later poems, satire became not a feather to tickle his audience, but a holy weapon, a hallowed scalpel to cut away corruption:

> O sacred weapon! left for Truth's defence,
> Sole dread of folly, vice and insolence!
> To all but Heav'n-directed hands deny'd,
> The muse may give thee, but the Gods must guide.[30]

For all the taxonomic specificity of theory, in practice one finds a considerable degree of eclecticism in the works of Augustan satirists. It is not that they ignore the formal categories and distinctions between

Horatian and Juvenalian models, but that often it is circumstances
which dictate a more or less serious tone. Also they recognised the ironic
benefits to be gained by unannounced shifts from a smiling to a snarling
tone; or from the provocative blending of rallery and railing. It is
perhaps indicative of this preference for an eclectic and empirical
approach to the questions of satiric taxonomy, that a favourite term to
describe the required quality of satiric wit was *raillery,* which hovered
conveniently between the railing of Juvenal and the rallery of Horace.

Perhaps the most important specific formal issue which divided
satirists was the matter of real names. Should satire be general and
universal, exposing only those vices which are common to all mankind;
or should it be specific and personal, holding up and exposing named
individuals to the ridicule and censure of their contemporaries and
posterity? Eloquent arguments were put forth on both sides of the
question. 'If men must not be told their faults,' wrote Gildon in 1694,
'they'll never mend 'em; and *general Reflections* will never do the
business, because the devilish good opinion ev'ry Man has of himself
furnishes him with an evasion from the last of general characters.'[31]
Swift agreed, declaring in the Preface to *The Battle of the Books* 'Satire
is a sort of glass, wherein beholders do generally discover everybody's
face but their own.' [32] Many years later, writing to Pope from Ireland,
where he had just had his first sight of *The Dunciad*, Swift insisted, 'I
would have the names of those scribblers printed indexically at the
beginning or the end of the poem, with an account of their works, for
the reader to refer to.' For, he explained, 'I have long observed that
twenty miles from London nobody understands hints, initial letters, or
town-facts and passages; and in a few years not even those who live in
London'[33] He need not have worried. Pope, too, in the later stages of
his career, was convinced that the sacred task of satire could only be
achieved by a fearless identification and exposure of the sinful: 'I am
afraid that all such writings and discourses as touch no man, will mend
no man,' he wrote to Gay in 1731.[34] Three years later he expanded this
belief: 'To reform and not to chastise, I am afraid, is impossible, and that
the best precepts, as well as the best laws, would prove of small use, if
there were no examples to enforce them. To attack vices in the abstract,
without touching persons, may be safe fighting indeed, but it is fighting
with shadows.'[35] It is worth noting Pope's explicit identification here of
satire with a kind of legal or judicial responsibility.

In this context a recent scholar has reminded us that eighteenth-
century legal punishments relied heavily upon two basic concepts: first,
the infliction of pain and, second, the public spectacle of these acts of

painful retribution: 'Punishment was public: it was directed in most cases at the body of the criminal; and it was meant not to reform or to correct the offender but to deter everyone, culprit and crowd alike, from criminal activity'.[36] This is the kind of quasi-judicial punishment that Pope intends in the pain and public exposure of the 'Sporus' portrait. And although the language of such satiric portraits may strike modern readers as cruel or extreme, they offer no match for the reality of the law's punishments. David Morris contrasts Titus Oates's 'punishment' by Dryden in the character of Corah in *Absalom and Achitophel,* with his real-life punishment from Lord Chief Justice Jeffreys.

> Jeffreys' sentence did not stop with provisions for public punishment on . . . five days but continued with an extraordinary provision for Oates's 'annual punishment'. Every year as long as he lived Oates was ordered—on appropriately commemorative dates—to stand in the pillory: on April 24 at Tyburn, on August 9 at Westminster Hall gate, on August 10 at Charing Cross, on August 11 at Temple Gate, and on September 2 at the Royal Exchange. What is most unusual about the annual progress through these stations of pain is the clarity with which it reveals how public punishment resembled a violent form of street theater. Like the paper over his head ('declaring your crimes'), Oates's body was meant to be read as a cautionary text. Jeffreys' ingenious punishment succeeded in transforming Oates into something like a living satire.[37]

The main voice raised loudly and repeatedly on the other side of this question of real names, was that of Addison. In *Spectator* No. 23 he launched the first of several attacks on slanderous satires:

> There is nothing that more betrays a base, ungenerous spirit, than the giving of secret stabs to a man's reputation. Lampoons and satires, that are written with wit and spirit, are like poison'd darts, which not only inflict a wound, but make it incurable . . . . It is impossible to enumerate the evils which arise from these Arrows that fly in the dark.[38]

For Addison the satirist is not a public-spirited judge, fairly and openly enquiring into the conduct of those in power, but a barbaric coward, a furtive, malicious and vengeful slanderer; exercising power without responsibility, spreading scandal to gratify personal spite. The satirist thus offends against all those tenets of polite behaviour, benign outlook and genteel conduct that *The Spectator* cherished. The utmost in the

way of social comedy that Addison would countenance was the finest
of fine raillery, aimed not at an individual but a type: In *Spectator* No.
34 (April 1711) he promised 'never to draw a faulty character which
does not fit at least a thousand people; or to publish a single paper,
that is not written in the spirit of benevolence, with love to Mankind.'
Finally, in *Spectator* No. 451, himself adopting the judicial metaphor,
Addison not only denied the right of any individual satirist to sit in
judgment like a magistrate and affect to pass sentence on his fellow-
citizens, but went so far as to describe the satiric sentences inflicted in
this way as themselves criminal acts:

> I cannot but look upon the finest strokes of satyr which are aimed
> at particular persons, and which are supported even with the
> appearance of truth, to be marks of an evil mind, and highly
> criminal in themselves. Infamy, like other punishments, is under
> the direction and distribution of the magistrate, and not of any
> private person.

It was, of course, precisely because of their scepticism at the
effectiveness—or impartiality—of the law in punishing highly placed
malefactors, that satirists like Pope wished to expose 'Crimes that
'scape or triumph o'er the law.'[39] In his later poems Pope saw himself
as the arbiter of an alternative tribunal from the Whig justice of the
courts under Walpole's administration:

> Hear this, and tremble! you, who 'scape the laws.
> Yes, while I live, no rich or noble knave
> Shall walk the world, in credit, to his grave.

Hence the name and identity which appears most prominently in
these later satires is that of Pope himself. He presents himself as a lone
crusader in the cause of virtue and truth; Pope *agonistes,* an em-
battled but fearless judge wielding with an awesome but unhesitant
authority the weapons of divine retribution:

> Yes, the last Pen for Freedom let me draw
> When Truth stands trembling on the edge of Law.[40]

For many modern readers the self-portrait which Pope creates in
these lines demonstrates an embarrassing and irritating vanity. But, by
placing himself centre stage in his own satires, Pope attempts to deny
Addison's charge of cowardice and irresponsibility. These are no

'secret stabs' or 'arrows that fly in the dark' but open, public accusations.

By contrast, the self-portraits which Swift composed in his satires are considerably more ambiguous and foxy. By which I do not imply that we should necessarily take Pope's idealised self-portraits as *true;* they are of course fictional constructs, versions of autobiography which serve an imaginative and rhetorical function in the adversarial structure of the satires. The 'strong antipathy of good to bad' becomes personified in the contrasting images between the dutiful filial Pope who rocks 'the cradle of reposing age' and the vile reptile Sporus, in Satanic posture 'half froth, half venom' who 'spits himself abroad'. Yet they are at least fictions in which Pope himself believed, and which he took as the embodiments of essential moral polarities. Swift's versions of autobiography are always more ambiguous and deceptive. Deliberate lies are interwoven with affectations of self-deprecation and indirect self-praise to create a teasing and ironic portrait. This is nowhere truer than in his *Verses on the Death of Dr Swift*. Towards the end of this poem he imagines an impartial commentator at the Rose tavern summing up his life and character. Among the many questionable claims advanced in this 'impartial' eulogy is this couplet:

> Yet malice never was his aim:
> He lash'd the vice but spar'd the name.
> (ll.459-60)

This would appear to be wrong—deliberately wrong, that is—on both counts. Not only does the poem in which this claim is made *itself* contain attacks on a dozen named individuals; but, even while composing this poem, Swift was simultaneously confiding to Lord Bathurst that 'revenge, malice, envy and hatred and all uncharitableness' provided the only stimulation for his work. In fact, Swift's attitude to the matter of real names varied according to the scope and purpose of each satire. While never reluctant to engage in *ad hominem* lampoons and 'libels', his major satires addressed themselves to wider and more general moral concerns. Those who labour to uncover the 'real' identity of Flimnap or Reidresal in the Voyage to Lilliput are in danger of falling into one of the many ironic traps with which Swift's satires are strewn.

Simply by adopting a 'no names' policy, however, a satirist could not ensure security from hostile reactions and false interpretations.

Not naming individuals brought its own dangers. 'Even those you touch not, hate you', Pope noted wryly.[41] General portraits could be misidentified by friends and enemies alike as Pope learned to his cost when his attack on 'Timon' in his *Epistle to Burlington* was generally taken to be based on the Duke of Chandos, despite Pope's vehement protests to the contrary. Not that such ambiguities always worked against the satirist's interests, though, since this element of doubt in the specific identity of a portrait could widen its application and increase public interest. 'Atossa' could be Sarah, Duchess of Marlborough or Katherine, Duchess of Buckingham; the vain patron Bufo (Latin for 'toad'), could be either Lord Halifax or Bubb Dodington. Often a deliberate ambiguity of this kind would be fostered, less to diminish the dangers of a personalised attack than to increase public speculation and fascination with the portrait. On the other hand, in the devious world of political satire, where any stray or ambiguous attribution might be seized on and exploited by an enemy, the use of named portraits did at least limit the damage possible from deliberately hostile misattributions.

For modern readers the problems posed by the use of real names in Augustan satires are not so much moral as practical. Who are all these people whose names litter the lines of *The Dunciad* and the pages of *A Tale of a Tub;* the Bentleys and Wootons, Theobalds, Curlls, Gildons Brevals, Cibbers and hosts more? And does it matter? How much does one need to know about them to understand the satire? The first point to remember is that—with the exception of simple Grub Street lampoons—any satire containing a portrait of a real person is actually creating its own fictionalised version of that person. This is not the same as saying—as some Victorian critics contended about Pope— that he simply misrepresented his opponents, lied about them or falsified their biographies. Rather it is an acknowledgement of the imaginative power of satire as an art which transforms local facts and incidents into universal images. Thus the Dunces of *The Dunciad,* although modelled on real people and bearing their names, are in fact characters of the poem; their beings are circumscribed by that work with its notes and Introduction. In attempting to understand their 'identities', it is important to see how they function in the poem, not in their 'real' lives outside the test.

Let us take the example of Theobald. The first thing that Pope does to distinguish the hero of his poem from the real-life Lewis Theobald is to spell his name as pronounced—Tibbald; or, more accurately, to play with his name (and identity) as if he himself were merely another of the variant texts that he took so much pride in correcting; Tibbald, Tibald, Tibbalds. Next, Tibbald's role as the mock-Aeneas of this mock *Aeneid* confers upon his character a whole range of obligations, though Pope is careful not to over-dignify his King Dunce by making the parallel with Aeneas too close. At those points where Pope's lines come closest to echoing Dryden's version of *The Aeneid,* it is often someone else's words that are reported by Aeneas. In Book I, Pope's hero bemoans the imminent destruction of Dulness's citadel in terms drawn from Books II and III of the *Aeneid*, where Aeneas describes the fall of Troy to Dido:

> Had heav'n decreed such works a longer date
> Heav'n had decreed to spare the Grubstreet state.

In the original, these were the words of Anchises, recalled by Aeneas:

> Had heav'n decreed that I should life enjoy,
> Heav'n had decreed to save unhappy Troy.[42]

Through these mock-heroic associations Tibbald acquires a twofold literary ancestry. The Anchises to his Aeneas, and hence his satiric 'father', being Elkanah Settle, the City poet (who was not, of course, the real father of the real Lewis Theobald). One might compare the creation of this mock-heroic ancestry with Fielding's device in *Jonathan Wild.* The biographical facts of the real-life Jonathan Wild, born in Wolverhampton, son of a carpenter were well known. But Fielding ignored all this and provided his Wild, a mock-heroic disciple of Greatness, with an appropriately heroic and completely fictitious ancestry stretching back to Wolfstan Wyld, 'who came over with Hengist' and including 'Wild, surnamed Longfinger' who 'flourished in the reign of Henry III'.[43] But, of course, Tibbald isn't only modelled on Aeneas. Milton's Satan provides another pattern; thus the opening of Book II: 'High in a gorgeous seat, that far outshone/Henley's gilt tub . . .' clearly echoes *Paradise Lost* (II. 1-2) 'High on a throne of royal state, that far/Outshone the wealth of Ormus and of Ind . . .'.

In addition to all this, the Tibbald of the poem is haunted and harried by a figure called Theobald, who appears as the author of several of the more pedantic notes to the poem. This Theobald, too, is of course another of Pope's fictional creations, but this further Theobald/Tibbald division between 'character' and 'editor' is part of

Pope's technique of undermining the identification of real life figures
with their fictional counterparts. While it remains true that many
elements in the fictional Tibbald's career are metaphorical elabor-
ations of literary and editorial features in the real-life Theobald's
works, the relationship is essentially literary rather than biographical.

The final proof of this is the ease with which Tibbald was replaced
by Cibber in the 1743 version of *The Dunciad*. For Pope the fortuitous
phonetic similarity between the two names solved what might
otherwise have been the most difficult part of the substitution. The
mock-heroic identity of the King Dunce role was so firmly
established that, although many appropriate minor alterations were
made, few descriptive changes were required. Great Tibbald, enthroned on his gorgeous seat is described thus:

> the proud Parnassian sneer
> The conscious simper, and the jealous leer,
> Mix on his look.

Great Cibber is described in exactly the same terms. The look, in other
words, goes with the role rather than the individual, and this is true of
much else in the poem.[44] This is not to say, however, that the
individuals don't matter. They do. But they matter as fictional
characters, not as biographical facts. These are not generalised
symbols but highly individualised fictional creations. To appreciate
the subtlety and depth of Pope's Tibbald it is necessary to attend to the
constant ironic interplay between poem and commentary. But it is
not necessary to go outside the work itself; that Tibbald is contained
within the world of Pope's satire. A study of the real-life Lewis
Theobald would be of as much, or as little, significance as a study of
John Dickens to an appreciation of Mr Micawber.

On other occasion names are used for their qualities as words,
their sonority or suffused puns, as much as for the identities they
proclaim. Following the urinating competition, the Dunces engage in
another childish sport to see who can make most noise.

> Twas chatt'ring, grinning, rumbling, jabb'ring all,
> And Noise and Norton; Brangling and Breval,
> Dennis and Dissonance; and captious Art,
> And snip-snap short, and Interruption smart.
>
> (ll. 229-32)

The names here become part of the general cacophony and were clearly chosen for their sound properties. 'And Noise and Blackmore' would hardly create the same effect, though in onomatopoeic lines elsewhere Pope makes clear his dislike of Blackmore's rumbling blank-verse epics. Naturally these names were not selected *solely* for their sound qualities; the alliterative association of Dennis with dissonance is also appropriate for this notoriously ill-tempered critic. What happens is that the individuals tend to merge into the sound, as if taken over by it. They are literally taken over by the ranting of their own rhetoric, and can only be differentiated by their various forms of din.

The case is similar with the 'mighty Mist'. Nathaniel Mist was the publisher of a Tory weekly paper, but his inclusion in *The Dunciad* owes more to the pun in his name than to his politics. When Tibbald announces, 'Yes, from this moment, mighty Mist! am thine!' (I.194) it signifies less a decision to write for the Tory press than an abandonment to the fogs of Dulness:

> All these and more, the cloud-compelling Queen
> Beholds thro' fogs that magnify the scene.
> (I. 77-8)

More (James Moore) ceases to be a person at all and becomes a pun, a printing error, a pseudonym, a phantom.

> She [the Goddess] form'd the image of well-bodied air,
> With pert-flat eyes she window'd well its head,
> A brain of feathers and a heart of lead,
> And empty words she gave, and sounding strain,
> But senseless, lifeless! Idol void and vain!
> Never was dash'd out, at one lucky hit,
> A Fool, so just a copy of a wit;
> So like, that critics said and courtiers swore,
> A wit it was, and call'd the phantom More.[45]

A lengthy note to these lines by Scriblerus 'proves' this More/Moore to be a mere plagiary—which was indeed the charge that Pope accused James Moore Smythe of committing. So once again the person *becomes* his own characteristic form of literary solecism. Tibbald becomes an editorial variant; Dennis becomes dissonance; Mo(o)re becomes a plagiarism. But in addition, Pope, whose satiric imagination throughout *The Dunciad* was clearly influenced by

Erasmus's *Praise of Folly* (Latin: *Encomium Moriae*), plays with the
More/Moriae pun just as Erasmus had done. Scriblerus quotes both
Erasmus's dedication of his book to Thomas More, and the Farewell,
'which may be our Author's to his plagiary. *Vale* More! & Moriam
tuam graviter defende. Adieu More, and be sure strongly to defend thy
own folly!'

After a while one realises that Pope can conjure as much satiric
magic out of a real name as out of any other noun. The difficulty for a
modern reader in appreciating these names is not that of knowing
who they 'really' are, but of keeping up with their bewildering
metamorphoses in his surreal imagination.

Political Satire

The use of real names was not the only— nor indeed the most
effective—way of designating individual satiric targets. One of the
advantages of the pervasive 'Augustan' iconography of the period was
that it afforded political satirists a ready-made system or code of
historical parallels that could be used to identify contemporary
targets while protecting the satirist from the reach of the libel laws.
Dryden's *Absalom and Achitophel* is an early example of this
technique, an extended series of satiric parallels with only the most
perfunctory pretence of historical authenticity more like a fancy-
dress pageant than a sustained analogy, hovering on the frontier
between political allegory and caricature.

Swift was particularly skilled in exploiting the potential of parallel
history in his political satires. In his *Examiner* papers, written on
behalf of Harley's Tory administration during 1710, he frequently
invoked Roman parallels to give an added force to his criticisms of
Whig grandees. In his 'Letter to Crassus' (*Examiner* No.27), Swift's
target is clearly the Duke of Marlborough, but the substitution of the
Roman general's name both disguises and dignifies the party-political
attack. In part the use of such Roman names was a subterfuge to evade
prosecution; in part it was an ironic assault upon the pseudo-
Augustan pretensions of the Whig nobility; but in part too it
represented a genuine attempt to invoke a sense of what were thought
of as Roman values—modesty, decorum, courage and integrity—in
contrast with their modern British travesties. This is most clearly seen
in Swift's *Examiner* No.16. The Whigs were loud in their complaints
against the alleged Tory ingratitude towards the victorious General

Marlborough, so Swift presents two contrasting bills, the first of British 'ingratitude', the other of Roman gratitude. In the British balance sheet we find Woodstock, Blenheim, gifts of jewels, pensions, and sinecures totalling 'a good deal above half a million of money', which has already been granted to the Duke, and 'all this is but a trifle in comparison of what is untold'. On the Roman side we find a triumphal arch, a statue, a sacrificial bull, a crown of laurel and some frankincense. In a meticulous display of fairness, the *Examiner* costs every item, from the laurel crown (2d) to 'casual charges at the triumph' (£150). Yet still the Roman bill only amounts to £944 11s 10d.[46] This is one of Swift's most accomplished uses of statistics to 'prove' a satiric point. The 'impartial' implication is that figures cannot lie, while the playful inclusion of such details as the twopenny laurel crown emphasises the gross discrepancy between the austere Roman ideal and the vulgar British imitation.

One politician achieved such a towering reputation for political management and patronage—otherwise known as corruption—in the two decades between 1722 and 1742, that it was possible for satirists to attack him without using either his name or an historical alias. It was sufficient merely for satirists to refer to a 'Great Man', or sometimes even simply to 'a statesman' for an audience to identify the target as Walpole. Gay's *Beggar's Opera* has always been accepted as an attack on Walpole, a fact implicitly acknowledged by Walpole himself when he banned the sequel, *Polly,* from the stage. Yet Walpole is never mentioned in the opera; nor can any one of the central characters, Macheath, Peachum or Lockit, be interpreted as a caricature of the Prime Minister. This lack of satiric specificity has sometimes puzzled commentators on the play. 'Does Walpole think you intended an affront to him in your opera?' Swift wrote in a letter to Gay, adding, 'pray God he may'.[47] In our own times, too, some well-informed readers have expressed sharp differences of opinion concerning the specific objects of Gay's political satire in the opera.[48]

In this case the very absence of a direct *ad hominem* attack is part of the subtlety of Gay's satiric technique. At one point the gang leader Peachum runs through his blacklist of villains to be sent to the gallows next sessions and concludes with the name 'Robin of Bagshot, alias Gorgon, alias Bluff Bob, alias Carbuncle, alias Bob Booty' (I.iii). A contemporary audience would have recognised in this list of soubriquets several of the nicknames used for Walpole in ballads and lampoons, though the character himself never appears. In fact, *The Beggar's Opera* is less concerned with pillorying an individual than with indicting a political system and with identifying the commercial expropriation of moral values. The Scriblerians easily adapted the mock-heroic technique of comic miniaturisation into an effective form of political *reductio ad absurdum*. In Lilliput the contests and dissensions between Whigs and Tories are transformed into vehement disputes between the high heels and the low heels; while controversies of principle and doctrine are reduced to the overwhelming question: which end of the egg should be broken open. In a similar spirit of satiric reductionism Gay transforms statesmen into gang leaders. In the Preface to his earlier burlesque comedy *The What D'Ye Call It,* he had ironically interpreted the pastoral convention which offers an idealised identification of shepherds with princes, as the basis for some satiric mock-egalitarianism. 'The sentiments of princes and clowns have not in reality that difference which they seem to have', he declares. As we shall see, Gay's poetry offers a series of comic and satiric versions of pastoral themes, constantly reducing courtiers to clowns, princes to peasants and statesmen to pickpockets and thieves. It was a formula enthusiastically imitated by Fielding in *Jonathan Wild* where the careers and ambitions of 'Great Men' (politicians) and 'prigs' (thieves) are constantly compared. But the metaphorical reach of these mock-heroic formulas means that these comparisons are not simply—or simplistically—two-dimensional. It is not a simple matter of comparing Walpole with Jonathan Wild, or Whitehall with Newgate. The classical echoes implicit in the mock-heroic style evoke a third level of comparison against which both politicians and prigs are to be judged. Fielding's Jonathan Wild consciously models himself on such classical examples of greatness as Alexander the Great and Julius Caesar. At school, we are told, 'He was a passionate admirer of heroes, particularly of Alexander the Great' (I.iii). In *The Beggar's Opera* the quarrel between Peachum and Lockit (II.x) over the question of honour was, according to one authority, 'so well understood at that time to allude to a recent quarrel between the two ministers Lord Townshend and Sir Robert, that the House was in convulsions of applause.' But behind this political allusion lay a literary one, in the quarrel between Brutus and Cassius in *Julius Caesar,* though Swift for one did not pick up the hint. 'I did not understand that the scene of Peachum and Lockit's quarrel was an imitation of one between Brutus and Cassius till I was told it', he confessed.[49] In other words, this form of political mock-heroic produces a two-way pressure, a dual perspective on the contemporary target. Above the modern statesman hovers the model of classical greatness, embodied by an Alexander or Augustus, a Brutus or Aeneas; while beaneath him swarms the underworld of thieves and whores whose activities parody his pretensions. Above Walpole is Alexander, beneath him Jonathan Wild; just as above Theobald there is Aeneas and beneath him the fairground freaks of Smithfield. The imaginative force of this form of satire lies in its ability to create scenes which constantly remind us of this dual perspective.

By far the majority of the political 'satires' of the period scarcely merit so dignified a title. Of the more than three thousand satirical pieces which survive from the years 1660 to 1678, the greatest number are ephemeral lampoons, crude squibs, ballads and broadsheets, repetitive, formulaic party-political invective, unrelieved by wit or imagination. Even those that rise above the predictable level of scatological similes and stereotyped sentiments of day-to-day political in-fighting, often disguise a straightforward party line under a bluster of Augustan objectivity and Olympian impartiality. Several of Swift's own political satires, despite his fierce protestations of strict impartiality and independence, are little more than propaganda for Harley's Tory ministry. In his first *Examiner* (2 November 1710) Swift declared, 'It is a practice I have generally followed, to converse in equal freedom with the deserving men of both parties.' Later he claimed to offer 'nothing more than the common observations of a private man' and asserted that, far from rewarding him, the ministry had 'never so much as sent to the printer to enquire who I was.'[50] These claims are frankly disingenuous, since it was Harley himself who had recruited Swift to write the *Examiner* as a champion of government policy. It is not easy, however, to decide how far Swift disbelieved his own claims of journalistic independence. It was important to him that he should not appear as a mere hireling scribbler, like the Whigs whom he derided. For the most part Harley was careful to sustain this illusion; it was an uncharacteristic lapse when, in July 1711, he sent Swift £50 for his services. Swift was deeply humiliated by this offer and angrily refused the money.

It has become common in recent years to discuss Swift's satires in terms of a narrative persona, and it may perhaps be useful to consider these early political satires too in this way. By which I do not mean the persona which Swift assiduously promotes as the 'author' of these pamphlets, that is the character of the impartial observer of affairs, discoursing disinterestedly above the heads of the squabbling party factions. I am thinking rather of the persona of the advocate, the man who argues a client's case with all the rhetorical force and guile at his disposal, yet who remains personally detached from its outcome. Such a role, more dignified than that of the Grub Street hack writing for money, and more independent than the party-man writing from prejudice, would seem to characterise Swift's position in many of these pamphlets. So, while it would be both rash and misleading to suggest that the indignation so forcefully expressed in many of Swift's political works is ever merely synthetic, there remains a sense sometimes of another 'Swift' watching and applauding with detached amusement, the satiric *coups* of this polemical persona.

The actual political outlook of the so-called 'Tory' satirists has become something of a vexed issue, and a detailed study of this subject lies outside the scope of this book. The conventional view, offered by Bredvold, Orwell and others, is that certain instinctive 'Tory' allegiances to ideals of authority, monarchy and hierarchy, which had been reinforced by lurid recollections of the turmoil of the Civil War, were subsequently undermined by an intense dislike of the new Hanoverian dynasty. The Tories were out of power from the death of Queen Anne in 1714 till the accession of George III in 1760. During that time their traditional political assumptions and attitudes underwent considerable revisions in reaction to the apparent monopoly of political power wielded by Walpole.

In 1680 the Tories were the Court party, the defenders of the royal prerogative, while the Whigs were the champions of Parliament against the powers of the executive. By the 1730s, under Walpole, all that had changed. Now it was the Whigs who were sustaining the rights and privileges of the Hanoverian Court, while the Tories fought to defend the 'country' interest and to preserve the independence of Parliament from the influence of royal patronage. The ambiguous significance of the party labels 'Whig' and 'Tory' during this period helps to account for some of the controversy concerning the political affiliations of individual satirists. Swift's politics, for example, have recently become the subject for fierce scholarly debate. According to F.P. Lock, Swift was a 'natural Tory' with a lifelong belief in order, hierarchy, stability and authority. J.A.Downie, on the other hand, sees Swift as a champion of the 'old Whig' tradition of individual liberty, and largely endorses Swift's own claim that 'Fair liberty was all his cry'.[51]

Both views are in a sense correct. The problem for traditional defenders of hierarchy such as Pope and Swift was that they were confronted by an authority which they could not respect. Defenders of monarchy, they were faced with a monarch—George II—with an avowed contempt for all those cultural and political values which monarchy should sustain. Champions of parliamentary freedom, they were appalled by a ministry which, in their view, devalued its own authority by being in the pockets of 'moneyed men' and Whig grandees. Hence the appeal of an alternative system of uncorrupted authority represented by the model of Augustan Rome.

Even that model, however, was not without its own ambiguities and ironies. Recent scholars have emphasised the 'dark' side of the Augustan parallel. While on the one hand it was portrayed as an era of political stability and flourishing literary achievements, on the other it could be viewed as a period of decadence and corruption. In a letter to Pope, Swift wrote of the first Augustan Age as an epoch of cultural greatness:

> I have often endeavoured to establish a friendship among all men of genius, and would fain have it done. They are seldom above three or four cotemporaries and if they could be united would drive the world before them; I think it was so among the poets in the time of Augustus, but envy and party and pride have hindred it among us.
>
> (20 September 1723)[52].

De Quincey, however, concentrated on the dark side, when he commented that 'the cruelties of Augustus were perhaps equal in atrocity to any which are recorded.' Even these ambiguities could serve the satirists' purposes, as Claude Rawson has argued:

> The discreditable elements of Augustus's traditional reputation, so far from being mainly fuel for anti-Augustan sentiments, were themselves a positive strength where panegyric needed to carry a latent reservation or monitory note, or where a high political idealism needed to be checked by a recognition of harsher realities.[53]

The long shadows of parallel history cast by the first Augustan Age represent not some simple utopian alternative but a complex pattern of political comparisons.

The literary schizophrenia which often resulted from this combination of belief in monarchy with contempt for the monarch, is perhaps best illustrated by Swift's frequent oscillation between

ideals of libertarianism and authoritarianism. He who attacked
Walpole's manipulation of Parliament through royal patronage as
bribery and corruption had openly applauded Harley's creation of
twelve new peers in 1712 in order to pack the House of Lords and pass
the government's business. He who objected vehemently to
Walpole's attempts at press censorship was the man who had called,
throughout Harley's administration, for just such repressive measures
to curb the scandalous libels of the Whig pamphleteers. In politics, as
we know, general principles are always in some tension with local
interests, and the political satires of the Augustan period are full of
reminders of this teasing relationship.

It should also be remembered that the political world of the
eighteenth century was remarkably intimate and circumscribed, so
that personalities would often exert a considerable influence on both
policies and principles. Swift in the period from 1708 to 1710 was
torn between the Whig group led by Halifax and the Tory group led by
Harley; in the end it seems that it may well have been the different
personal treatment that he received from these two men, as much as
any matter of principle, that decided his allegiance. In the same way, a
few years later, Pope was undecided between the Whigs' literary
clique presided over by Addison, and the Tory group, now led by
Swift. Again it was largely Swift's assiduity in cultivating the younger
poet's friendship at that time which influenced Pope's political
orientation. Both men of course, throughout their lives, denied
belonging to either 'faction'. Swift described the party-man thus: 'He
hath neither thoughts, nor actions, nor talk, that he can call his own,
but all conveyed to him by his leader, as wind is through an organ. The
nourishment he receives hath been not only *chewed,* but *digested*
before it comes into his mouth.'[54] Pope made a positive virtue of his
own political ambiguity:

> In moderation placing all my Glory,
> While Tories call me Whig, and Whigs a Tory.[55]

Given this ambiguity or, as they would see it, even-handedness of
approach, it may be useful, instead of concentrating on specifically
political issues, to examine a range of satirical responses to underlying
social changes which shaped the politics of the period. Apart from
their abiding concern wth ministerial corruption, satirists were
greatly exercised by two related forms of subversion which seemed to
threaten the stability of society. One was the misuse and apparent

decay of the language; the other, the growth of a capitalist culture, serviced by banks, joint-stock companies and paper money. I call these related phenomena since both money and language are linked by the central concept of *currency.*

Those who, like Pope, opposed paper money and clung to a gold standard of known intrinsic monetary values had clear affinities with those, like Swift, who wished to fix the terms of language 'for ever'. Critics of linguistic corruption often expressed themselves in terms of coin-clipping, and *vice versa*. Chesterfield described how his 'fair country-women', 'take a word, and change it, like a guinea into shillings for pocket-money, to be employed on the several occasional purposes of the day.'[56] The satirists were not alone in wishing to see some kind of linguistic Bretton-Woods to put a stop to this process of devaluation. But both Locke at the start of the century and Johnson fifty years later were equally contemptuous of such Utopian desires. 'To enchain syllables', Johnson wrote emphatically in his Preface to the *Dictionary,* 'and to lash the wind are equally undertakings of pride, unwilling to measure its desires by its strength'. The marketplace must settle both linguistic and financial values; there was no supreme court of linguistic jurisdiction with authority to oversee usage. Yet to Swift the idea of sanctioning usage to determine meaning implied enfranchising the mob to pervert language in a hand-to-mouth process of devaluation. His *Proposal for Correcting, Improving and Ascertaining the English Tongue* (1712) aimed at restricting this anarchic democratic power of 'one man, one voice' by 'fixing our language for ever'. The irony of this authoritarian attempt is that Swift thereby aligns himself with the materialists, like the bishops Sprat and Wilkins of the Royal Society, whom his satires elsewhere constantly ridicule. Indeed, the contradiction between his instinctive belief in intellectual freedom, and his equally instinctive defence of the benefits of social conformism, are vividly illustrated in his ridicule of linguistic reformers in the Academy of Lagado:

Many of the most Learned and Wise adhere to the new scheme of expressing themselves by Things, which hath only this Inconvenience attending it; that if a Man's Business be very great, and of various Kinds, he must be obliged in Proportion to carry a greater Bundle of Things upon his Back, unless he can afford one or two strong servants to attend him. I have often beheld two of those Sages almost sinking under the Weight of their Packs, like Pedlars among us; who when they met in the Streets would lay down their Loads, open their Sacks, and hold Conversation for an Hour together; then put up their Implements, help each other to resume their Burthens, and take their Leave.

Swift makes fun of this absurdly materialistic 'scheme' for fixing language, and thereby reduces Sprat's recommendation that members of the Royal Society should concentrate their philosophical investigations on things rather than words, to a kind of grotesque pantomime. This is truly an example of 'enchaining syllables'. Yet Swift can offer no realistic alternative to suggest how language may be more acceptably controlled. The crucial point about the currencies of language and finance is that they are enabling forces; they are the fluids which animate a society and make it dynamic. Yet as currencies they acknowledge no master, and are at the service of the highest bidder, whether philosopher or politician, Man of Ross or Jonathan Wild. Defoe saluted this enabling power of money:

O Money, Money! What an influence hast thou on all the affairs of the quarrelling, huffing part of this world, as well as upon the most plodding part of it! Without thee parliaments may meet, and councils sit, and Kings contrive, but it will all be to no purpose, their councils and conclusions can never be put into execution! Thou raisest armies, fightest battles, fittest out fleets, takest towns, kingdoms, and carries on the great affairs of the war; All power, all policy is supported by thee, even vice and virtue act by thy assistance; by thee all the great things in the world are done. Thou makest heroes, and crown'st the actions of the mighty; By thee in one sense, Kings reign, armies conquer, princes grow great, and nations flourish.[57]

By contrast, the pictures drawn by Swift and Pope celebrate a *dis*abling force in society. Swift pictures conversations fatally hampered by these pedlars' packs full of things. Pope, in his *Epistle to Bathurst,* reduces bank-bills back to their collateral objects, and his imagery introduces a vein of surrealistic fantasy.

> Astride his Cheese Sir Morgan might we meet,
> And Worldly crying coals from street to street.
>
> (ll.49-50)

For Pope, paper credit is like an Aeolist fantasy—insubstantial, yet of potentially limitless powers. A crisp bank-bill sanitises and disguises all those awkward realities of property and power for which it stands as cipher. The form is ludicrously out of proportion with the value, and it is this mock-heroic discrepancy which frequently provides the satirists with their best effects. A bank-bill is adaptable to all men's wishes and ruling passions; yet it is out of touch with reality, with *things*. It is a promise written upon the air, and will stand as readily a cipher for a million as for a hundred pounds. It is an image of anarchy to be so frail and yet so powerful; this discrepancy violates those natural laws of harmony so dear to the classical mind.

> Pregnant with thousands flits the Scrap unseen,
> And silent sells a King, or buys a Queen.

In Swift's *Drapier's Letters* one finds a similar picture of a society disabled by the damming up of its currency. Swift imagines that if Wood's inferior half-pence were allowed to circulate in Ireland, they would soon drive out all the country's gold and silver:

> The common Weight of these HALF-PENCE is between four and five to an Ounce; suppose five, then three Shillings and four Pence will weigh a Pound, and consequently Twenty Shillings will weigh Six Pounds Butter Weight. Now there are many hundred Farmers who pay Two hundred Pounds a Year Rent: Therefore when one of these Farmers comes with his Half-Year's Rent, which is One hundred Pound, it will be at least Six hundred Pound weight, which is Three Horses Load.[58]

However, while Swift's imagery of horses laden with rent money has clear similarities with Pope's fantasy of gambling clubs blockaded with wagers of hops and hogs, the underlying themes of these two satires point in diametrically opposed directions. Swift's satire, addressed to a readership of shopkeepers, merchants and craftsman, exploits the notion of free trade as a symbol of political independence and a healthy society. His exaggerated portrait of a society reduced to barter with sackloads of brass farthings is a graphic metaphor for the effects of political corruption and profiteering by absentees. For Pope, on the other hand, this magical disabling process whereby money is reduced to its collateral origins in hops and hogs is a form of moral awakening, a sobering dose of reality to chase away the over-heated fantasies released by paper money. He presents paper credit as a volatile contagion, feeding the vanities and vices of weak minds.

It is highly revealing that these two Scriblerian satirists should employ the same metaphorical formula for such divergent purposes, since it reminds us that we should not seek for any consistent or clearly defined political 'line' in their writings. Both men were fascinated by certain antithetical formulations, and the dynamic charge in their works often derives from a rapid alternating tension between the sublime and the ridiculous, freedom and control, the mind and the body. Images of volatility and Aeolist idealism alternate with images of leaden dulness and corporeal bathos. Often a materialist analogy will be used to deflate some visionary pretension, as when the 'inspiration' of the Aeolists is transformed into a grotesque pantomime of 'several hundreds linked together in a circular chain, with every man a pair of bellows applied to his neighbour's breech'.[59]

Elsewhere, though, the muddy antics of Pope's Dunces offer not a correction but a distortion of an ideal. Their vulgar and obscene displays befoul the heroic classical models which they parody. So there is no simple or uniform way of interpreting the contrasts between high and low, mind and body, in their satires. Instead, what we notice is a consistent tendency to view all human experience on a sliding scale between balanced and polarised extremes. Throughout most of Pope's writing one can detect the notion of a grand providential antithesis, most frequently expressed in the concise paradoxical formula *concordia discors*. The prose, just as much as the verse of the period, expresses through its balanced and symmetrical phrasing a system of values based on comparison rather than revelation. When an Augustan writer offers us a maxim ('True Wit is Nature to advantage dress'd'; 'Happiness is a perpetual possession of being well deceived') we instinctively hold our breath, waiting for the qualification or irony in the following line that will restore this lonely assertion to its appropriate niche in a dialectical balance. Even the aphorisms of Johnson, too often regarded as a man of maxims, function not like the epigrams of Wilde as brilliant one-liners, but as rhetorical overtures to a synthetical and moral analysis. An emphatic proposition such as, 'Nothing can please many and please long but just representations of general nature', is weighed and qualified in a series of balancing clauses in succeeding sentences. And the most characteristically Johnsonian judgements are all expressed in terms of comparisons: 'Human life is everywhere a state in which much is to be endured, and little to be enjoyed'; 'Marriage has many pains, but celibacy has no pleasures.'[60]

It follows that we should consider the politics of the Augustan satirists less in terms of party labels than through the expression of certain instinctive patterns of association or antithesis. Political question cannot be divorced from literary, cultural and moral preoccupations; those perennial tensions between the individual and society, liberty and authority, conscience and consensus are presented as symptomatic of deeper ambivalences in human nature which find their most tormented expression in the Houyhnhnms and Yahoos.

THE RHETORIC OF FINAL SOLUTIONS

I would like to conclude this section by returning to a question raised in the previous chapter: what, for the modern reader, is the literary significance of eighteenth-century political satire? In an attempt to offer at least a partial answer to this question, I should like to contrast two of the most well-known and widely read of eighteenth-century political satires—Swift's *Modest Proposal* (1729) and Defoe's *Shortest Way with Dissenters* (1702).

I have often tried the experiment of presenting Defoe's *Shortest Way with Dissenters* as an anonymous piece of polemic to a group of students who are ignorant of its status and 'meaning'. On the whole, rather less than half the students take the pamphlet 'seriously' as a genuine recommendation of a policy of extermination. The others sense something 'ironic' in the work. When pressed to identify this irony and indicate its specific manifestation in the text, they will usually point to such a passage as the following, with its grotesque animal imagery, describing the tone of brutal, gloating menace as repulsively exaggerated and hyperbolic:

'Tis cruelty to kill a snake or a toad in cold blood, but the poison of their natures makes it a charity to our neighbours to destroy those creatures, not for any personal injury received, but for prevention; not for the evil they have done, but the evil they may do.

Serpents, toads, vipers &c. are noxious to the body, and poison the sensitive life; these poison the soul, corrupt our posterity, ensnare our children, destroy the vitals of our happiness, our future felicity, and contaminate the whole mass.

Shall any law be given to such wild creatures: Some beasts are for sport, and the huntsmen give them advantages of ground; but some are knocked on head by all possible ways of violence and surprise.

I do not prescribe fire and faggot, but as Scipio said of Carthage, *Delenda est Carthago,* they are to be rooted out of this nation, if ever we will live in peace, serve God, or enjoy our own.

Such a reaction undoubtedly does credit to the humanity and moral sensitivity of the students who express it; however, it less admirable as a demonstration of literary critical skill. Compare Defoe's language of serpents, toads and vipers with this polemical description of a subhuman species:

> The sub-man—that creature which looks as though biologically it were of absolutely the same kind, endowed by nature with hands, feet and a sort of brain, with eyes and mouth—is nevertheless a totally different, a fearful creature, is only an attempt at a human being, with a quasi-human face, yet in mind and spirit lower than any animal. Inside this being a cruel chaos of wild, unchecked passions: a nameless will to destruction, the most primitive lusts, the most undisguised vileness. A sub-man—nothing else! . . . And this underworld of sub-men found its leader: the eternal Jew![61]

This passage is taken from a tract issued by Nazi SS headquarters, and its violent language of racial purification is typical of the work of most of the leading Nazi propagandists. In 1936 *Der Sturmer* looked forward to a worldwide cleansing operation: 'The mobilization of the German people's will to destroy the bacillus lodged in its body is a declaration of war on all Jews throughout the world. Its final result will decide the problem whether the world is to be redeemed by German virtues or to perish by the Jewish poison'. Again, in 1938, *Der Sturmer* described the Jews: 'bacteria, vermin, and pests cannot be tolerated. For reasons of cleanliness and hygiene we must make them harmless by killing them off'.[62] Hitler himself was obsessed by the notion of the Jewish 'virus'. 'The discovery of the Jewish virus', he told Himmler in 1942, 'is one of the greatest revolutions that have taken place in the world. The battle in which we are engaged today is of the same sort as the battle waged, during the last century, by Pasteur and Koch. How many diseases have their origin in the Jewish virus!'[63]

Now when we re-read Defoe's description of the Dissenters as noxious vermin, poisoning the sensitive life of the nation, the phrases may seem rather less exaggerated and sensational. For the language of hygiene, purification and cleansing is common to both campaigns, and we know only too well that the Nazis were not engaging in irony or hyperbole. The violence of their vocabulary was meant as an incitement to, not an indictment of, a corresponding violence of political action. Yet what is there in the language to distinguish between the genocidal earnestness of Streicher and the cautionary irony of Defoe? Hyperbole of itself is clearly not sufficient to signal a lack of seriousness; nor, regrettably, is the advocacy of genocide always merely a form of sick joke. Here is Goebbels, at the Nuremburg party rally of 1937:

> Europe must see and recognise the danger . . . We shall point fearlessly to the Jew as the inspirer and originator, the one who profits from these dreadful catastrophes. . . . Look, there is the world's enemy, the destroyer of civilisations, the parasite among the peoples, the son of Chaos, the incarnation of evil, the ferment of decomposition, the demon who brings about the degeneration of mankind.[64]

Rhetorical exaggeration here reaches a pitch of apocalyptic intensity. The imagery performs a tattoo of dark and light forces, civilisation and chaos. The demagogue is a hero of racial purity, wielding the surgeon's scalpel and the crusader's lance against a dark, inchoate verminous mass of poison and contagion. Violence becomes noble and holy, and murder an affirmation of life and health. Defoe's persona, too, has a demagogue's skill in manipulating and nursing a reaction of outrage into hysteria:

> If the gallows instead of the counter, and the gallies instead of fines, were the reward of going to a conventicle to preach or hear, there would not be so many sufferers, the spirit of martyrdom is over; they that will go to church to be chosen sheriffs and mayors, would go to forty churches rather than be hanged.

The neat rhetorical pairing of gallows and gallies; the sneering aside concerning the hypocritical dissenting practice of 'occasional conformity', and the comically exact exaggeration 'forty churches', all demonstrate an accomplished skill in political propaganda.

Placed beside these Nazi tracts, the language of Defoe's *Shortest Way* seems not exaggerated and extreme but modest and reasonable. Its anger proceeds from grievances which are eloquently described; its fears are grounded upon historical precedents which are also graphically expounded. By contrast with this controlled polemic, the Aryan fantasies of Goebbels and Streicher seem like grotesque and macabre examples of self-parody. Yet tragically we know that their savage melodrama was transformed into a hideous reality. The barbarity of a political creed is, unfortunately, no obstacle to its popularity.

What internal literary evidence then is there in this tract which recommends the extermination or imprisonment of all Dissenters to suggest that Defoe, a Dissenter himself, may not entirely have 'meant' all that he seems to say in it? There is an obvious comparison to be made with Swift's *Modest Proposal*. It is often asserted that Swift's satiric suggestion for solving the economic problems of Ireland by a policy of cannibalism deceives the reader with its earnest well-intentioned tone and plausible financial arguments. I have to say, however, that when attempting the same practical 'unseen' experiment on a group of students, I have never yet encountered one who did not identify the pamphlet as ironic. In part this may be on account of Swift's general reputation as a satirist, so that even those students who have not read *A Modest Proposal* are alerted to expect some form of irony or deception. But, more importantly, I feel it confirms that Swift's satiric strategy in this work is significantly different from Defoe's in *The Shortest Way*. Swift goes to considerable trouble to build up a coherent character for his Modest Proposer. He is not completely obtuse to the hideous implications of his proposal, and there is a nervous cough in his voice when he hopes it will 'not be liable to the least objection'. We sense a guilty conscience in his stereotyped declarations of humanity which entreat us into a conspiracy of silence concerning the reality of what is proposed. His language shifts between the cattle market and the counting-house, but the real note of obscenity occurs when he begins to introduce the language of luxury, describing the cooked babies as tasty dainties to tempt jaded English appetites: 'a young healthy child, well nursed, is at a year old a most delicious, nourishing and wholesome food, whether stewed, roasted, baked or boiled, and I make no doubt that it will equally serve in a fricassee or a ragout.' Yet at two points in the pamphlet Swift clearly and deliberately violates the integrity of the narrative voice so carefully created. The first is when, acknowledging that this food will be 'somewhat dear', he suggests it will be 'very proper for landlords, who, as they have already devoured most of the parents, seem to have the best title to the children.' This is far too direct and bold a comment for the Proposer, whose tone otherwise is obsequious and acquiescent. The other is when he declares: 'Therefore let no man talk to me of other expedients' and proceeds to list ten practical expedients for remedying Ireland's economic plight, all of which had been championed by Swift himself in a series of pamphlets during the preceding nine years. At these two points we clearly hear Swift's voice bursting through the character of his persona; and any 'belief' we may have been tempted to grant to the seriousness of the proposal is dissipated.

Swift was too consummate an ironist not to have recognised the effect of these intrusions, which immediately alert us to another level of interpretation, a voice behind the narrative voice. *A Modest Proposal* and *The Shortest Way*, for all their similarities as ironic defences of genocide, illustrate two very different methods of political satire. One possible tactic for the satirist is to set about the deliberate deception of an audience. According to Kierkegaard, the true end of irony was not utility but the private satisfaction of the ironist. 'Should he wholly succeed in leading people astray, perhaps to be arrested as a suspicious character', he wrote, 'the ironist has attained his wish.'[65] This was exactly Defoe's fate after the publication of *The Shortest Way* on 1 December 1702. Its purpose was to satirise the high Tory hints conveyed in Dr Henry Sacheverell's sermon, preached at Oxford in June, which had urged the Church to 'hang out the bloody flag of defiance against the Dissenters'. However, Defoe's plan misfired. His pamphlet was hailed by Tories as a forthright expression of their secret desires and condemned by the Dissenters as a vicious and inflammatory attack. Both sides apparently failed to discern any irony in his creation of the persona of a High Church zealot, and Defoe was arrested and imprisoned for sedition. Yet Kierkegaard is surely wrong to assume that the private satisfaction of the ironist in deceiving his audience is necessarily at odds with utility. The paradoxical triumph of Defoe's irony in this pamphlet is achieved at the expense of his audience; by fanning their prejudices and reinforcing their stereotypes, his satire had the political effect of bringing this issue to a head. The effect of this kind of irony works like a hoax or practical joke. The satiric impact is contained not in the reading of the text but in the political follow-through; in those feelings of foolishness, discomfiture and political exposure which resulted from the subsequent realisation by High Church enthusiasts for this pamphlet, that they had been 'had'.

Swift too was a great practical joker; many of his literary satires had their origins in April Fools' Day pranks or 'bites'. On one occasion he placed an advertisement in the *London Post Boy* for a totally fictitious auction of books and prints to be held at a shop in the Strand on 1 April, apparently for the simple delight of watching a group of frustrated bibliophiles gather for this non-event. His Bickerstaff papers too developed out of the most elaborate of his April Fool 'bites' at the expense of the almanac-maker John Partridge. Tricks of this

kind reveal a curiously childlike pleasure in teasing and deception that
lies at the heart of many of Swift's more sophisticated ironic strategies.
Yet, despite appearances, *A Modest Proposal* is not a 'bite'. Instead, it
works by a kind of double-bluff, pretending to try to deceive us, but
actually flattering our intellectual powers of discrimination as we
identify the mollifying tones and plausible arguments ostensibly
calculated to tempt us into cannibalism.

In fact, the satire here works not by deception but by confrontation,
drawing our attention to a violent analogy. The effects of English
economic policies towards Ireland had reduced that country to such a
state of destitution that its only saleable commodity appeared to be its
people, as slaves to the West Indies, mercenaries for the armies of France
or as oven-ready delicacies for the tables of the great in England. The
literary shock-effect of the satire works at the level of metaphor and
analogy. We are not meant to be deceived into accepting the proposals,
but roused to indignation by its daring. Anger at government policy
mingles with admiration for Swift's ingenious wit. The following year
Swift's friend in England Lord Bathurst sent him a facetious letter in
praise and imitation of the *Modest Proposal*. A father of nine children,
Bathurst wrote that it was 'reasonable the youngest should raise
fortunes for the eldest' or, that in the case of twins, 'the selling of one
might provide for the other.'[66] Several more jokes of this kind indicate
that Bathurst had relished the wit of Swift's satire, but remained
relatively unaffected by its political message.

Yet Bathurst should not be too readily accused of political
insensitivity. Unlike the *Draper's Letters, A Modest Proposal* is not a
campaigning work, a call to arms or a programme of action. Its satiric
impact is contained within the text; its political effect is literary rather
than practical. The brilliant intermingling of horror and delight which
Swift achieves—horror at the suggestion, and delight at the confident
irony of its treatment—turn this pamphlet into a literary masterpiece.
Defoe's work on the other hand, viewed as a piece of literary irony was,
and often still is regarded as a failure. Modern readers, not so much
deceived as impatient, round on Defoe, accusing him of clumsiness,
incompetence, naivety and a fundamental failure to understand the
ironist's craft. Yet as a political work, Defoe's satire was far more
effective than Swift's, successfully exposing the violence of High
Church prejudices that sheltered behind evasive euphemisms. Thus one
might regard the literary quality of the pamphlet as merely the surface
level, or first act of a sustained political hoax: Defoe's real satire is a
practical assault, with a direct impact on events.

We are dealing then with two different kinds of satiric success. *A Modest Proposal* offers us a paradoxical blend of tones which draw attention to the teasing mind of their creator, full of humanity's moral ambiguities. Defoe's cruder satire develops a voice which so closely counterfeits the hyperbole of a Sacheverell or a Goebbels that it can trick its antagonists into revealing their own inhumanity. Both satirists play with their audiences, revelling in the power of the printed word to confuse and confront the authority of governments. Yet underlying Defoe's satire we can detect a practical confidence in remedial measures, and an optimism concerning the capacity of common humanity to reject barbarity and butchery. Swift's satire leads us to contemplate a greater complicity between popular instincts and the barbarity of tyrants. He invites us to acknowledge that all man's institutionalised inhumanity to man finds its origins and legitimation in some concept of the good of the people.

The World of Augustan Humanism

More important in many ways than those explicitly political works in which the attitudes of the satirists are inevitably subject to the ephemeral considerations which affect the day-to-day realities of party-politics, is an underlying ideology shared by a great many of the satirists of the period. The label usually attached to this ideology is 'Augustan humanism': its defining characteristics are a veneration for the past allied to and predicated upon a fundamental belief in the historical uniformity of human nature. When in his *Preface to Shakespeare* Johnson describes Shakespeare's characters as 'the genuine progeny of common humanity', his judgement clearly expresses some central axioms of Augustan humanism. The passage is worth quoting in full:

> Shakespeare is above all writers, at least above all modern writers, the poet of nature; the poet that holds up to his readers a faithful mirrour of manners and of life. His characters are not modified by the customs of particular places, unpractised by the rest of the world; by the peculiarities of studies of professions, which can operate but upon small numbers; or by the accidents of transient fashions or temporary opinions; they are the genuine progeny of common humanity, such as the world will always supply, and observation will always find.[67]

It is not, one notes, the uniqueness of Shakespeare's insight, nor the brilliance of his language which attracts Johnson's praise, but the generality, the universal negotiability of his portraits of humanity.

More specifically, Augustan humanism may be regarded as the final flowering of a Renaissance tradition which blended together Christian morality and classical wisdom. In recent times several scholars have pointed to the strong affinities which link the Scriblerian group of satirists with the Renaissance humanist group of Erasmus, More and Colet. One has argued that the qualities of the Scriblerus Club

> recall nothing so much as the circle of More and Erasmus: not only literary cultivation and critical stringency but an almost conspiratorial intimacy and high spirits. The admiration in which Swift held More, and the reverence which Pope more than once expressed for Erasmus are too well known to need insisting on: *Gulliver's Travels* is of course, an example of Utopian fiction, while in one or two respects . . . Pope's *Praise of Dulness,* the *Dunciad,* recalls the *Praise of Folly* (and was dedicated to Swift just as *The Praise of Folly* was to More)[68]

Yet, while acknowledging the important links between Renaissance and Augustan humanism, we should also recognise the differences between them.

Erasmus, More and Colet represented a pioneering group who enthusiastically welcomed the insights into both Christian and classical learning afforded by the recently discovered Greek manuscripts from the East. Erasmus's 'Philosophia Christi' was an ideal which sought to unite the best of classical wisdom with the spiritual revelations of the New Testament:

> Two essential traits, inseparable and interrelated, distinguished the Christian humanists. They were as ardently devoted to the literature of Christian antiquity—the Early Fathers and the New Testament—as to the literature of pagan antiquity; and they passionately believed that embedded in both of these literatures was a wisdom that could both improve individual men, but more important, renovate the moribund Christian society of their own day temporally and spiritually in head and members.[69]

The elements of this 'philosophy of Christ' are well displayed in Erasmus's *Colloquies.* In one of these, 'The Godly Feast', he describes a banquet set in a garden that is both beautiful and fruitful, uniting the imagery of the Platonic Symposium with that of the Last Supper. Statues from both classical and Christian antiquity decorate the house and garden, and discourses at table range over both fields of reference with equal erudition and tolerance.[70]

The imagery of the garden reappears in Sir William Temple's essay *On the Gardens of Epicurus,* a key work in explaining those changes in the tone of humanist defences of learning which occurred between the sixteenth and eighteenth centuries. Temple begins by drawing the customary analogy between a garden and the paradise of Eden: 'God Almighty esteemed the life of a man in a garden the happiest he could give him.' However this garden, like that of Voltaire some years later, is quite consciously a retreat, a place of retirement.

The epistemological corollary of this retreat is a delimitation of the area of learning that is considered valuable:

> As to that part of philosophy which is called natural, I know no end it can have but that of either busying a man's brains to no purpose, or satisfying the vanity so natural to most men of distinguishing themselves, by some way or other, from those that seem their equals in birth . . . I know of no advantage mankind has gained by the progress of natural philosophy.[71]

These ideas reach their climax in Temple's *Essay on Ancient and Modern Learning,* in which he challenged both the accuracy and the usefulness of Harvey's discovery of the circulation of the blood, and Copernicus's cosmology.

Something important had happened in the intervening years between the optimistic openness of Erasmus and More and the defensive suspicions of Temple. The province of learning had expanded to such an extent, and particularly in the area of 'natural' philosophy (i.e. science) that a man of 'polite' learning no longer felt secure with the total admission of all knowledge. Temple's garden is a secluded haven, far away from the storms of empirical discovery, whereas Erasmus's garden was a place of education dominated by the beliefs that all knowledge brought Man closer to God. Between the two periods of Renaissance and Augustan humanism fall the shadows of Calvin and Luther. The influence of seventeenth-century Puritanism, with its strong emphasis upon man's fallen state, may account for those differences of tone which, despite their many similarities, clearly distinguish *The Praise of Folly* from *The Dunciad,* and *Utopia* from *Gulliver's Travels.* Coleridge once described Swift as *'anima Rabelaisii habitans in sicco;* the soul of Rabelais dwelling in a dry place.' It is a description which perfectly crystallises the differences I have in mind. Many of Swift's finest comic effects are influenced by, or even stolen from, Rabelais, but the tone of his humour is quite different. Where Rabelais is exuberant and festive, Swift is ironic and biting. Rabelais does not hesitate to link images of excrement with the name of God; indeed, their combination is one of the most forceful ways of expressing fertility, as in the phrase 'si Dieu y eust pissé'. The inundations of urine which flow through his works are parodic floods completely free of the sense of shame occasioned when Gulliver extinguishes the fire in the Queen of Lilliput's appartment. Rabelais concluded *Le Quart Livre* with a celebratory peroration including twelve synonyms for excrement: 'Appellez-vous cecy foyre, bren, crottes, merde, fiant, déjection, matiére fécale, excrément, repaire, laisse, emeut, fumée, stront, scybale, ou spyrathe? C'est, croy-je, sapphran d'Hibernie. Ho, ho, hie! C'est sapphran d'Hibernie! Sela! Beuvons!' Swift's notorious 'excremental vision', however, tends to view such human end-products as satiric daubs and missiles. He seems determined to rub our faces in the dirt in order to have us acknowledge ourselves at least as much (if not more) Yahoo as Houyhnhnm.

In the same way, the infinite ironies of Erasmus's paradoxical style which proclaim the total interdependence of wisdom and folly, represent an affirmation of the inclusiveness of God's creation. The paradoxes of his style are, as one critic notes, 'a logical and rhetorical application of the orthodox dictum that the last shall be first.'[72] With the Augustan satirists, however, one often feels that these same paradoxical tropes and formulas are manipulated as defensive devices. There is a patterned structure of antitheses, and an ordered system of pseudo-logical arguments that keep such problems as the mutability of language, or the corrupting power of money, at a negotiable distance in the face of an opposition forging its own weapons. As Denis Donoghue writes, 'Much of Augustan literature is a series of strategic withdrawals, retreats in good order from positions deemed too Faustian or metaphysical to be held.'[73]

The most obviously Faustian element in the intellectual world of the late seventeenth and early eighteenth centuries was represented by the growth and development of experimental science. The establishment of the Royal Society in 1662, followed by the discoveries of Newton (*Principia,* 1687, *Opticks,* 1704;) gave rise to

notions of progress, with Wootton boasting, as we have noted, that all
the physical myseries of the universe would soon be solved and 'the
next age will not find very much work of this kind to do'. The
Augustan satirists have often been portrayed as classicists reacting
with a mixture of panic and contempt to the emergence of a rival
scientific 'culture'. Yet it would be a serious over-simplification, and
indeed an error, to suggest that they were merely hostile to the 'new
science'. One member of the Scriblerus group, Dr John Arbuthnot,
was himself a Fellow of the Royal Society and an enthusiastic
experimenter. In 1732 he published a lengthy scientific study on *The
Nature of Aliments,* and earlier had published learned essays on the
usefulness of mathematics, the laws of chance and probability, and
the natural history of the earth. Indeed, in many ways the ethos of the
Scriblerian enterprise, which set out to ridicule 'all the false tastes in
learning'[74] had much in common with the Baconian ideology of the
Royal Society itself. In his *New Atlantis* and *Novum Organum* Bacon
had consistently championed practical, as opposed to speculative
science, stressing usefulness as the true goal for all enquiries. From the
first, however, satirists of the Royal Society either wilfully or
carelessly confused this Baconian philosophy with a penchant for
crack-brained schemes and ludicrous experiments. In Shadwell's play
The Virtuoso, first produced in 1676, the hero, Nicholas Gimcrack is
presented performing several of the experiments recorded in the
Society's *Philosophical Transactions,* or in Sprat's *History of the
Royal Society.* Yet, in what is probably the funniest scene in this satiric
drama, Gimcrack is shown 'swimming' on the drawing-room table.
He is asked if he has ever tried swimming in water.

Gimcrack: Never Sir. I hate the water. I never come upon the water,
            sir.
Longvil: Then there will be no use of swimming.
Gimcrack: I content myself with the speculative part of swim-
            ming, I care not for the practise. I seldom bring
            anything to use; 'tis not my way. Knowledge is my
            ultimate end.[75]

In this scene, then, the character who is being used to personify all the
attitudes and activities of the Royal Society flatly contradicts its
fundamental philosophy. Shadwell's comic misrepresentation of
scientific methodology is typical of much of the satire on science
published during the following century. While applauding and

approving the Baconian emphasis on useful knowledge, satirists like
Swift frequently viewed the scientists in practice as cranks and
fetishists, forever dabbling with lice and grubs and fleas, blowing up
dogs or transfusing a sheep's blood into a man.[76] Like latterday
alchemists, they were at best mad, at worst fraudulent, with their
grandiose schemes for transforming the detritus of their experiments
into panaceas for the ills of mankind, or for extracting sunbeams from
cucumbers.

In *The Battle of the Books* the essential distinction between
learning as a benefit to humanity and learning as a manifestation of
personal vanity is drawn in the emblematic contrast between the
spider and the bee. The spider 'swollen up to the the first magnitude
by the destruction of an infinite number of bees' boasts to the
'freebooter' bee that he is 'furnished with a native stock within
myself'. 'This large castle, (to show my improvements in the
mathematics) is all built with my own hands, and the material
extracted altogether out of my own person.' At the end of their
lengthy debate, the bee is given this final word:

> So that in short, the question comes all to this—which is the nobler
> being of the two, that which by a lazy contemplation of four inches
> round, by an overweening pride, feeding and engendering on
> itself, turns all into excrement and venom, produces nothing at last
> but fly-bane and a cob-web; or that which, by an universal range,
> with long search, much study, true judgement and distinction of
> things, brings home honey and wax.[77]

These were very much the terms in which the Augustan satirists
viewed the divisions between themselves and their intellectual
opponents, the virtuosi, experimenters and utopians. They were the
bees, carefully studying nature and the classics to enrich humanity;
their opponents were the spiders, spinning only confusion and
destruction out of their own vain pretensions.

Similar imagery is to be found in the third book of *Gulliver's
Travels,* when Gulliver visits the island of Balnibarbi. At the Academy
of Lagado he finds one man 'of a meagre aspect, with sooty hands and
face, his hair and beard long, ragged and singed in several places. . . .
He had been eight years upon a project for extracting sunbeams out of
cucumbers.' In another room Gulliver is 'almost overcome with a
horrible stink'.[78] Stopping his nose he encounters another experimenter, 'his hands and clothes daubed over with filth', engaged in

attempting to reduce human excrement to its original food, by separating the several parts, removing the tincture which it receives from the gall, making the odour exhale, and scumming off the saliva.' Yet another experimenter, in a room 'hung round with cobwebs', is working with spiders to replace silkworms. Throughout the kingdom of Balnibarbi which is governed according to modern experimental principles, Gulliver 'could not discover one ear of corn or blade of grass'. Except, that is, when he visited the estate of the lamentably old-fashioned Lord Munodi, who has been dismissed from office for 'insufficiency' and for his 'low contemptible understanding'. Here at last Gulliver encounters 'a most beautiful country: farmers' houses at small distances, neatly built, the fields enclosed, containing vineyards, corn-grounds and meadows.' Munodi confirms that 'his countrymen ridiculed and despised him for managing his affairs no better, and for setting to ill an example to the kingdom, which however was followed by very few, such as were old and wilful and weak like himself.'

Munodi goes on to explain that 'about forty years ago' certain persons spent some time up in the Flying Island of Laputa and came back 'full of volatile spirits acquired in that airy region'. They procured a royal patent for erecting an Academy of *Projectors* of Lagado and set about revolutionising all the arts and sciences so that, for example, 'all the fruits of the earth shall come to maturity at whatever season we think fit to choose, and increase an hundredfold more than they do at present'. The only inconvenience is that none of these projects has yet been brought to perfection, and in the meantime 'the whole country lies miserably waste, the houses in ruins, and the people without food or clothes.'

Fairly obviously, the Academy of Lagado is largely intended as a parody of the Royal Society, and several scholars have detailed specific parallels between the experiments witnessed by Gulliver and those recorded in the Society's *Philosophical Transactions*.[79] More recently it has also been suggested that the crack-brained projects and experimental mania that accompanied the South Sea Bubble may have provided an alternative model for the crazy utopian schemes of the projectors of Lagado:

the wild schemes of Book III can be related to something far more direct and close at hand than the elitist science of the 1690s. In fact, the best location for sources and analogues, as far as projects go, is not the *Philosophical Transactions* but the columns of newspapers in the Bubble era and the patent applications of the day. *Gulliver's Travels* was written at a time of exuberant commercial expansion and fertile practical invention. Its cultural matrix can be defined as the Age Of Projectors—a bustling uncerebral world of entrepreneurs and inventors. . . . Swift, I shall argue, meant to site Lagado nearer Exchange Alley than Gresham College.[80]

Pat Rogers goes on to cite a number of the more bizarre patent applications from the Bubble years which bear a striking resemblance to the projects of the Academy of Lagado. Among them James Puckle's machine-gun, with a special attachment for firing either round or square cannon balls 'according to whether the enemy were Christian or Turks'; and a scheme—real or fantastic—for extracting butter from beech-trees. However, in this case, as in so many others, we are not required to make an 'either/or' judgement: was Swift's 'real' target the Royal Society or the South Sea Bubble. The likelihood is that he had both in his sights. The absurd projects filling the advertisement columns of the papers in the early 1720s may no doubt have triggered off memories of those earlier scientific experiments gleefully compiled during the first Scriblerian meetings in 1714.

What all such projects have in common is a combination of enthusiastic zeal and bathetic raw materials. They represent a quasi-alchemical dream to find a short-cut to a Nirvana of happiness, riches or enlightment; a desire to synthesise a golden future out of a pile of material dross. As such they are symptomatic of that millenarian or Faustian dream of human perfectibility that, in the eyes of the Augustan humanists, not only inspired the fanatical sects of the Civil War period but also fatally threatened those notions of balance, moderation and restraint which offered the only real hopes for the amelioration of human ills. The humanists believed in a patient philosophy based on observing and following the harmonious patterns of nature, rather than seeking out some esoteric panacea or attempting to transcend nature by short-circuiting the seasons. 'Great works', observes Imlac in *Rasselas,* 'are performed, not by strength, but perseverance: yonder palace was raised by single stones, yet you see its height and spaciousness. He that shall walk with vigour three hours a day will pass in seven years a space equal to the circumference of the globe.'[81] Here we see a consistent Augustan tendency to de-sublime ambitions, retrieving them from the volatile regions of enthusiasm and despair, and rooting them in the empirical world of practical quotidian experience. In Book II of *Gulliver's Travels* the

King of Brobdingnag gives voice to one of the few unequivocal positives to be found anywhere in Swift's writings: 'He gave it for his opinion, that whoever could make two ears of corn, or two blades of grass to grow upon a spot of ground where only one grew before, would deserve better of mankind and do more essential service to his country, than the whole race of politicians put together.'[82] Such a sentiment may seem so unexceptionable as to verge on the banal, yet in that it effectively conveys the humanist distrust of dramatic solutions or revolutionary improvements. Down-to-earth and practical, it sets the patient husbandry of the bee far above the political web of the spider. It is no coincidence that the revolutionary experiments and speculative theories of Balnibarbi have resulted in a landscape where Gulliver could 'not discover one ear of corn or blade of grass'.

The humanist criticism of those who exploited their learning for personal vanity rather than for general use was not confined to scientists. It applied equally to those literary scholars who sought to transform the masterpieces of the past into their own private fiefdom, rather than opening them out for the pleasure and edification of all polite readers. Foremost among those in this category was the remarkable philologist Richard Bentley. Bentley's pre-eminence as a literary scholar has been described thus: 'Never have the pursuits of scholars been so dominated by a single influence as those of the eighteenth century were dominated by Bentley.' The secret of this superiority was the new professionalism which Bentley brought to the study of ancient texts: 'Bentley systematized his knowledge. He constructed a Hexapla, in the first column of which he inserted every word of the Hebrew Bible, and in other columns, the corresponding word in Chaldee, Syriac, the Vulgate, Latin and the septuagint.'[83] The first and decisive conflict between this new professional style of philology and the older more intuitive tradition of classical exegesis took place over the *Epistles of Phalaris,* which William Temple had unwisely cited as examples of the superiority of ancient culture over that of the moderns. Bentley, in his *Dissertation* on these Epistles devastated Temple's modest arguments with several hundred pages of detailed etymological analysis of Greek dialects, sources, analogues and history. Thereafter his authority in such matters was unassailable, and he proceeded to produce editions of Aristophanes, Cicero, and most controversially of Horace, in 1711, in which he became ever more imperious in his style of emendatory scholarship. Familiar readings of these texts were replaced by new Bentleian emendations which, he asserted, represented the true meanings which had been lost in corrupt and damaged manuscripts.[84] His example inspired a number of disciples and imitators; most notable among whom was Lewis Theobald. In his *Shakespeare Restored,* modelled on the example of Bentley's *Horatius Reformatus,* Theobald sought to apply the Bentleian style of emendatory criticism to the text of *Hamlet.*[85] He prefaced his scholarly remarks with this declaration, 'The alteration of a letter, when it restores sense to a corrupt passage in a learned language, is an achievement that brings honour to the critic who advances it.' It was this combination of vanity and pedantry in the work of these new philological critics, preening themselves on the alteration of commas and pronouns in great literary works, which annoyed the more traditional humanists. William King, in a poem entitled *Bibliotheca* (1712), wrote mockingly:

> Bentley immortal honour gets
> By changing Que's to nobler Et's

Pope in several places attacked 'Each Word-catcher that lives on syllables', each pedant 'who reads not, and but scans and spells'.

> Pains, reading, study, are their just pretence,
> And all they want is spirit, taste and sense.
> Comma's and points they set exactly right,
> And 'twere a sin to rob them of their mite.[86]

It was the contention of those who distrusted this new 'scientific' approach to literary scholarship, that the obsessive attention to petty details of punctuation and spelling frustrated, rather than enhanced, a true sense of the poetic qualities of great works. And their arguments seemed to receive a considerable confirmation with the publication in 1732 of Bentley's version of Milton's *Paradise Lost.* Fired by his successes with classical authors, Bentley's rage for emendation led him to postulate various errors and corruptions in the text of Milton's great poem. Milton had, after all, been blind, and Bentley chose to assume that the poet's manuscript had been seen through the press by an incompetent friend. In setting out to correct the 'errors' that had crept into the text, Bentley's was able not only to show off his knowledge of English philology but to demonstrate his superior understanding of science over that of the poet. Here, for example, in rejecting a famous line from Book I of the poem, he parades his reading of Newton's *Opticks:*

> 'No light, but rather darkness visible' (I.63)
> Darkness visible and darkness palpable are in due place very good expressions; but the next line makes visible here a flat contradiction. Darkness visible will not serve to discover Sights of Woe through it, but to cover and hide them. Nothing is visible to the eye, but so far as it is opake, and not seen through; not by transmitting the rays, but by reflecting them back.

Instead of Milton's majestic paradox, Bentley offers this correction, in order to 'come up to the author's idea':

> No light but rather a transpicuous gloom.

The 'transpicuous gloom' of Bentley's emendatory method, engulfing the familiar features of literary classics in a web of pedantic annotations, was a favourite satiric target. In his very first annotation to *The Dunciad* Pope ridicules all such arrogant nit-picking with a little parodic display of mock erudition laced with vanity, complacency and prejudice.

> The *Dunciad.* Sic M.S. It may be well disputed whether this be a right reading. Ought it not rather to be spelled *Dunceiad,* as the etymology evidently demands? Dunce with an *e,* therefore *Dunceiad* with an *e.* That accurate and punctual Man of Letters, the Restorer of Shakespeare, constantly observes the preservation of this very letter *e,* in spelling the name of his beloved author, and not like some common careless editors, with the omission of one, nay sometimes of two *ee*'s (as Shak'spear) which is utterly unpardonable. Nor is the neglect of a *Single Letter* so trivial as to some it may appear; the alteration whereof in a learned language is an *achievement that brings honour* to the critic who advances it . . . THEOBALD.
> I have a just value for the letter E, and the same affection for the name of this poem, as the forecited critic for that of his author; yet cannot it induce me to agree with those who would add yet another *e* to it, and call it the *Dunceiade;* which being a French and foreign termination, is no way proper to a word entirely English, and vernacular. One *E* therefore in this case is right, and two *E*'s wrong; yet upon the whole I shall follow the manuscript, and print it without any *E* at all; mov'd thereto by authority, at all times with critics equal if not superior to reason . . . SCRIBLERUS.

To some modern readers this parody may seem merely an exercise in petty point-scoring, a self-indulgent and esoteric piece of literary tit-for-tat. Yet the parodic wit of annotations like this subtly prepare and evoke the playful mock-heroic style of the poem itself. Long before the entrance of the King Dunce Tibbald we are here harried and hectored by the phantom presence of a mock-Theobald as editor in the footnotes. This is Theobald the conqueror of commas and liberator of letters, the squab insect-like asterisk lurking in Shakespeare's lines and even boring his way into Shakespeare's name. The vain-glorious achievements of his pedantry, evoked in the footnotes, establish the satiric context of Pope's surreal transform-ations in the poem itself.

Perhaps the most eloquent evocation of the humanist ideal of learning is to be found in *Windsor Forest,* where Pope describes the life of retirement, meditation and study.

> Happy the Man whom this bright court approves,
> His sov'reign favours and his country loves;
> Happy next him who to these shades retires,
> Whom Nature Charms, and whom the muse inspires,
> Whom humbler joys of home-felt quiet please,
> Successive study, exercise and ease.
> He gathers health from herbs the forest yields,
> And of their fragrant physic spoils the fields:
> With chymic art exalts the min'ral pow'rs,
> And draws the aromatic souls of flow'rs.
> Now marks the course of rolling orbs on high;
> O'er figur'd worlds now travels with his eye.
> Of ancient writ unlocks the learned store,
> Consults the dead, and lives past ages o'er.
> Or wandring thoughtful in the silent wood,
> Attends the duties of the wise and good,
> T'observe a mean, be to himself a friend,
> To follow Nature, and regard his end.
>
> (ll. 235-52)

What is noticeable here is that each of the several intellectual disciplines—history, botany, astronomy, chemistry, literature—is revealed as merely a branch of the central study and celebration of nature. They are like different languages all expressing the same meaning. The vein of a leaf, the skein of history, the kinship of metaphors and the nebulae of the stars all express the same pattern, the same controlling harmony of nature. They are different narrative codes articulating the providential structure of *concordia discors:*

> Where order in variety we see,
> And where, tho' all things differ, all agree.
>
> (ll. 15-16)

This unity, the integration of human science with divine purpose, informs the humanist conception of learning. Human institutions are subject to the same laws as natural phenomena; human hopes and fears are metaphors for the diversity of the created universe. At the heart, then, of the humanist opposition to new trends in scholarship, science and learning was a hostility to the fragmentation of this wholeness into a series of exclusively specialised and profes-sionalised territories. In particular, the jargon of the various 'learned' disciplines, from the pedestrian materialism of the *Philosophical Transactions* to the pedantic arrogance of Bentleian annotations, seemed calculated, like the mumbo-jumbo of the legal profession, to privatise and incorporate the various territories of human knowledge into esoteric preserves. The humanists tended to identify specialisation itself as the first dangerous step towards that distorted simplification of complex human and natural phenomena which characterised the views of all factions and fanatics.

In a famous passage in his *Defence of Poetry,* Sir Philip Sidney argued that the world of the poet, though imitated from nature, might offer an idealised image that would surpass the original: 'Nature never set forth the earth in so rich tapestry as divers poets have done; neither with pleasant rivers, fruitful trees, sweet-smelling flowers, nor whatsoever else may make the too much loved earth more lovely. Her world is brazen, the poets only deliver a golden'.[87] But if the world of the classical and Renaissance poets was golden, the world of the new scientists and professional scholars seemed, in the eyes of the Augustan satirists, to be made of a very inferior metal. In a key conceit in *The Dunciad*, Pope plays with the double meaning of the word 'Saturnian'. In the coronation of his king Dunce Theobald, Pope echoes the language of Virgil in *The Aeneid* ushering in a new Golden Age.

> This, this is he, foretold by ancient rhymes
> Th'Augustus born to bring Saturnian times.
>
> (III. 317-8)

But in a note to the opening section of the poem Pope explains the full satiric implications of the use of the Augustan parallel here. 'The Golden Age', he tells us, 'is by poets stiled Saturnian; but in the chymical language, saturn is lead.' Nothing could better crystallise the reverse alchemy of the modern dunces who turn heroic idealism into childish posturing and golden themes into leaden projects. The golden world of classical values is debased into a world of leaden dullness. The analytical chemist becomes the true decipherer of the age, exposing the fool's gold of its Augustan metaphors as mere dross.

Style as Meaning

The same tendency towards specialisation can be seen in the literary developments of the period. In a sense, the gradual eclipse of satire by the novel indicates a shift away from a literature of universal types and forms towards one dealing with individual experience. Indeed, in this respect Johnson's fiercely expressed preference for Richardson over Fielding is somewhat surprising. There was, he declared, as great a difference between the literary talents of Richardson and Fielding 'as between a man who knew how a watch was made, and a man who could tell the hour by looking on the dial-plate.'[88] Yet it was Fielding who shared with Johnson the confident humanist style of literary generalisation. 'The business of a poet', Imlac reminds us, 'is to examine not the individual but the species; to remark general properties and large appearances: he does not number the streaks of the tulip, or describe the different shades in the verdure of the forest.'[89] Fielding's terminology in *Joseph Andrews,* which Johnson boasted of never having read, is almost identical. 'I declare here once for all, I describe not men but manners; not an individual but a species.'[90] It was Richardson who, filling several hundred pages with a detailed and breathless examination of the momentary fluctuations within the mind and breast of an adolescent servant girl, developed the art of enumerating and delineating each separate streak in the youthful bloom of a sensibility. This is in sharp contrast with Fielding's urbane narrator who, with modest deference to good taste and his reader's native intelligence, prefers to leave some of the more tender moments in his story to our imagination:

As to the present situation of [Sophia's] mind, I shall adhere to a rule of Horace, by not attempting to describe it, from despair of success. Most of my readers will suggest it easily to themselves; and the few who cannot, would not understand the picture, or at least would deny it to be natural, if ever so well drawn.

(*Tom Jones,* IV.xiv)

Fielding's fictional style assumes that Sophia's emotional state belongs to an identifiable type of human response. Whereas for Richardson it is precisely such moments as these, where the stress of heightened emotions produces conflicts of loyalties, that put moral and social values at risk, that form the heart of his narrative. Indeed, the central difference between Richardson and Fielding is as much a matter of style as of philosophy or morality. By which I do not simply mean literary style, though that is important, but style as the denomination of an attitude to life; style not simply as the dress of thought, but as the visible embodiment of morality in action. For those, like Fielding, who attacked *Pamela,* it was not simply the complacent materialist implications of the subtitle 'Virtue Rewarded' that dismayed them. It was the combination of prurient voyeurism and vulgar moralising which in their view disfigured the style of the book throughout. When Fielding follows his characters into the bedroom he does so in a style of slapstick comedy or mock-heroic burlesque; there is always some form of literary detachment or narrative self-consciousness which turns the intimate space into a little theatre for a comedy of errors:

> This inclosed place exactly fronted the foot of the bed, to which, indeed, the rug hung so near, that it served, in a manner, to supply the want of curtains. Now, whether Molly in the agonies of her rage, pushed this rug with her feet; or, Jones might touch it; or whether the pin or nail gave way of its own accord, I am not certain; but as Molly pronounced those last words, which are recorded above, the wicked rug got loose from its fastning, and discovered everything hid behind it; where among other female utensils appeared—(with shame I write it, and with sorrow will it be read)—the philosopher Square, in a posture (for the place would not near admit his standing upright) as ridiculous as can possibly be conceived.

> (*Tom Jones,* V.v)

Yet when Richardson enters his characters' bedrooms, the first-person epistolary style makes this an unguarded introduction to a private and intimate domain. It is we, the readers, who find ourselves

'among the female utensils'. The unsophisticated and apparently
often undiscriminating rush of Pamela's narrative, sometimes teasing,
sometimes pious, sometimes coy, sometimes hysterical, traps us into a
claustrophobic drama of unsophisticated below-stairs intensity.

Undoubtedly there is a class aspect to some of the attacks of the
Augustan satirists on their 'modern' opponents and rivals, and this
aspect reveals itself most clearly in the matter of style. When at the
start of *The Dunciad Variorum* (1729) Pope writes:

> Books and the Man I sing, the first who brings
> The Smithfield Muses to the Ear of Kings.

he envisages the polite neo-classical culture of the court being
supplanted by the raucous huckstering puritanism and side-shows of
Bartholomew Fair. The writings of City poets such as Settle or
Blackmore were often described in terms which evoked the sectarian
rantings and militant metaphysics of the Civil War period. The
grammatical licence of the Poet Laureate Cibber, who made a habit of
'improving' Shakespeare in order to provide himself with bigger
acting parts, seemed suited to an age when the King of England
himself had problems with the English language. The popularity of
Richardson's pious and coy social climber, Pamela, indicated the
spread of a vulgar preference for voyeurist titillation and smug
moralising rather than the more urbane and sophisticated values of
classical literature. Richardsonian fiction seemed to offer the self-
absorption of literary identification rather than the self-knowledge of
literary irony.

The very terminology of eighteenth-century literary criticism,
with its emphasis upon order, decorum, correctness and politeness, is
redolent with social assumptions. Words themselves were carefully
differentiated and categorised according to class. Men of taste had
clear and somewhat inflexible notions concerning the social status of
words. A great many of the terms which are now as happily used by
the *Tatler* as by the *News of the World* were then regarded as 'low', a
kind of proletarian vocabulary inadmissible in polite society or
literature. Simple words such as 'knife' or 'blanket' carried such
powerful suggestions of lower-class origins that could not be
admitted to the salon of serious literature. Unfortunately, Shakespeare
had been lamentably un-class-conscious in his language, mingling
together high and low terms in a most promiscuous manner. For this,
of course, he was not entirely to blame. 'The English nation in the time

of Shakespeare', wrote Johnson, 'was yet struggling to emerge from barbarity.'[91] It was hardly surprising therefore if Shakespeare's vocabulary should contain some residual barbarisms. The task, as many of his Augustan admirers saw it, was to rescue his plays from such unfortunate lapses of taste. One of the most indefatigable of the 'improvers' of Shakespeare was William Davenant, who assumed a unique authority for his revisions by claiming to be Shakespeare's illegitimate son. Working together with Dryden, Davenant turned *The Tempest* into *The Enchanted Isle,* a sentimental romance of young love. But his most interesting attempt at improving his 'father's work was his version of *Macbeth*. Apart from drastically reducing the cast and simplifying the theme into a homily on the evils of ambition, Davenant paid particular attention to refining Shakespeare's language. Take these lines:

> Come, thick night!
> And pall thee in the dunnest smoke of hell,
> That my keen knife see not the wound it makes;
> Nor heaven peep through the blanket of the dark
> To cry, Hold! Hold!

In Davenant's version this becomes:

> make haste, dark night,
> And hide me in a smoke as black as hell,
> That my keen steel see not the wound it makes
> Nor heaven peep through the curtains of the dark
> To cry hold! hold!

'Knife' we see has been generalised to 'steel', and 'blanket' has been changed to 'curtain'. Curtains, possibly through their association with the theatre, are apparently more dignified, or at least more dramatic than blankets. Later critics have found the notion of any kind of fabric here, however noble, quite wrong. One editor is convinced the line should read 'blankness' of the dark. Coleridge, too, felt that draperies were altogether too lacking in sublimity for such a moment of infernal invocation and suggested something far more awesomely abstract—'the blank height of the dark'. But the most revealing discussion of the language of this passage is by Johnson in *The Rambler.* Written nearly a century after Davenant's adaption, Johnson's comments indicate how long-lasting were the prejudices against 'low' vocabulary in serious literature:

> We cannot surely but sympathise with the horrors of a wretch
> about to murder his master, his friend, his benefactor, who
> suspects that the weapon will refuse its office and start back from
> the breast which he is preparing to violate. Yet this sentiment is
> weakened by the name of an instrument used by butchers and
> cooks in the meanest employments; we do not immediately
> conceive that any crime of importance is to be committed by a
> *knife;* or who does not at last, from the long habit of connecting a
> knife with sordid offices, feel aversion rather than terror.

But if 'knife' is bad, the next line is quite insupportable.

> Macbeth proceeds to wish . . . that he may in the involutions of
> infernal darkness escape the eye of Providence. This is the utmost
> extravagance of determined wickedness; yet this is so debased by
> two unfortunate words that, while I endeavour to impress on my
> reader the energy of the sentiment, I can scarce check my risibility,
> when the expression forces itself upon my mind. For who,
> without some relaxation of his gravity, can hear of the avengers of
> guilt peeping through a blanket?[92]

When it comes to high drama, clearly the blanket and knife are no
substitute for the cloak and dagger.

This class consciousness of eighteenth-century vocabulary
corresponds to the social preoccupations of the literature itself. A
dignified tone and polite style were the hallmarks of a civilised
culture in which manners and morality went hand in hand. The ethos
of *The Spectator,* made explicit by Addison in its tenth number, was
designed to foster a spirit in which fashion and etiquette underpinned
rather than undermined morality and study:

> It was said of Socrates that he brought Philosophy down from
> Heaven, to inhabit among Men; and I shall be ambitious to have it
> said of me, that I have brought Philosophy out of closets and
> libraries, schools and colleges, to dwell in clubs and assemblies, at
> tea-tables and in coffee-houses.

In place of the fierce antagonism of the seventeenth century, when
the fashionable pursuits of a Cavalier court stood in apparent
opposition to the dour spiritual fundamentalism of puritan morality,

Addison proposed a civilised synthesis in which morality itself could become as fashionable as periwigs or patches.

The relationship between manners and morals could not, of course, be as easily resolved as that, and most of the satirists took a far more sceptical view of the 'civilising' effect of fashion than *The Spectator.* The pages of Swift and Fielding are filled with instances of the social process of refinement as a deformation, rather than an enhancement of a natural or innocent morality. Tailors and dancing-masters, those purveyors of fashionable accomplishments, figure prominently in their satires, almost invariably as tutors in the politic skills of hypocrisy. At the heart of almost all Fielding's work is a simple contrast between the spontaneous good nature of a Joseph, a Parson Adams or a Tom Jones, and the practised hypocrisy of a dedicated follower of fashion such as Beau Didapper or Lady Bellaston. In the endemic cultural confrontation between art and nature which runs right through eighteenth-century literature, the satirists give their vote emphatically on the side of nature. But it is in their style that we recognise the triumph of art, or even artifice, over the supposed innocence of their morality. Part of the satisfaction of a novel like *Joseph Andrews* comes from the successful intermingling of philosophies of art and nature. While we applaud the charming Christian innocence of Parson Adams, who instinctively takes each person he meets at their word, the narrator's ironic tone constantly invites us to contemplate the discrepancy between public statements and private motives. It is the combination of these two elements, the ingenuous morality and the ingenious style, which gives the novel its characteristic humour. For to express, as the narrator does, a love of unworldly innocence in a tone of urbane irony, is itself richly, and stylishly ironic.

Similar ambiguities can be found in the satirists' reactions to bad writing. Fielding is merciless in his exposure of Cibber's grammatical lapses. In one issue of *The Champion* he created a vivid court-room comedy with Cibber arraigned before a Court of Censorial Enquiry on a charge of murdering the English language.[93] Similarly, Swift in his *Public Spirit of the Whigs* makes great play with Steele's 'illiteracy', treating him like an errant schoolboy who has produced a rather shoddy essay. 'He hath a confused remembrance of words since he left the university, but hath lost half their meaning.[94] Yet, on the other hand, the Moderns were equally attacked for their pedantic and punctilious correctness on matters of grammar and syntax:

> Comma's and points they set exactly right,
> And 'Twere a sin to rob them of their mite.[95]

Correctness of this kind is the mark of the pedant, obsessed with minor details, but blind to the wider artistic harmony of a great literary work. The same kind of double standard can be seen in the satirists' reactions to modern versions of Shakespeare. Theobald was ridiculed for his presumption in burrowing his way like some noxious grub into the very text of Shakespeare's plays with his copious emendations; Cibber was attacked for foisting his own 'improved' version of *Richard III* on the public. Yet Pope himself, in his own edition of Shakespeare, showed an equally arrogant, and even more arbitrary judgement in excluding from the text 'low' material and 'nonsense'. In his edition of *Othello*, for example, he omits 'a great deal of nonsense' from one of Friar Lawrence's speeches, and relegates several of Iago's remarks to the margin, with the note, 'No hint of this trash in the first edition.'[96] In this area too, therefore, it would be fruitless to seek for any consistent theoretical position behind the satirists' remarks on style. Swift's admirably concise definition of a successful style, 'proper words in proper places',[97] is an intuitive judgement which corresponds to a wider sense of proprieties, both perceived and desired in the world beyond the written work. In his *Essay on Criticism* Pope offers a more explicit description of the necessary correspondence between literary and natural proprieties:

> First follow Nature, and your judgement frame
> By her just standard, which is still the same:
> Unerring Nature, still divinely bright,
> One clear, unchang'd, and universal light,
> Life, force and beauty, must to all impart,
> At once the source, and end, and test of Art.
>
> (ll.68-73)

The 'rules' of art 'discovered' by Aristotle and subsequently refined by such neo-classical critics as Boileau and Rapin, are not, in Pope's view, arbitrary laws or mere conventions:

> Those rules of old discover'd not devis'd,
> Are Nature still, but Nature methodiz'd;
> Nature, like Liberty, is but restrained
> By the same Laws which first herself ordain'd
>
> (ll.88-91)

They are, in fact, merely a codified formulation of the same rules or laws by which the universe itself is governed. The harmony of created nature is the model for all human creativity and sets the standards by which all artistic works must be judged. It follows that those who offend against these rules are not merely breaking some critical shibboleth, but denying, through ignorance or iconoclasm, the laws of nature. Bad writing thus becomes a form of rebellion, and solecism a sin. When in *The Dunciad* Pope describes how 'a mob of metaphors advance', he makes the satiric link between unruly images and a political revolt. Bad style represents a refusal to acknowledge one's own modest place in the natural order. At best it may be a piece of ignorant *lèse-majesté* or pretentious vulgarity in bringing the Smithfield muses to the ear of kings; at worst, it implies an assault upon the natural rhythms and cycles of creation:

> Realms shift their place, and Oceans turn to land.
> Here gay description Aegypt glads with showers;
> Or gives to Zembla fruits, to Barca flowers.[98]

The fact that it was those in power—the Hanoverian monarchs, with their laureates and eulogists, who were most responsible for these acts of verbal rebellion—indicated how far the corruption had already proceeded. The sovereignty and laws which Pope invokes are those of Nature, implying that the authority of the Hanoverians is itself a kind of illiterate metaphor of bad pun, which bears as much relation to true sovereignty as a pantomime by Heidegger bears to a natural scene.

The satirists, of course, did not have a monopoly of the language of nature whose laws, like those of men, could be subject to a variety of interpretations and constructions. To contrast with Pope's ringing principles, equally emphatic statements could be cited form the works of Dennis, Blackmore or Addison, all invoking Pope's own authorities—nature, reason and the ancients—in order to arrive at conclusions quite different from his. In the end one is forced to concede that those elliptically expressed axioms to 'follow nature' or to put 'proper words in proper places' add up not to a systematic statement of critical principles, but to a code for a patrician sense of decorum. In Fielding the civilised tones of the narrator represent the perfect congruence of good nature and good breeding. Presenting himself as our host, he assumes all the social obligations of the role to entertain and divert us. He would never presume so far upon good manners as to preach to us in the manner of Richardson, nor insult our intelligence by

implying our ignorance of any aspects of human nature. Instead, he
modulates his patrician tone of mock-deference to congratulate us on
our perspicacity in observing some ironic detail, while actually
manipulating our responses as comprehensively as he controls both
plot and characters.

In a sense the fictional relationship between narrator and reader in
a novel like *Tom Jones* represents an extension of the idealised
community of intelligent and civilised figures that Pope sought
assiduously to cultivate in his verse epistles. The friends and patrons
whom Pope celebrated and addressed in these poems, including
Bathurst, Burlington, Bolingbroke, Cobham, Swift and Arbuthnot,
personified and embodied those Augustan values. Their tastes in books,
architecture and landscape gardening, their moral and political
judgements, amounted to a virtual definition of Augustan style. They
were the alternative aristocracy, an aristocracy of Horatian retirement
who, on their own landed estates, maintained and observed the true
harmony between art and nature. While the court of a philistine
monarch and his illiterate laureates could best be represented and
entertained in forms derived from pantomime and masquerade, these
Tory lords and satirists maintained a kind of Augustan regime in exile.

CHAPTER THREE

Pope

> I have not the courage to be such a satirist as you, but I would be as
> much, or more, a philosopher. You call your satires, libels; I would
> rather call my satires, epistles: they will consist more of morality
> than wit, and grow graver, which you will call duller.
>
> (Pope to Swift, 1733)[1]

Pope remains one of the most difficult and least appreciated of the
great English poets. Byron was in no doubt of his pre-eminence,
calling him 'the moral poet of all civilisation.'[2] Yet until the last fifty
years the expression of such unqualified approval has been rare
indeed. Throughout his life Pope was subject to sustained campaigns
of vilification by his enemies. From the time of his death until the
early decades of the present century he was normally treated with a
blend of civilised disparagement and polite neglect—exactly the kind
of critical condescension that Pope himself so admirably
encapsulated in the phrase 'damn with faint praise'. Matthew Arnold's
praise was one of the most damning variety when in 1880 he
declared, 'Dryden and Pope are not classics of our poetry, they are
classics of our prose.'[3] Lytton Strachey was scarcely more enthusiastic
when he wrote in 1925: 'Pope's poetic criticism of life was, simply
and solely, the heroic couplet.'[4]

Alongside, and often providing an unacknowledged motive for
such faint praise of Pope's poetry, ran a dislike of Pope the man. This is
how Strachey began his essay.

> Among the considerations that might make us rejoice or regret that
> we did not live in the eighteenth century, there is one that to my
> mind outbalances all the rest—if we had, we might have known

Pope. At any rate, we have escaped that. We may lament that flowered waistcoats are fobidden us, that we shall never see good Queen Anne taking tea at Hampton Court: but we can at least congratulate ourselves that we run no danger of waking up one morning to find ourselves exposed, both now and forever, to the ridicule of the polite world—that we are hanging by the neck, and kicking our legs, on the elegant gibbet that has been put up for us by the little monster of Twit'nam.

During the past fifty years we have heard less of the little monster of Twit'nam and more of the master of mock-heroics. We no longer think of Pope as a classic of our prose, but as a subtle poet of allusion, whose satires have a unique facility for blending modern facts with ancient myths, and fusing classical heroes with contemporary hacks. In particular, the 'monster' taunt loses much of its force when one compares the tone of Pope's invective, in for example the 'Sporus' portrait of Hervey, with the language of the attacks which he suffered himself. Physically, Pope, who had caught a tubercular infection in childhood, was badly crippled, only four foot six inches tall, with a humped back and twisted spine. He also suffered serious social disabilities since, as a Catholic, his education, employments and place of residence were all subject to restrictions.[5] During times of Jacobite unrest—notably in 1715 and 1722—his activities came under close government surveillance. Yet, in a less sentimental age than our own, when a visit to Bedlam to laugh and stare at the lunatics was considered an agreeable afternoon diversion, Pope's enemies did not hesitate to parade his disabilities in print. His *Essay on Criticism*, published when Pope was just twenty-three, was described by the critic John Dennis as the work of a 'stupid, impotent . . . hunchback'd toad'. Some years later, in the midst of another violent harangue, Dennis offered this justification for his sadistic language:

But if any one appears to be concern'd at our upbraiding him with his natural deformity, which did not come by his own fault, but seems to be the curse of God upon him; we desire that person to consider, that . . . the deformity of this libeller, is visible, present, unalterable, and peculiar to himself. 'Tis the mark of God and Nature upon him, to give us warning that we should hold no society with him, as a creature not of our original, nor of our species . . . 'Tis certain at least, that his original is not from *Adam,* but from the *Divel.* By his constant and malicious lying, and by that angel face and form of his, 'tis plain that he wants nothing but horns and tail, to be the exact resemblance, both in shape and mind, of his infernal father.[6]

'Half-man, half-monkey', wrote another critic, arguing, as many did, that the deformity of Pope's body provided an indication of the perversions of his mind:

> Composed of malice, envy, discontent,
> Like his limbs crooked, like them impotent.

And so on: such attacks could be, and were, duplicated at length. Beside such sustained vilification, Pope's lines on 'Sporus' seem relatively mild and infinitely more inventive.

> This painted child of dirt that stinks and stings;
> Whose buzz the witty and the fair annoys,
> Yet wit ne'er tastes, and beauty ne'er enjoys,
> So well-bred spaniels civilly delight
> In mumbling of the game they dare not bite.[7]

Yet if we are less likely now to dismiss Pope as a bitter and malicious libeller, there remain other serious obstacles to a full appreciation of his poetry. There is the problem of his allusions, as already noted. There is the formality of his poetic style with its end-stopped couplets and antithetical rhythms which are uncongenial to modern poetic tastes. But perhaps most difficult of all is the tone of personal selfrighteousness and moral infallibility that often results from Pope's desire to combine the roles of satirist and moral philosopher. 'Ask you what provocation I have had?' he enquires in the *Epilogue to the Satires*, replying with this ringing declaration: 'The strong antipathy of Good to Bad'.[8] There is something disconcerting—even disturbing—to many modern readers about a writer who can, not only so confidently identify and divide the world into these two antithetical camps, but also unhesitatingly parade himself as the standard-bearer of Goodness. Midway through the *Epistle to Bathurst* Pope pauses, and then announces in vatic tones, 'Hear then the Truth'. Nothing could better indicate the instinctive differences in style and approach between Swift and Pope as satirists than this. If we were ever to encounter the phrase 'Hear then the Truth' in a work of Swift's, we should know we were about to be told a lie. For Swift, who naturally adopted the role of the 'hypocrite reversed', the man who wears his principles on his sleeve is at best a fool, at worst a knave. Pope's uncompromising direct claims of moral and philosophical absolutism in satiric poems which simultaneously require us to uncover the devious motives of his enemies, have led generations of readers to detect a taint of disingenuousness in Pope's own attitudes. When the conduct of others is held up to the detailed inspection of satire, there sometimes seems something unbalanced about the heroic figure which Pope allows himself to cut in these epistles.

Moreover, the very conciseness of his couplets, and the clarity of his expression, often appear to encapsulate aphorisms by which Pope can be conveniently summed up and marked down. One famous couplet would seem to 'prove' the complacency of his traditional and derivative view of poetry:

> True wit is Nature to advantage dress'd
> What oft was thought, but ne'er so well express'd.[9]

Another shows him to be narrow and timorous in his philosophy, recommending a trite and unquestioning acquiescence to the ways of Providence:

> Know then thyself, presume not God to scan,
> The proper study of mankind is man.[10]

A third seems to reveal that he considered women as far beneath rational consideration as God was above it:

> Nothing so true as what you once let fall,
> 'Most women have no characters at all.'[11]

However, this image of Pope as a man of maxims belies the process of creative thought that lies behind those couplets. The formal precision and symmetrical elegance of Pope's couplets create the impression of a sequence of perfectly formed and finished gems. Yet the apparent ease of this effect is deceptive—the result of careful literary revisions and reformulations as much as of a knack for 'lisping in numbers'. Pope, we know, was an indefatigable reviser who continued to make alterations, both major and minor, to such poems as *The Rape of the Lock* and *The Dunciad* throughout his life. 'Poems were rarely finished' observes one recent critic, 'but were perpetually finishing'.[12] What appears to us as a kind of formal perfection, an absolute fixity of expression, was in fact for Pope always provisional. 'After writing a poem', he told Spence, 'one should correct it all over with one single view at a time.[13] Even his readers were required to revise and refine their own first impressions of his poems. Swift's reaction to the *Essay on Man* was to tell Pope that 'in some few places I was forced to read twice', and Pope himself told his friend John Caryll that he was eager to hear his opinion of the poem 'after twice or thrice reading'.[14]

What this emphasis upon revision and rereading indicates is that Pope's couplets do not yield up their full meaning at a first reading. Initially, one may be dazzled by the glitter of the couplets and the surface wit of the antitheses. Only when one allows the full range of connotations to sink in does one come to recognise that Pope's wit is not merely a dance of rhetorical effects: the subtle verbal patterning enacts a careful analysis of meanings.

In his *Essay on Human Understanding* Locke writes at length on imperfections of language and in particular of those dangers that arise when words are used without clear and distinct ideas: 'I may have the ideas of virtues or vices, and names also, but apply them amiss: v.g. when I apply the name frugality to that idea which others call and signify by this sound, covetousness.'[15] The manipulation of just such a misapplication of names and ideas is part of the instinctive technique of Augustan satirists. To us, Pope's use of abstract nouns may seem to exude an unchallengeable confidence and authority. In his book *The Providence of Wit,* Martin Battestin discusses much of the literature of the period in terms of such abstract certainties, a practice for which he has been rightly censured by Claude Rawson. 'These terms', writes Rawson, 'are deployed across [Battestin's] pages like an occupying army pressing every author into service, and subjecting every literary text to a stunned and restrictive obedience.'[16] If, instead of being mesmerised by the formal uniforms of these confident abstractions, we venture, as the satire invites, to dissect them, we will recognise a process of careful ironic discrimination at work. A passage like the following is like a satiric version of Locke, analysing the distinctions between deceptively similar ideas, covetousness and frugality, meanness and thrift:

> Perhaps you think the Poor might have their part?
> Bond damns the Poor, and hates them from his heart:
> The grave Sir Gilbert holds it for a rule,
> That 'every man in want is knave or fool;'

'God cannot love (says Blunt, with tearless eyes)
The wretch he starves'—and piously denies:
But the good Bishop, with a meeker air,
Admits, and leaves them Providence's care.
    Yet, to be just to these poor men of pelf,
Each does but hate his neighbour as himself:
Damn'd to the mines, an equal fate betides
The slave that digs it, and the slave that hides.[17]

Such a passage demonstrates Pope's satire as its best—detailed, yet direct; allusive, yet imaginatively forceful; controlled, yet full of passionate anger. He constructs a neat crescendo of uncharitable attitudes, deftly moving from Bond's percussive sole to the bishop's sanctimonious chorus. Bond's reaction has at least the virtue of frankness; it is straightforwardly and unambiguously brutal.

'Bond damns the Poor, and hates them from his heart'—There is a specific allusion behind this line. Denis Bond, a director of 'The Charitable Corporation for the Relief of Industrious Poor', was found guilty of embezzling some of the corporation's funds, and was alleged to have retorted, 'Damn the poor!' But 'Bond' here belongs to the same class of semi-metaphorical personae as Mist and More. 'Bond' appropriately suggests the callous financial world of stocks and bonds, and this is the association conveyed to readers unaware of the specific target. The harsh monosyllables of the line are like repeated hammer blows, and this effect of brutality is reinforced by the alliterative antithesis of hate and heart, where the similitude of sounds ironically reverses the conventional emotional associations of the heart. 'Bond' further suggests bondage and slavery; the tyranny of money. For all these reasons Bond stands as the unfeeling base for this little vignette of uncharitable attitudes. His frank callousness is repudiated by the figures who follow, though their milder vocabularies imply no greater generosity of spirit.

Unlike Bond, whose meanness proceeds from undisguised self-interest, the 'grave' Sir Gilbert (Sir Gilbert Heathcote, Governor of the Bank of England) seeks to justify his lack of charity as a social philosophy. The careful framing of his opinion, with the adjective 'grave' (suggesting deathly seriousness) indicates that he has arrived at his conventional evasion as the result of some considerable thought. Poverty, in his considered view, is the badge of knavery and fecklessness, and hence charity would merely be a subsidy for these social evils.

Blunt indulges a similar vein of sophistry to justify his lack of charity, but whereas Sir Gilbert merely invokes his own brand of natural law philosophy, Blunt goes further and cites God's own precedent and example for his meanness. Here too a specific reference jostles the general one. Sir John Blunt, one of the directors of the South Sea Company, is the particular target here, but as with Bond, the harsh monosyllable 'Blunt' suggests a more general sense of callousness. The neat parenthesis—'(says Blunt, with tearless eyes)'—which interrupts Blunt's pious denial, is a masterstroke of understatement and delay. Our expectation, from the rhythm, is that this detail will convey some choking of emotion, and we instinctively anticipate tear*ful* eyes. The unnecessary information that Blunt is indeed tear*less* (as, one presumes, are all the others, though Pope does not tell us so) only raises the suggestion of tears in order to deny it, thus confirming the bluntness of Blunt. Then examine what he says: 'God cannot love'. This pious belief would seem to contradict the central New Testament doctrine that God is Love. While that sly final formulation 'and piously denies' neatly encapsulates the kind of casuistry which preserves the forms of Christian observance while inverting their meaning. Thus far the progress of self-interest through philosophical complacency to religious hypocrisy is evident. The next couplet, however, seems rather different.

> But the good Bishop, with a meeker air,
> Admits . . .

Those benign adjectives suggest a complete contrast with the tearless, if pious, Blunt. Yet what exactly is the difference between these two?

> . . . and leaves them, Providence's care.

With that insidiously overrun line, Pope goes out of his way to hint that the bishop will contradict all the uncharitableness that has gone before. The rhythm strains towards a refutation. Yet these expectations merely strengthen the irony when it comes that the bishop's refutation is of a theological rather than practical kind. Whereas Blunt believes that God punishes the wrong-doers by starving them, and therefore that it would be blasphemous to interfere with such a divinely ordained system, the bishop believes in a much more benign Providence. God, in his view, can be relied upon to love and care for the poor, which conveniently absolves human beings from any responsibility to do so. So what at first appears as a contradiction of uncharitableness, in fact supplies a neat climax to it. At this point Pope intervenes in judgemental tones which emphasise the pattern of Christian imagery that runs throughout the passage:

> Yet to be fair to these poor men of pelf
> Each does but hate his neighbour as himself.

'Poor men of pelf', a neat if unremarkable oxymoron (pelf = riches) is used to point up the contrast between material poverty and poverty of spirit. The absence of charity which leads Blunt to deny God's love, returns to plague him in a world where counting has replaced compassion and hate has taken the place of love. Pope offers us a characteristic vignette of the providential balance operating in the world:

> Damn'd to the mines, an equal fate betides
> The slave that digs it, and the slave that hides.

The mines here clearly have two meanings: in a physical sense they are the gold or coal mines where the poor are condemned to labour for the enrichment of others. But they are also the mines of Hell whither those, like Bond, Blunt and Sir Gilbert, who had led unchristian and uncharitable lives, will be damned for all eternity. Thus Bond's initial 'Damn the poor' is neatly turned against him. This equal fate has both a comic and a tragic face. Comically, Pope offers us a mirror image; on one side the literal slave, labouring to dig the gold from the earth; on the other, the slave to his own greed, burying the gold away in vaults underground to keep it safe. While in tragic terms the cupidity which will take these callous misers to Hell for all eternity, condemns the poor to a hell on, or under, the earth for all their working lives. The passage is a subtle exposure of all those gradations of polite euphemism by which self-interest is disguised as social responsibility and low greed masquerades as high moral principle. Pope's style here in fact has precisely that deftness of touch of which Lady Mary Wortley Montagu denied him to be capable:

> Satire should, like a polish'd razor keen,
> Wound with a touch, that's scarcely felt or seen.
> Thine is an oyster-knife, that hacks and hews.[18]

As one grows accustomed to reading Pope's verse the initial impression of unvaried formality and symmetry disappears, and one develops an ear for those nuances of tone and inflexion which point to comic effects. Often quite small technical shifts, such as an internal rhyme, the reversal of poetic feet, or the postponement of the caesura, act as signals for corresponding ironic disjunctions of meaning; such as the elision of parsimony into thrift, or the glide from liberty into licence. Yet this emphasis upon nuances and subtleties, revisions and refinements, should not be misinterpreted to suggest that Pope is merely a skilled craftsman, a poetic technician. If we read Pope's satires merely as versifications of Locke, then we will find ourselves back on the path which led to Arnold's description of him as a 'master of our prose'. Joseph Warton, writing in 1756, was one of the originators of this idea when he described Pope as 'a most excellent *improver,* if no great original *inventor.*'[19] Keats, too, saw Pope's poetry as a triumph of technique, but a denial of the poetic spirit:

> ye taught a school
> Of dolts to smooth, inlay and clip and fit . . .[20]

In recent years some critics, anxious to re-emphasise the importance of Pope's imagination and poetic inspiration, have shied away from such terms as 'reason' and 'judgement' as if contamination by rationality must inevitably imperil the fragile flow of the imagination.[21] Yet the remarkable fact about Pope is that his poetic imagination draws its strongest inspiration from raw facts; his flights of fantasy are grounded in, and guided by, specific satiric detail. It is this rare, indeed unique, combination of satiric specificity and visionary invention that leads to the surrealistic quality of his major satires. By using the term 'surreal', I do not refer merely to the mock-heroic poems with their mythopoeic patterns of allusion, but also to a characteristic blend of fact and fiction in the moral epistles. For an example, we might return to the *Epistle to Bathurst.* Throughout this poem Pope presents the power of money as a subversive quasi-Satanic force; it becomes a false God of creation, supplanting the natural order with its own values and standards, and replacing the natural rhythms of the seasons which fulfil the needs and appetites of men with its own market-forces and unequal divisions of wealth. The same providential power which bids 'the oceans ebb and flow' also ordained a reciprocal harmony in the affairs of man and nature.

Money destroys this subtle ecology of harmonious reciprocities by
intruding its cruder rhythms of supply and demand, and creating
unnatural polarities of penury and excess, dependence and
domination. Under the guise of smoothing out irregularities in the
natural cycle, it creates new and harsher inequalities:

> What Nature wants, commodious Gold bestows,
> 'Tis thus we eat the bread another sows:
> But how unequal it bestows, observe,
> 'Tis thus we riot, while who sow it, starve.
> What Nature wants (a phrase I much distrust)
> Extends to Luxury, extends to Lust:
> And if we count among the needs of life
> Another's toil, why not another's wife?[22]

As an indication of the irresponsibility of money, Pope shows not
only its mesmeric and subversive powers, but its fundamental
violation of the natural correspondence between form and content.
The power of a bank-note is out of all proportion with its physical
form: it thus becomes a perfect metaphor for the millenialist fantasies
of a modern acquisitive society. Its promises of riches contained in a
tiny, flimsy slip of paper belong to the same delusory world as those
utopian projectors caught up in the South Sea Bubble with their
schemes for making salt water fresh, or for creating a perpetual
motion machine. The bank-bill, with its heroic powers located in
such a flimsy form, represents a kind of mock-heroic. It has the
transformational powers of high art, but the vulnerability of mere
paper. It is a kind of magic, and Pope plays with it as a magician:

> Blest paper-credit! last and best supply!
> That lends corruption lighter wings to fly!
> Gold imp'd by thee, can compass hardest things,
> Can pocket states, can fetch or carry kings;
> A single leaf shall waft an army o'er,
> Or ship off senates to a distant shore;
> A leaf, like Sibyl's, scatter to and fro
> Our fates and fortunes, as the wind shall blow:
> Pregnant with thousands flits the scrap unseen,
> And silent sells a king, or buys a queen.
>
>   (ll.69-78)

The visual fantasy here has the vividness of a cartoon, and focuses on those incongruous liaisons that money can so neatly conceal. Note how the chiming assonance of the line 'Blest paper-credit! last and best supply!' has an insinuating, lisping charm. 'Imp'd' in the next line, the glossary informs us, is a term of falconry, meaning to insert a feather into a hawk's damaged wing to increase its power of flight. The image then is of a gold coin borne aloft, its power extended by the aid of this more buoyant currency. Yet the other associations of 'imp'—'a little devil or demon, an evil spirit' (*OED*)—continues the Satanic implications of this power. *Compass* means 'to contrive, devise, machinate a purpose' but also 'passing into the bad sense of craft, subtilty, cunning' (*OED*), strengthening the malign or mischievous suggestion. Moreover, this idea of encircling and encompassing conveys the chameleon-like flexibility and malleability of money—at one moment open like a wing, the next, folded round like wrapping paper. This suggestion continues in the next line: 'Can pocket states, can fetch or carry kings.' There is a furtive insolence in this image of a state or nation wrapped up in a bank-note and slid into some banker's pocket. The phrase a 'pocket-borough' was a familiar description of the power of bribery and patronage in local elections. Pope here domonstrates that the power of money is not restricted to the parish level, but works on an epic scale. The mock-heroic quality of this elliptical phrase 'to pocket states' reduces a nation to the size of a pack of cards. Money has the same power as the satirist's imagination to reduce empires into Lilliputs, and turn monarchs into menials. 'Fetch and carry' is what the lowest household servants are required to do. Here the phrase is used to indicate the contemptuous ease with which money has utterly replaced the traditional authority of monarchs, who are unceremoniously trafficked like any other commodity.

There are two possible interpretations of the imagery in the next line. The single leaf may be seen as a kind of magic carpet 'wafting', that is flying, armies from one mercenary loyalty to another. Alternatively, it can be seen as a kind of fan, a single 'waft' from which will cause a whole army to collapse, like toy-soldiers on a table. Then the bank-bill becomes a little paper boat, carrying away the Blefuscudian fleet. The next comparison, with the sybilline leaves, perfectly encapsulates the irresponsible, non-providential pagan forces at work in the money-God. Like Sibyl's leaves—tantalisingly frail, at the mercy of the winds—yet containing the destinies of humans, so these skimpy pieces of paper have the power of life and death over thousands of individuals. 'Pregnant with thousands' . . .

here we note the imaginative affinity between the subversive powers
of money and the unruly wit of the Dunces in *The Dunciad,* both
producing a parody of creation. The image 'pregnant with
thousands' is of a bank-bill covered with noughts, that is thousands of
pounds. Yet each nought is like a little egg, a little potential imp-like
being, a monetary sylph with power to damn the lives of humans who
fall under its sway. Dulness, too, is pregnant with such thousands,
even millions of parodic souls:

> Millions and millions on these banks he views,
> Thick as the stars of night, or morning dews,
> As thick as bees o'er vernal blossoms fly,
> As thick as eggs at Ward in pillory.
> *(Dunciad* 1729, III. 23-6)

The final mock-heroic cadence 'And silent sells a king' is a neat
summation of Pope's satiric attack on a society where traditional
power, values and authority have been subverted by money; where all
that remains is a pantomime of regal authority, while the real
controlling forces are in 'Change alley, pocketing states and buying
queens. Here too we can detect a specific allusion: there was a
widespread rumour that Queen Caroline had accepted a large present
from the cashier of the South Sea Company. Yet this specific detail is
only one small component in a total satiric vision. Pope's poetic
imagination emulates the transformational powers of money itself.
Like a magician presenting the bank-bill as a wing, a magic carpet, a
wrapping-paper, a leaf, a toy boat, a fan, it domesticates the financial
subversion of natural relationships. The capitalist has the power to do
in fact what the satirist can only do in fiction—overturn hierarchies
and transform landscapes. The surrealism of Pope's metaphors
catches the buoyant animation of that process. One might compare
this effect with Belinda's toilette in the *Rape of the Lock.*

> And now, unveil'd, the Toilet stands display'd,
> Each silver vase in mystic order laid.
> First, rob'd in white, the nymph intent adores
> With head uncovr'd, the cosmetic pow'rs.
> A heav'nly image in the glass appears,
> To that she bends, to that her eyes she rears;
> Th'inferior priestess, at her altar's side,
> Trembling, begins the sacred rites of pride.
> Unnumber'd treasures ope at once, and here

The various off'rings of the world appear;
From each she nicely culls with curious toil,
And decks the goddess with the glitt'ring spoil.
This casket India's glowing gems unlocks,
And all Arabia breathes from yonder box.
The tortoise here and elephant unite,
Transform'd to combs, the speckled and the white.
Here files of pins extend their shining rows,
Puffs, powders, patches, bibles, billet-doux.
Now awful beauty puts on all its arms;
The fair each moment rises in her charms,
Repairs her smiles, awakens ev'ry grace,
And calls forth all the wonders of her face,
Sees by degrees a purer blush arise,
And keener lightnings quicken in her eyes.[23]

Here the poetic opulence seduces us into an implicit endorsement
of Belinda's narcissism. The practical heresy of this ritualistic event,
in which the language of religion is perverted to gratify worldly
vanity, is never in doubt. Yet the censorious note of that phrase 'the
sacred rites of pride' is lost in the swelling and swooning of sensuous
adjectives which inspire the reader with the same reverential awe that
Belinda herself expresses when contemplating her own 'heavenly'
image. Here too we are offered another parody creation, a pastiche of
order. Her worship of the 'cosmetic' powers—a phrase which neatly
catches an echo of its alternative, the *cosmic* powers—implies a
sympathy for the elaborate facade. Pope's poetry joins in the make-
believe, and through metaphors from India and Arabia enhances the
sense of Belinda as a deity presiding over the world. Fashion, like
money, has the power to miniaturise the whole world into a domestic
toy. The dressing-table, like the gaming-table, becomes a mock-heroic
tableau; a model world in which vanity and utopian dreams usurp the
place of nature. In both cases Pope's poetry breathes imaginative life
into the hedonist illusions it attacks. It allows us to become
intoxicated with the power of money, the delight of conspicuous
expenditure and of absolute command. He strokes us and delights us
with an iridescent bubble of such dreams, without ever forgetting to
instruct us in the dangers of these illusions. Nothing is more vain than
a metaphor; no one enjoys the self-indulgence of artifice more than
the poet. Pope's poetry rises to heights of surrealism as he combines
the roles of dreamer and judge, conjuror and censor.

Passages like these, inventive set-pieces, clearly offer evidence of rich poetic imagination. Yet this is less obviously true of the more philosophical sections of the *Moral Essays* or of the *Essay on Man*. Sometimes such passages are presented as vivid *arias* in works which otherwise consist of long sections of dry recitative. Even in the less obviously 'imaginative' passages in Pope's poetry, however, there is a level of visual imagery that sometimes goes unnoticed. As Byron declared, 'I will show more imagery in twenty lines of Pope than in any equal length of quotation in English poesy, and that in places where they least expect it.'[24] Thrown into prominence by his rhetorical formulas and antithetical structures, Pope's fondness for abstract nouns seems to confirm a prosaic, colourless, rational texture in his verse. Yet even the most limpid abstractions have concrete sources; and as a classicist Pope was keenly aware of the physical origins of many of his metaphysical generalisations. As an example I'd like to look at these lines from the *Epistle to Cobham:*

> There's some peculiar in each leaf and grain,
> Some unmark'd fibre, or some varying vein:
> Shall only Man be taken in the gross?
> Grant but as many sorts of mind as moss.
> That each from other differs, first confess;
> Next, that he varies from himself no less:
> Add Nature's, custom's, reason's, passion's strife,
> And all opinion's colours cast on life.
> Yet more; the diff'rence is as great between
> The optics seeing, as the objects seen.
> All manners take a tincture from our own,
> Or come discolour'd thro' our passions shown.
> Or fancy's beam enlarges, multiplies,
> Contracts, inverts, and gives ten thousand dyes.
>   (ll.15-28)

Pope's argument here is clear enough; generalisations about human nature are useless. Yet at first sight he may appear to labour his point by repetition, tautology and by the deployment of that occupying force of fierce abstractions—mind, custom, nature, reason, passion, opinion, manners and fancy. When one examines these terms more closely, however, one finds the lines as richly crowded with flora and fauna as a virtuoso's study. Each couplet proceeds like an experiment in natural philosophy. The 'peculiar in each leaf and grain' invites us to imagine the 'fingerprint' of each leaf as seen under a microscope. Pope adds his own learned note to the analogy 'as many sorts of mind as moss'. There are, he notes 'above 300 sorts of moss observed by naturalists'. The alliteration emphasises the ironic parallelism which encourages us to see the brain's grey matter as some species of fungus or lichen.[25]

Pope's optimistic argument proceeds with images drawn from two sources: the first is Newton's *Optics,* as fancy's beam is described in the language of the prism, and the effect of passion presented as Newtonian rainbow. But in addition, Berkeley's concept *esse est percipi* has its influence on that neat formulation 'the optics seeing as the objects seen'. It is noticeable here that the antithesis creates a mirror effect; the shimmering near identity of sound producing a refracted rather than a reflected image. Thus the abstractions here are rich both in specific allusions and in physical images drawn from the natural world. Less exuberant than the passages noted above, it is this analytical imagery of nature expressed in the lineaments of stamen and pistil which makes Pope's formality not merely a mannered artifice, but a serious attempt to recreate the inner patterns and codes of the natural world. 'He preferred the artificial to the natural', declared Hazlitt, quite wrongly.[26] For Pope the only art of any value was based on the harmony of nature; but he found nature not on mountaintops or in waterfalls, but in the shape of a leaf, the ebb and flow of tides and in the minds of men.

JOINT-TENANTS OF THE SHADE

One particular vein of imagery may be worth exploring further. The lines of Pope's verse are crowded with references to animals and insects. Sporus, for example, is called a bug, a butterfly, a spaniel, a toad, a reptile, an 'amphibious thing' and a 'curd of ass's mild'. Elsewhere in the same poem (*Epistle to Dr Arbuthnot*) Pope refers to his enemies as spiders, grubs, worms and rabid dogs. In *The Dunciad* we find a teeming mass of maggots, spawn, bears, monsters, apes, monkeys, dab-chicks, cows, asses, dogs and wolves; the farmyard and the menagerie meet in this fairground.

There is more to this imagery than the kind of casual abuse that we might employ calling someone a bitch or a louse. It is clearly very different, too, from the animal imagery of D.H.Lawrence or Ted Hughes, with their associations of power and physical force. Pope's use of animal imagery carries with it an implied allusion to the natural hierarchy of all created things now over-familiarly referred to as the 'Great Chain of Being'. Within that hierarchy, as he argues in his *Essay on Man,* each species has its own appropriate form of limited perfection—limited by its role and place in the universe as a whole:

> Then say not Man's imperfect, Heav'n in fault;
> Say rather, Man's as perfect as he ought;
> His knowledge measur'd to his state and place,
> His time a moment, and his point a space.
>
>   (I.69-72)

Pope's vision of the immense heterogeneity of the universe is based upon this clear and confident assertion of a divine plan in which every grub and bug, every comet and star, has its own appointed place on some vast mathemtical grid:

> Why has not Man a microscopic eye?
> For this plain reason, Man is not a fly.
>
>   (I.193-4)

The use of the word 'plain' here is a tell-tale sign of insecurity; just as when he asserts, 'One truth is *clear*, 'Whatever IS, is RIGHT.' Whenever Pope tells us that something is plain or clear, and seeks to confirm that clarity with the emphatic closure of his couplet, we sense a momentary panic—a reaching for the rhetorical drum-roll to drown out the little voice of doubt. Pope swats away this impertinent fly, but the very impatience with which he does so betrays the anxiety of a man who, having peeped through the microscope at the teeming world of formication, steps back abruptly to assert, 'Whatever is, is right', as an antidote to the monstrous nightmares glimpsed in *The Dunciad*, where Dulness, like a vast queen bee, launches her buzzing hordes upon the world. Man's position, placed on this isthmus of a middle state, is a precarious one, imposing responsibilities as the corollary of privileges. Blessed with reason and a soul, it is man's duty to exercise both in accordance with the divine plan. Pope's use of animal imagery, like Swift's use of Houyhnhnms and Yahoos, is an ever-present reminder of the failures of humanity to live up to its own appointed place. While he is prepared to indulge and entertain us with a display of social butterflies and Grub Street maggots, he constantly reminds us that such charlatan impostures reduce individuals to a subhuman mob, like specimens on a slide, or a menagerie of *lusus naturae*.

For Pope the animal world existed as far more than a thesaurus of analogies. He had an unusual respect and sympathy for animals of all kinds, and his pioneering attack on hunting in the *Guardian* shows him as an early animal liberationist.

> We should find it hard to vindicate the destroying
> of anything that has life, merely out of wantonness;
> yet in this principle our children are bred up, and
> one of the first pleasures we allow them, is the
> licence of inflicting pain upon poor animals: Almost
> as soon as we are sensible what life is ourselves, we
> make it our sport to take it from other creatures.[27]

He was equally hostile to the experiments which his neighbour at Twickenham, the Rev. Stephen Hales, performed on rats and dogs. 'How do we know', Pope protested, 'that we have the right to kill creatures that we are so little above as dogs, for our curiostity, or even for some use to us?'[28] In the *Essay on Man* he gave a sentimental image of the original state of nature in which 'Man walk'd with beast, joint-tenant of the shade.'[29] The blend of Arcadian idyll and contractual formality in that phrase 'joint-tenant' (not *sub*-tenant or lessee) represents a typically Augustan fusion of idealism and regulation. In *Windsor Forest* Pope showed how man violated this partnership with beasts, initiating a war against nature with reverberations all down the 'great chain':

> Beasts urg'd by us, their fellow beasts pursue,
> And learn of Man each other to undo.
>
> (ll.123-4)

Though specifically referring to gun-dogs, trained to track down and trap their prey, Pope's lines go further, suggesting Man's intrusive capacity for disturbing the carefully balanced moral ecology of nature. His description of the killing of a lark or a lap-wing, is not mock-heroic but anti-heroic:

> He lifts the tube, and levels with his eye;
> Strait a short thunder breaks the frozen sky.
> Oft, as in airy rings they skim the heath,
> The clam'rous lapwings feel the leaden death:
> Oft as the mounting larks their notes prepare,
> They fall, and leave their little lives in air.
>
> (ll.129-34)

The 'tube' has a chilling functional anonymity; this is no heroic lance, sabre or cannon, but a featureless killing machine. There is an obvious hint of presumption in the 'thunder' produced—thunder being the sound of gods. Man is attempting to arrogate a godlike role to himself, but can do so only in a negative, destructive sense. Similarly, the leaden death, like the tube, is grey, anonymous, unheroic. There is an evocative movement in these lines, rising with the 'mounting larks' only to fall again as they do. Yet as their bodies drop, heavy with lead, their 'little lives', a phrase which beautifully associates their echoing songs with their souls, seem to soar above human lead and tubes, the paraphernalia of death.

The criticism of hunting in *Windsor Forest* works by analogy as an attack on war, specifically on the war policies of William III. In his fierce hostility to the Norman forest laws which had turned Windsor into a 'gloomy waste/To savage beasts and savage laws a prey,/And kings more furious and severe than they', Pope employs a kind of coded (and potentially Jacobite) arithmetic, namely William I + William II = William III. Other critics have demonstrated the political iconography of the early sections of this poem which contrast the 'peace and plenty' of a Stuart reign with the gloomy desolation of a 'foreign master's rage'.[30] Yet we should not be tempted to read Pope's attack on hunting merely as a coded metaphor for the war of the Spanish Succession. His observations on the relationships between man and beasts exist in their own right as central motifs in his moral philosophy. The way in which humans treat animals becomes for Pope a test, as well as a metaphor, for moral behaviour in general. Cutting up rats is as much a violation of nature, though on a smaller scale, as razing a town to the ground.

An important key to a full appreciation of Pope's satiric poetry may be the recognition that the apparent antithesis between art and nature in his works is often in fact a form of metaphor. 'Nature and Homer were, he found, the same', he writes in his *Essay on Criticism*. Nature is as much to be found in a mathematical equation, or in the symmetry of a couplet as in the song of the lark or the ebb and flow of the tides. His couplets embody the polarities of the created universe; unity and chaos, light and dark, reason and passion, art and nature, revealing them not as antitheses but as veiled metaphors or misunderstood analogies: 'All Discord, Harmony not understood'. His 'philosophy', then, is not comprised of a series of glib aphorisms, to be memorised like mottoes, but is a process of imaginative exegesis. It is true, however, that his knack for versifying sometimes led him to be guilty

of an ad-man's flourish in producing dazzling tautologies or trite half-
truths. At the heart of his moral and poetic dilemma is the problem of
reconciling the heterogeneous chaos of experience with the ordered
universe of his deepest convictions. In *Windsor Forest* he finds his
resolution in the characteristic form of a paradox, with a vision of the
world harmoniously confus'd;

> Where Order in Variety we see,
> And where, tho' all things differ, all agree.

In the *Essay on Man* he produces a similar paradox, but the rhetorical
imperatives betray a greater sense of strain:

> All Nature is but Art, unknown to thee;
> All Chance, Direction, which thou canst not see;
> All Discord, Harmony, not understood;
> All partial Evil, universal Good:
> And, spite of Pride, in erring Reason's spite,
> One truth is clear, 'Whatever IS, is RIGHT.'
>
> (ll. 289-94)

In place of the leisurely perspective of the landscape painter, we have
here the rhetorical and hieratic imperatives of a high priest. In
rhythmic terms, all the power of these lines is concentrated in the
mystical paradoxes of each first hemistich as polar opposites are
magically proclaimed as synonyms. After each caesura the line is
allowed to dribble away, enacting the condescension of the
hierophant for the uninitiated. Pope's metaphors, pitched midway
between calculus and a conjuring trick, constantly produce order out
of chaos. His lifelong friend and physician, Arbuthnot, had once
sought to prove the benign workings of divine providence on the
evidence of the equal distribution of births of boys and girls. Pope
sought to do much the same when he described a form of moral
calculus producing equal numbers of misers and spend-thrifts, getters
and spenders:[31]

> Extremes in Nature equal good produce,
> Extremes in Man concur to gen'ral use.
> Ask we what makes one keep and one bestow?
> That POW'R who bids the Ocean ebb and flow.[32]

Yet the strain of maintaining this tolerance of 'partial evil' as part of some 'universal good' finally proved too much for Pope's philosophy, though not for his poetry. The formulas held fast; the heroic couplets held like whalebones while the philosophy they were formulated to expound was extinguished in the universal darkness of *The Dunciad*. Consider the final lines of Book IV:

> Lo! thy dread Empire, CHAOS! is restor'd;
> Light dies before thy uncreating word:
> Thy hand, great Anarch! lets the curtain fall;
> And Universal Darkness buries All.

The pattern, we should note, is the same as before; this is another form of harmonious confusion in which 'tho' all things differ, all agree'. The heterogeneous forms of Dulness still compose themselves into an overall unity—though this time it is the unity of universal darkness. These lines confirm Denis Donoghue's description of much Augustan literature as 'a series of strategic withdrawals, retreats in good order from positions deemed too Faustian or metaphysical to be held.'[33] That element of 'good order' is important. Even in defeat and disillusionment the art of rhythmic and structural *trompe l'oeil* by which this apocalypse is rendered to us in the most symmetrical and ordered couplets, is an irony which proclaims the triumph of the artist, the satirist, over the world. He remains a godlike artificer and his work alone does not disintegrate into the miscegenation of Dulness.

That detachment, maintained till the end, is the cutting edge of Pope's satire. The peculiar force of his satire comes from his unique combination of the roles of insider and outsider. Marked out by religion, politics and physical deformity as an outsider, he contrived to make a virtue of necessity, converting his Twickenham retreat into an Horatian shrine, embodying the values of an uncorrupted classicism. Yet he was also a man whose unique versifying talents had from an early age made him an intimate of coffee-houses and aristocratic homes. His satiric portraits constantly blend the inside knowledge of a social habitué with the detachment that comes from the implementation of classical models and humanist themes. As an illustration, we might consider this portrait of Chloe:

> Say, what can Chloe want?—she wants a heart.
> She speaks, behaves, and acts just as she ought;
> But never, never, reach'd one gen'rous thought.

> Virtue she finds too painful an endeavour,
> Content to dwell in decencies for ever.
> So very reasonable, so unmov'd,
> As never yet to love, or to be lov'd.
> She, while her lover pants upon her breast,
> Can mark the figures on an Indian chest;
> And when she sees a friend in deep despair,
> Observes how much a chintz exceeds mohair.
> (*Epistle to a Lady*, ll. 160-70)

Chloe is presented as essentially static. Her life affects the perfect stasis of a work of art rather than the activity of nature. Note the sense of strain in the phrase 'But never, never *reached* . . .'; generosity is seen as some form of vulgar exercise, the kind of strenuous exertion that one's servants should perform for one. Virtue is presented as a painful 'endeavour', rather like hiking, another vulgar activity calculated to discompose the artistic effect of style. This sense of stasis culminates in the visual pun of her unmoved state during lovemaking. Unmoved, both physically and mentally, we see her like a statue, elegant and cold, while her lover 'pants' upon her breast. The contrast between those two verbs—*pants,* with its association of lap-dog activity, and *marks,* suggesting precise mental calculation—is excellently judged. And the symmetry of this antithetical image is held fast by the punning rhyme, breast/chest. Chest is of course a synonym for breast, but while he pants upon her body, she is calmly considering a wooden object on the far side of the room. The irony is further heightened as the Indian chest would probably be decorated with carvings of naked figures. This further emphasises the total separation between Chloe's appearance of artistic cultivation and her utter vacuity of feeling. Now, this portrait may quite possibly be based on Henrietta Howard, later Countess of Suffolk, but this identification is less significant than the clear sense conveyed by the portrait of Pope's intimate familiarity with the idioms and tones of the world he describes. The voice of this description carefully counterfeits the tone of court gossip, yet merges with this an outsider's judgemental inflexions.

The problem that remains, particularly for modern readers, is one of tone. There is often an apparent self-righteousness, a gloating censorious exultation in the authority which Pope assumes for himself:

> Yes, I am proud; I must be proud to see
> Men not afraid of God, afraid of me.
> (*Epilogue to the Satires,* Dia.II, 208-9)

It's precisely here, at the moral core of his satires, that Pope abandons his self-deprecating ironies and presents himself as a lone avenger. Where Swift is content to portray himself as a rueful, rather ridiculous pedagogue, aiming one last lash at the world's posteriors, Pope truly feels himself entrusted with a divine mission:

> Yes, the last pen for freedom let me draw,
> When Truth stands trembling on the edge of Law.
> (*Epilogue to the Satires,* Dia. II, 248-9)

Pope's most recent biographer has demonstrated his obsession with the creation of flattering self-images. Not only did he sit for a remarkable number of portraits but also, as has long been well known, he tampered with his own early correspondence to present his career in a more sympathetic light. This meant not only removing awkward or inelegant phrases, but also editing out awkward or inelegant friends, and reassigning letters originally sent to these un-persons to more prestigious acquaintances. So early letters sent to Pope's unsung friend John Caryll reappeared in the printed version of his correspondence as if sent to Congreve or Addison. Taking a charitable view of these alterations, one might argue that they represent no more than a logical extension of Pope's normal processes of literary revision and correction. Why should replacing Caryll's name with Addison's in a letter be any more reprehensible than replacing Theobald's name with Cibber's in successive versions of *The Dunciad*? But letters are more than literary artefacts. They are the records of a relationship. And Pope's motives for making these changes were less aesthetic than biographical. He wished to project his own fictionalised version of his vexed relationship with the now dead Addison. And, while one can no doubt infer reasons for Pope's obsession with the creation of flattering self-images from his own physical deformity, there remains something unpleasant about his tendency to rewrite history in order to protect his own moral positions. Ironically, it has been this very tendency that has done most to damage Pope's moral reputation in the eyes of posterity. Yet it is just arguable that we should regard the 'Pope' presented to us in the *Epistle to Arbuthnot,* or in the *Epilogue to the Satires* as a fictional character akin to the 'Theobald' of *The Dunciad*. Pope's 'Pope', in other words like Pope's Man of Ross, is a deliberate blend of biography and classical myth. They stand as the imaginative antagonists to 'Sporus' and 'Theobald' in the poetic texture of these satires. Truth, in these satiric poems, is not a matter of biography or documentary evidence but an effect of the poetic imagination and a product of creative faith.

CHAPTER FOUR

John Gay

Shepherds and Chimeras

A few years ago, in the laboratories of Cambridge University a fabulous beast was conceived and born. That creature, as reported in the press, was a cross between a sheep and a goat, known variously as a 'shoat' or a chimera. The biology of this shoat is, I readily confess, a mystery to me. But in this chapter I wish to present the literary ancestry of just such a curious hybrid in the poetical works of John Gay.

Gay was a pastoral poet. It's worth reminding ourselves what that means, since 'pastoral' has become a word of almost infinite elasticity. It is now applied to anything from a pretty landscape picture to the responsibility for attempting to dissuade young people from committing suicide. The word, of course, derives from *pastor,* shepherd, and refers specifically to the keeping of sheep. The moral, spiritual and literary connotations of lost sheep, sacrificial lambs, the Lamb of God and the good shepherd, have been part of our religious iconography for centuries. But John Gay, who came from the pasture country of Devon, never forgot the animal origins of the pastoral motif. He never fails to remind his readers that all this complicated superstructure of literary, moral and spiritual connotations derives from the care of beasts whose fells, as Corin remarks in *As You Like It,* are greasy.

Interestingly enough, the symbolic and physical associations of sheep and sheepishness were curiously intermingled in the first recorded attempt to create a living ovine hybrid. In November 1667 Pepys reported that a 'poor debauched man' had been hired by the Royal Society for twenty shillings 'to have some of the blood of a sheep let into his body'. According to Pepys, the members of the Society differed 'in the opinions they have of the effect of it; some think that it may have a good effect upon him as a frantic man, by cooling his blood; others that it will not have any effect at all. ' The man himself, when asked why he had consented to the transfusion, replied, 'Sanguis ovis symbolicam quandam facultatem habet cum sanguine Christi; quia Christus est agnus Dei' (The blood of a sheep has a certain symbolic affinity with the blood of Christ, for Christ is the Lamb of God).[1]

The sadly absent shoat, that modern spatch-cocked hybrid, successor to the mythological beasts of classical antiquity, is the appropriate mascot for Gay's literary hybrids, ironic versions of pastoral which are all combinations of sheep and goats, blends of pastoral and parody. *The Shepherd's Week* is a mock-pastoral; *The Beggar's Opera* was inspired by Swift's suggestion for a 'Newgate pastoral'; *Dione* is a pastoral-tragedy; The *Tea-Table* and the *Toilette* are town-eclogues, that is, town-pastorals. The *Fables* are introduced by a pastoral dialogue between a shepherd and a philosopher. *The What D'Ye Call It,* the most chimerical of all these hybrids, is a tragi-comi-pastoral-farce.

Gay was not alone in recognising the potential ironies implicit in the fashionable Arcadian affectation which led Court ladies to dress up as shepherdesses, and Court poets to disguise themselves as rustic clowns or swains. Indeed, the intense self-consciousness that one finds in the eighteenth century to define the precise form of the pastoral genre is an indication of a loss of confidence in its literary force, and of a certain embarrassment at the potential bathos implicit in an urbane and sophisticated pose of bucolic naivety.

In April 1712 the *Guardian* devoted a series of issues—probably by Tickell—to the subject of pastoral poetry.[2] These acknowledged that the pastoral was a kind of literary make-believe, based on the depiction of an historical never-never-land (or fairy-land, as they call it). In a tone of urbane, metropolitan condescension he offers to lay down rules for those attempting to 'follow the shepherds and shepherdesses of ancient times'.

Pastoral poetry, we are told, derives from the 'first ages of the world . . . before mankind was formed into large societies or cities' and when 'the wealth of the world consisted chiefly in flocks and herds. . . . The tending of these we find to have been the employment of the first princes, whose subjects were sheep and oxen. . . . It was a state of Ease, Innocence and Contentment; where plenty begot pleasure, and pleasure begot singing, and singing begot poetry, and poetry begot pleasure again.'[3]

One might contrast this with what Rasselas discovers about the lives of shepherds: 'Their hearts were cankered with discontent . . . they considered themselves as condemned to labour for the luxury of the rich, and looked up with stupid malevolence towards those that were placed above them.'[4] 'Thus happy was the first race of men', The *Guardian* continues, 'but rude withal, and uncultivated.' This lack of cultivation was an essential ingredient in the folkloric charm of the pastoral form. For as Tickell (I call him Tickell) explains,[5] 'before any considerable progress in arts and sciences' could be achieved, the tranquillity of the rural life had to be destroyed by 'turbulent and ambitious spirits; who, having built cities, raised armies, and studied policies of state, made vassals of the defenceless shepherds, and rendered that which was before easy and unrestrained, a mean, laborious, miserable condition.'[6] By this historicised version of the expulsion from an Arcadian Eden, Tickell represents the price of civilisation as being the divorce between princes and shepherds, Court and country, power and pleasure. Hence, he concludes, 'if we consider the pastoral period before learning, we shall find it unpolished; if after, we shall find it unpleasant.'

The consequence is that any author who 'would amuse himself by writing pastorals' must engage in a kind of make-believe. He must 'show only half an image to the fancy . . . let the tranquillity of that life appear full and plain, but hide the meanness of it; represent its simplicity as clear as you please, but cover its misery.'[7] Pastoral does not involve holding a mirror up to nature, but rather pulling a little decorative wool over the eyes of the readers.

Pastoral itself is a kind of hybrid, part country life, part urban fantasy. Only the most conventional and stylised of misfortunes can be allowed to disturb the general ease and tranquillity of the bucolic world. 'I will allow shepherds to be afflicted with such misfortunes as the loss of a favourite lamb, or a faithless mistress. He may, if you please, pick a thorn out of his foot, or vent his grief for losing the prize in dancing.' What is most evident in all these prescriptions is a tone of condescension. This is the voice of a sophisticated Modern, addressing his coffee-house readership and recommending the affectation of rustic innocence as an amusing diversion, but constantly implying, by his tone, that this is a paradise well lost in favour of the modern benefits of irony and city life. It is a far cry indeed from a later version of the shepherd's life, in Wordsworth's poetry.

Pastoral swains are thus neither princes not shepherds, but a fictitious hybrid of the two whose chief appeal should be a total lack of historical authenticity. Arcadia is neither ancient nor modern but an idealised Disneyesque confection of the two where Court and country are one. As the *Guardian* articles continue, it is made evident that the language, beliefs and activities of the swains should all sustain this fake quality. The only clear requirement of pastoral poetry is that it must convey 'innocence and simplicity'. These terms, together with 'tranquillity and ease' are repeated ten times in the five short articles: simplicity of manners; simplicity of diction; simplicity of thought.

I do not propose to discuss here the historical and biographical relationship between these *Guardian* articles, Pope, Gay and *The Shepherd's Week*, which is already well documented;[8] Pope was annoyed that throughout the series, Philips' pastorals were taken as the only model for modern pastorals, while his own were ignored. So in *Guardian* No.40 he produced his own paper on pastoral, ostensibly a continuation of the series, but actually parodying everything that had gone before.[9] Dwelling on those key terms 'innocence and simplicity', he produces a definition of pastoral which, as J.V. Curran argues in his excellent edition of *The Art of Sinking in Poetry,* converts 'the beautiful simplicity of the Greeks and Romans' (as Addison called it in *Spectator* No.62) into the straw-chewing vacancy of the village idiot.[10]

Pope's parody is at its best when he simply quotes some of Philips' lines out of context, to reveal the bathetic inanity of this kind of simplicity:

> Ah me the while! Ah me! the luckless Day,
> Ah luckless lad! The rather might I say;
> Ah silly I! More silly than my sheep,
> Which on the flowry plain I once did keep.

Pope comments, 'How he still charms the ear with these artful repetitions of the epithets; and how significant is the last Verse! I defy the most common reader to repeat them without feeling some motion of compassion.'[11]

What I think is more interesting is to consider some of the quotations from Philips' pastorals that are presented in the *Guardian* articles, since these are clearly in the nature of appetisers in what is partly designed as a piece of puff copy. There is something rather curious about the actual passages chosen to illustrate the natural innocence and simplicity of Philips' swains:

>As I to cool me bath'd one sultry day,
>Fond Lydia lurking in the sedges lay.
>The wanton laughed, and seemed in haste to fly,
>Yet often stopp'd and often turned her eye.

Or again:

>Once Delia slept, on easie moss reclin'd,
>Her lovely limbs half-bare, and rude the wind:
>I smooth'd her coats, and stole a silent kiss;
>Condemn me shepherds, if I did amiss.[12]

In both extracts what we have, surely, is a kind of coy erotic hinting; not real innocence at all, but a form of rustic play-acting, a bucolic bo-peep. Arcadia here is a setting for some semi-naturist frolics, a kind of licensed play-area, and these coy nymphs belong to the same sort of teasing fantasy which in later literature is filled with French maids and naughty schoolgirls. This is definitely a post-Eden nakedness; a world of eyeing and spying.

Notice how the adjectives carry over from the objects of external nature to which ostensibly they refer, to the human agents. 'On easie moss reclined'; that word 'easie' seems to carry over to Delia herself, with her 'lovely limbs' displayed, suggesting not so much easy moss, as an easy miss. Similarly, the rude wind teases and seems to justify a corresponding 'rudeness' of the swain (and the ambiguity in that word 'rude' encapsulates the kind of knowing irony here). The phrase 'I smoothed her coats' cries out to be read by contraries, and the hidden pun in 'condemn me shepherds if I did amiss' all combine to make this a little voyeuristic fantasy, a kind of masque in *déshabillé*. In recommending his friend's work on the strength of this extract, Tickell is actually inviting an amused worldly reader to indulge himself at the expense of real innocence. We have entered the world of the *Ploughman's Lunch,* where bucolic motifs are reduced to tit-bits for worldly appetites.

'It is to this management of Philips that the world owes Mr Gay's pastorals', declared Pope.[13] I don't want to debate whether this is a sufficient explanation of the genesis of *The Shepherd's Week*. But obviously, particularly in the Proeme and first two eclogues, Gay makes his parody of Philips' work explicit; the fake archaic language; the coy pretensions; the use of superstitious lore, the glossary, are all deliberate attacks, designed to draw attention to the costume-drama

bathos of Philips' lines. In the hands of Philips, pastoral ceased to be a
splendid myth of human innocence in which shepherds are princes;
but became a tawdry masquerade in which some off-the-peg scenes
and phrases provided a bucolic backdrop for some fun and games for
wolves in sheep's clothing.

Like Pope, Gay seized upon and parodied the voyeurism implicit in
such lines. Thus in 'Monday' Cuddy boasts:

> As my Buxoma in a morning fair,
> With gentle finger stroak'd her milky care
> I queintly stole a kiss. [14]

Gay's footnote to the word 'queint' is a model of what was to become
the Scriblerian method of mock-annotaion. 'Queint has various
significations in the ancient English authors. I have used it in this place
in the same sense as Chaucer hath done in his *Miller's Tale*: 'As clerkes
been full subtil and queint' (by which he means arch or waggish) and
not in that obscene sense wherein he useth it in the line immediately
following.)' This is a typical Scriblerian trick. By drawing attention to
what the word doesn't mean (and by going out of his way to tell us
where we can find that other, obscene meaning), he outfaces the coy
voyeurism of Philips with an explicitly sexual parody which recalls
the technique of Rochester's mock pastoral, 'Fair Chloris in a pig-sty
lay'.

More importantly, Gay exploits the 'never-never-land' aspect of
pastoral as the basis for literary, social and, later, political satire.
Pastoral is his way into the anarchic world of literary and social
hybrids which deliberately defy the unities of time, place and status.
Thus he boasts of the never-never-land artificiality of his language in
The Shepherd's Week: 'which is, soothly to say, such as is neither
spoken by the country maiden nor the courtly dame; nay, not only
such as in the present times is not uttered, but was never uttered in
times future.' [15] It is an easy step from this to the form of the *What
D'Ye Call It,* a play which contradicts all attempts at categorisation. In
the Preface to the play, Gay asks all would-be critics to consider that
'when they object against it as a tragedy, that I designed it something
of a comedy; when they cavil at it as a comedy, that I had partly a view
to pastoral; when they attack it as a pastoral, that my endeavours were
in some degree to write a farce; and when they would destroy its
character as a farce, that my design was a tragi-comi-pastoral.' [16]

It is also in the Preface that he argues, taking his cue from the pastoral conventions, that 'the sentiments of princes and clowns have not in reality that difference which they seem to have'. Pastoral thus provides him with the basic pattern for his satiric works in which shepherds are compared with noblemen, clowns with courtiers, and highwaymen with statesmen.

In his Prologue to *The Shepherd's Week,* Gay represents his own move from Devon to London as a progress from clown to courtier.

> I sold my sheep and lambkins too
> For silver loops and garment blue.[17]

The emphasis upon selling his sheep is important, since it indicates two forms of reality—agricultural and financial—which reappear in the poem. In return, what Gay gains is a mere costume, 'silver loops and garments blue'. Not only does this seem trivial, but it also suggests a livery—the costume of a dependant. Gay thus reverses the conventional movement of the pastoral. Instead of the metropolitan world (as represented in the tones of the *Guardian*) standing for reality, with the pastoral world a kind of pretty masquerade, he presents the rural world as the real world, and the Court as a fancy-dress assembly of ribbons, loops, liveries and lace, sword-knots and wigs.

In a short but well-known article ten years ago, Arthur Sherbo asked whether Gay was a lightweight or a heavyweight, tough or tender, social critic or gentle miniaturist.[18] The advantage, for Gay, of his chosen hybrid world of pastoral parody, is that it enables him to maintain a permanent ambiguity, or duality of outlook. In both *The Shepherd's Week* and *The What D'Ye Call It* he see-saws happily from style to style, creating a satiric territory of his own out of the stylised formulas of contrasting literary genres. Sometimes satiric, sometimes indulgent, his poetry constantly detects and deflates the inherent implausibilities and inflexibilities in any of the formal genres which tend to reduce the experiences of life to costume pageant. Versatility, virtuosity and the *volte-face* are the hallmarks of a style that constantly likes to stay one jump ahead of expectations.

The most pervasive ambiguity, or hybridisation of tone comes from the insistent use of homely physical farmyard analogies and domestic details. Take this, from 'Tuesday, or the Ditty':

> Whilom with thee 'twas Marian's dear delight
> To moil all day, and merry-make at night.

If in the soil you guide the crooked share,
Your early breakfast is my constant care.
And when with even hand you strow the grain,
I fright the thievish rooks from off the plain.
In misling days when I my thresher heard,
With nappy beer I to the barn repair'd;
Lost in the musick of the whirling flail,
To gaze on thee I left the smoaking pail;
In harvest when the sun was mounted high,
My leathern bottle did thy drought supply;
When-e'er you mow'd I follow'd with the rake,
And have full oft been sun-burnt for thy sake . . .
When hungry thou stood'st staring, like an oaf,
I slic'd the luncheon from the barley loaf,
With crumbled bread I thicken'd well thy mess.
Ah, love me more, or love thy pottage less![19]

That last line is a good example of the *volte-face* effect, the final ironic descent into bathos, that I want to come onto later. But the general effect of these lines is not bathetic or ironic, but rather lyrical in their richly sensuous evocation of the tastes and smells, the sights and sounds of rural life. The suggestion of dialect in the words 'moil', 'misling', 'nappy' is not a self-conscious piece of parody or a deliberate literary slumming to draw attention to the affected archaisms and regionalisms of Philips' verse. There are no mock-learned footnotes to them as there are to *kee* = cows, and *ken* = know. They are part of a genuinely affectionate portrait as Gay strives, briefly, to recreate the authentic character of rural life; before abruptly undermining that, too, with an ironic shift, as though laughing at himself, and us, for having enjoyed this little piece of wool-pulling. The touch of the pastoralist's pen turns everything into stereotype.

The bathetic effect of this 'love in a pottage' motif is repeated several times throughout the eclogues. Usually the analogy is between the direct physical appetites of the livestock cattle, sheep, pigs, unmodified by the forms and conventions of art—and the more stylised desires of the swains, which are expressed in appropriately rustic versions of neo-classical formulas.

But let's return to the question of satire. In 'Wednesday' we find a vignette which, if taken out of context, would certainly seem to place Gay in the heavyweight category. His characters are as starkly distinguished as in any Victorian melodramas. Sparabella declares:

Ah! didst thou know what proffers I withstood,
When late I met the squire in yonder wood!
To me he sped, regardless of his game,
While all my cheek was glowing red with shame;
My lip he kiss'd, and prais'd my healthful look,
Then from his purse of silk a guinea took,
Into my hand he forc'd the tempting gold,
While I with modest struggling broke his hold.
He swore that Dick in liv'ry strip'd with lace,
Should wed me soon to keep me from disgrace;
But I nor footman priz'd nor golden fee,
For what is lace or gold compar'd to thee?[20]

There is the hunting metaphor, as the predatory squire 'regardless of his game' switches from an animal to a human quarry. The 'glowing red with shame' emphasises not only her embarrassment and terror, but also continues the suggestion of a blood sport. 'Healthful' nicely catches a tone of threatening euphemism in this compliment from a depraved superior to a young, vital prey. The violence in the woods forced and struggling is undisguised. To complete the humiliation, the squire promises to fix up a marriage for Sparabella with his footman, whose bondage is indicated by his livery, 'in liv'ry strip'd with lace'. The echo of Gay's description of his own trappings at Court—lace, loops and garment blue—is not coincidental. This livery is the uniform of humiliation. 'Strip'd' also conveys the suggestion to me of stripes, lashes, continuing the suffused sense of violence and blood, throughout the passage.

That, as I say, is what one *might* argue, taking the passage out of context. *In* context, however, all this satiric force is controlled and contained by the generic hybridisation which recognises all set-piece literary forms and styles as potentially self-parodic, and verging on stereotype. So Sparabella's description of her plight takes on the cliché style of a familiar motif: the country maiden seduced by the wicked squire. There is anger here, certainly; but it is a self-conscious anger qualified by its own stereotypical quality.

At the start of the *Ars Poetica,* Horace offers a graphic illustration of what, for him, constitutes bad art. I quote Ben Jonson's translation:

If to a woman's head a painter would
Set a horse-neck, and divers feathers fold
On every limb, ta'en from a several creature,
Presenting upwards, a faire female feature,

> Which in some swarthie fish uncomely ends:
> Admitted to the sight, although his friends,
> Could you contain your laughter?[21]

Gay, and later the Scriblerians as a whole, seized on this monstrous hybrid, this chimera of dulness, as the mascot for their satiric displays of *The Art of Sinking in Poetry.* In *The Dunciad,* Pope describes

> How tragedy and comedy embrace
> How farce and epic get a jumbled race.[22]

The works of the Scriblerians are filled with examples of this jumbled race—a progeny of prodigies; literary shoats, What D'Ye Call Its and Siamese twins, in which the irresponsible and meretricious powers of art are seen triumphing over nature. In this way they outface their antagonists, the Moderns or Dunces, by seizing upon their imaginative solecisms—such as Tickell's 'snow of blosssoms' in *Kensington Garden*—and turning them into triumphant symbols of a world of anarchy. They present the classical pretensions of modern culture as a series of incongruous hybrids; like bungled conversion jobs on magnificent old buildings by cowboy operators; grotesque botched attempts at cosmetic surgery; or crude, spatch-cocked, pre-Frankenstein attempts at anatomical joinery.

To conclude this section I would like to consider what I take to be the characteristic—almost the defining—device of *The Shepherd's Week,* the *volte-face.* For if zeugma is the key to the kind of antitheses one finds in *The Rape of the Lock,* the *volte-face* is the key device in these eclogues.

Apart from the use of the device within the various eclogues, five of the six eclogues conclude with one of these neat ironic twists. These closing couplets throw a wry backward glance over what has gone before. It is, of course, an explicitly literary device, an ostentatious flourish of wit which places a frame around the foregoing tragi-comi-pastoral elements, and leaves them with a clear authorial signature, which is knowing and ironic. Yet what precisely is the tone of that final irony? In 'Monday', Cloddipole suddenly appears and puts an end to the rival boasting of Cuddy and Lobbin Clout:

> Forbear contending louts . . .
> But see the sun-beams bright to labour warn,
> And gild the thatch of goodman *Hodge's* barn.

> Your herds for want of water stand adry.
> They're weary of your songs—and so am I.
>
>   (ll.121-4)

In 'Tuesday', Marion's lovesick ditty is interrupted by a cruder form of copulation:

> Thus *Marian* wail'd, her eye with tears brimfull,
> When Goody *Dobbins* brought her cow to bull.
> With apron blue to dry her tears she sought,
> Then saw the cow well served, and took a groat.
>
>   (ll.103-6)

In 'Wednesday', Sparabella's tragic fantasies are cooled by commonsense:

> The sun was set; the Night came on a-pace,
> And falling dews bewet around the place,
> The bat takes airy rounds on leathern wings,
> And the hoarse owl his woeful dirges sings;
> The prudent maiden deems it now too late,
> And 'till tomorrow comes, defers her fate.
>
>   (ll.115-20)

In 'Thursday', Hobnelia's piteous and superstitious lament for her lost love Lubberkin, is stilled as Lubberkin suddenly returns:

> But hold—our *Lightfoot* barks, and cocks his ears,
> O'er yonder stile see *Lubberkin* appears.
> He comes, he comes, *Hobnelia's* not bewray'd,
> Nor shall she, crown'd with willow, die a maid.
> He vows, he swears, he'll give me a green gown,
> Oh dear! I fall adown, adown, adown!
>
>   (ll.131-6)

In 'Friday', 158 lines of elegy, as humans, animals and all creation lament the death of Blouzelinda, are suddenly undercut by six lines reaffirming the continuity of life:

> Thus wail'd the louts in melancholy strain,
> Till bonny *Susan* sped across the plain;
> They seiz'd the lass in apron clean array'd,
> And to the ale-house forced the willing maid;

In ale and kisses they forgot their cares,
And *Susan, Blouzelinda's* loss repairs.

(ll.159-64)

Certain motifs, it will be noted, reappear in these concluding couplets. One is the antithesis of wet and dry. 'Excessive sorrow is exceeding dry' is Gaffer Treadwell's convivial motto in 'Friday', as he recommends a cheering autumnal beverage of 'cyder mulled with ginger warm'. The prolongation of any formal or conventional stylisation of feeling leads to a certain aridity which is at odds with natural inclinations and appetites. In 'Monday' it's the herds that are dry; in 'Friday' it's the louts. But in both, the promptings of nature are used to undermine the hyperboles of art. In 'Tuesday' the balance of nature works the other way; Marian's tears produce an excess of dampness; but this is soon dried as she is brought back from fanciful self-indulgence to the facts of financial and agricultural life which, as I noted before, Gay uses as a norm throughout the poem.

There's a sense in which the suddenness or glibness of these *volte-face* effects may appear condescending, or even cynical. The ease with which 'bonny Susan' can fill the place of Blouzelinda may seem to go beyond a parody of elegiac conventions and imply a certain brutishness or insensitivity in rural mirth and manners. But perhaps we should recall these lines from Swift's *Verses on the Death of Dr Swift*:

Here shift the scene to represent
How those I love my death lament.
Poor Pope will grieve a month; and Gay
A week, and Arbuthnot a day.

(ll.205-8)

Arbuthnot's brevity of mourning here represents not indifference, but a cheerful love of life. In the same way, Gay implies that a true celebration of Blouzelinda would take the form not of some hyperbolic invocation to all creation to cease in sympathy with her passing, but rather in a cheerful continuation of all those practical life-affirming values—the world of cakes and ale and kisses—that she represented and embodied.

Enjoyment is the essence of all these concluding couplets—a physical enjoyment that implies continuity. In 'Tuesday' and 'Thursday' we have copulation; in 'Monday' and 'Friday' the quenching of thirst with, in 'Friday', the hint of copulation to follow. In 'Wednesday' we have the continuation of life itself in the deferment of the tragic choice of suicide.

The effectiveness of these concluding *volte-faces* comes from the fact that while rhythmically and artistically they enclose the eclogues which they conclude, they simultaneously open them out in terms of feeling. They provide a final chink of light, or life to disturb the comic stereotypes and pastoral parodies. For the urban artist, country subjects present themselves all too easily in a series of familiar motifs, vignettes and charming cameo shots: 'rural sports', 'country life', 'pastoral scenes', 'the hay-wain', 'Ambridge', 'Lymeswold—there's a whole set of off-the-peg bucolic characters and roles from straw-chewing gaffers to pert milkmaids to decorate urban day-dreams. These final couplets confirm the control and self-conscious artistry of an author who knowingly switches from style to style, from stereotype to stereotype. Like the mock-learned footnotes and glossary, they are Gay's disclaimer of the fancy-dress imposture. He refuses to dress up either in a clown's smock, or in a courtier's ribbons and loops. But in addition, they remind us of the real underlying facts and rhythms of rural life which give a sustaining animation to what would otherwise be a meretricious display of parodies. The rhythms of birth, copulation, death; the rising and setting of the sun; the alternation of happiness and despair, summer and winter.

Pastoral in Gay's hands becomes a metaphor for a kind of cultural exchange in which both sides—the clowns and the courtiers—are engaged in play-acting, and in rituals of mock-deference. In one sense the idealised swain is an example of nature methodiz'd, like a human parterre, or a walking topiary-work. In another, the shepherd whose sentiments are no different from those of princes, is one of those tolerated exceptions from the rules of hierarchy—like a boy-bishop or a beggar-king. But the artful counterfeiting of this privileged simplicity is a dangerous kind of hypocrisy. In attempting to preserve the genuine article of rural innocence, and rescue it from the play-acting affectations of Philips, Gay confronts the same problem as Malcolm in *Macbeth:*

> Though all things foul would wear the brows of grace
> Yet grace must still look so.[23]

Or, as Pope wrote in his first *Guardian* article, 'Even Truth itself in a dedication is like an honest man in a disguise or a vizor-masque and will appear a cheat by being dressed like one.'[24] It is the problem of the fool among knaves, of the good-hearted innocent in a world of courtiers and corruption. Gay's solution to the problem offers a model for others, like Fielding, to follow. Just as the urbane sophistication of Fielding's narrative voice allows him to indulge us with the childlike simplicity of an Adams or a Heartfree, so Gay's self-conscious manipulation of a range of parodic devices enables him to safeguard a central belief in a form of Arcadian simplicity which lies at the heart of his own morality.

Businessman, Beggar-man, Thief

The Beggar's Opera is by far the best known of Gay's works with modern readers and theatre-goers. Indeed, there are many who are quite familiar with this opera who might be hard pressed to name another single one of his works. Consequently, productions of *The Beggar's Opera* represent the most reliable evidence of modern attitudes to Gay's status as either a serious social satirist or a charming lightweight entertainer. Satiric productions tend to view the opera through the hindsight of Brecht's *Threepenny Opera*, treating Gay's work as an interesting anticipation or prototype of the German classic of bitter-sweet social ironies. The lightweight school, exemplified by Nigel Playfair's celebrated production at the Lyric in the 1920s, with musical arrangements by Frederic Austin, amplifies the Arcadian elements in this Newgate Pastoral, providing lush orchestrations of the airs, and turning the low-life settings into charming Cinderella grottoes.

Naturally, the enduring success and fascination of the opera is due in part to the fact that it can sustain and attract both interpretations. Its initial triumph, enjoying an unprecedented opening run of sixty-two nights, was a result of this successful combination of commercially attractive elements. For some it was a kind of daring political cabaret; for others, a hit musical, full of sentimental songs and comic ballads. Many commentators, both at the time and since, have tended to associate the opera's triumph with its provocative social and political satire. Writing from Ireland, Swift enquired of his friend Gay, 'Does Walpole think you intended an affront to him in your opera? Pray God he may.'[25] In fact, Walpole artfully affected ignorance, or at least unconcern, towards any possible political allusions in the opera.

According to one report, he attended one of the first performances of
the opera. Lockitt's song caused a particular stir:

> When you censure the age,
> Be cautious and sage,
> Lest the courtiers offended should be:
> If you mention vice or bribe,
> 'Tis so pat to all the tribe;
> Each cries, that was levelled at me.

The greater part of the audience, we are told 'threw their eyes on the
stage-box where the minister was sitting and loudly encored it'.[26] But
the astute politician Walpole promptly 'encored it a second time
himself, joined in the general applause, and by this means brought the
audience into so much good humour with him, that they gave him a
general huzza from all parts of the house'. Modern scholars are
divided in their opinions of whether Gay did indeed intend an affront
to Walpole in his opera.[27] What is beyond dispute is that when Gay
followed up this success with the sequel, *Polly,* Walpole made his real
displeasure evident by having the play banned from performance and
causing Gay to be evicted from his lodgings in Whitehall. 'The
inoffensive John Gay is now become . . . the terror of ministers',[28]
reported Dr Arbuthnot. It was natural enough that Swift, who
confessed that he appreciated music 'like a Muscovite' (that is, not at
all), should emphasise the opera's political character, and give less
weight to its musical charms. However, it is equally clear that much of
the work's popular appeal relied less upon its political daring than
upon its lyrical airs and melodies, and in particular upon the talents of
the leading lady, Lavinia Fenton, in the role of Polly. Her performance
so captivated the Duke of Bolton, who came to see the opera every
night, that at the end of the run he made her his duchess. Amid all the
commercial exploitation of Gay's success, which included *Beggar's
Opera* fans, screens, songs and playing cards, it was Polly's picture
which figured most prominently. 'I am in doubt', commented Gay,
'whether her fame does not surpass that of the opera itself.'

Even if they recognised the opera as a satire, it is probable that those
first audiences would have regarded Gay's main target as Italian opera
rather than political corruption. The vogue for Italian opera in
London, beginning with *Arsinoe* in 1705, had recently grown into a
fashionable craze. In 1723 Gay wrote to Swift ridiculing this new
musical style:

There's nobody allowed to say, I sing, but an eunuch or an Italian woman . . . and folks that could not distinguish one tune from another now daily dispute about the different styles of Handel, Bononcini, and Attilio. People have now forgot Homer and Virgil and Caesar, or at least they have lost their rank, for in London and Westminster, in all polite conversations, Senesino is daily voted to be the greatest man that ever lived.[29]

In fact, the castrato Senesino had recently signed a contract to sing his first London season for the immense sum of £2,000. It was in part the huge sums paid to the stars of Italian opera, as well as what seemed the inherent effeminacy or puerility of the genre itself, which led moralists to condemn its malign influence on British culture. These verses, printed in Steele's *Miscellany* in 1714 following the return of the castrato Nicolini to Italy, are typical of many similar attacks:

> Begone, our nation's pleasure and reproach!
> Britain no more with idle trills debauch;
> Back to thy own unmanly Venice sail,
> Where luxury and loose desires prevail.

Yet it is equally difficult to identify any specific parodies of Italian opera in Gay's work as it is to point to any undisputed lampoons of Walpole. In his introduction to the opera the Beggar boasts, 'I have observed such a nice impartiality to our two ladies, that it is impossible for either of them to take offence.'[30] His words here clearly look beyond Lucy and Polly and are designed to remind us of a notorious row between the claques of the two rival leading prima donnas, Cuzzoni and Faustina, the previous summer. The row had been headlines for several weeks, and as Pat Rogers remarks, 'Apart from the death of George I a week later, it was the biggest news story of 1727'.[31]

The rapid medley of ten songs in Act 3 Scene13 of *The Beggar's Opera* may be taken as a burlesque of certain Italian styles, but in the main Gay attempted to challenge the taste for Italian opera less by parody than by contrast. There are in fact sixty-nine songs in *The Beggar's Opera*. The melodies are mostly old ballads and dance tunes, old English, Scottish and Irish airs, including such familiar favourites as *Greensleeves* and *Lillibulero*. The overall effect is of a wonderful vitality, of a patriotism rooted in a love of song, and the evocation of certain enduring values. Boswell described the effect of these songs: 'The airs in ''The Beggar's Opera'', many of which are very soft, never fail to render me gay, because they are associated with the warm sensations and high spirits of London.'[32]

I mention all this because I think there's a danger that modern students, reading the opera as a play on the page, may underestimate its musical effects as a work in performance. When we consider the opera verbally as a play-text, we are inevitably likely to concentrate on the social and political satire implicit in its prose. The remarks that follow examine in detail some of the social ironies revealed by the language of the opera. But we should always remember that Gay's satire achieves its peculiar subtlety and force from being grafted onto the charming lyrical vitality of these simple ballads. Hence his criticisms seem to emanate not from some rival politician or disgruntled courtier, but take on the tone and humour of a broader humanity, which transform the attacks upon individual politicians into a festival of traditional values.

Still one of the best-known and influential interpretations of *The Beggar's Opera* is that offered by Empson in *Some Versions of Pastoral*. There he presents the work as celebrating an ironic collaboration between aristocrat and swain in the character of the heroic rogue, at the expense of the bourgeois. 'I should say then that the essential process behind the Opera was a resolution of heroic and pastoral into a cult of independence'.[33] According to this view it is those bourgeois figures Peachum and Lockit who are the villians of the piece, not the cavalier Macheath. 'Gay meant Peachum to be the villain . . . Gay dislikes him as a successful member of the shopkeeping middle class, whereas Macheath is either from a high class or a low one.'[34]

What is surprising, however, is how much the language and idioms of this despised shopkeeping class permeate the play and colour the motives and behaviour of all its characters. As a title *The Beggar's Opera* retains the notion of the rogue outsider, the beggar-as-judge, the comic reversal whereby the last in society affects to pass sentence on the first. But to judge by the tone and sentiments at work it might more appropriately be called the *Business Man's Opera*. The word 'business' occurs fifteen times in the play. 'Money' occurs nineteen times, as well as its variants and synonyms—'fees', 'guineas', 'price', 'garnish', and so on. 'Account' is used nine times, and other financial words—'interest', 'perquisite', 'profit', 'debt', and 'credit'— run all through it. But it is not simply the frequency of these words but rather the specific usages of them which is interesting. As Rogers remarks, 'in fact the method of the entire *Opera* is to make language spill the beans—betray the hidden attitude and the real drives'.[35] He also notes a typical process by which 'Persons often become the objects of commercial verbs' and gives the example of Peachum and Lockit's agreement 'to go halves in Macheath'. This tendency to treat people and relationships in commodity terms deeply permeates the opera and is the key to its satiric tone. The most epigrammatic examples are well known; such as Peachum's 'Money, wife, is the true Fuller's Earth for Reputations, there is not a spot or a stain but what it can take out' (I.ix), or Macheath's declaration that 'a man who loves money might as well be contented with one guinea as I with one woman'. Such phrases draw attention to themselves as satiric one-liners, and are meant to provoke and challenge us with their neat antitheses of money and reputation, or money and love. More powerful though, because more insidious than these high-profile epigrams is the steady drip of unnoticed commercialising nouns and verbs, etching in the financial atmosphere of the opera.

We might start with the most obvious. Characters are often valued in strictly commercial terms, that is according to how much may be 'got' by them or for them. In the first three scenes, Peachum uses this formula three times. He promises to save Betty Sly from transportation, 'for I can get more by her staying in England'. He adds that 'there is nothing to be got by the death of woman—except our wives' (I.ii). He remarks that he hates 'a lazy rogue, by whom one can get nothing'. Later in Act 2 his resentment against Macheath is somewhat lessened when he recalls 'how much we have already got by him' (I.xi).

All this is very straightforward; but perhaps a more surprising usage is the word 'account'. This word occurs several times in the opera and usually refers directly to financial accounts. Yet it is interesting to observe how, when the word is ostensibly used in an abstract sense, as in the phrase 'on account of' it remains an ironic suggestion of commercial origins. Thus Mrs Slammekin claims the *credit* (another financial term to which we shall return) for the hanging of three men: 'I am sure at least three men of his hanging, and in a year's time too, (if he did me justice) should be set down to my account.' Though primarily an abstract term here, the pervasive commercial values of the opera imply that Mrs Slammekin actually has in mind Peachum's ledgers in which, in Scene 3 of the opera we see him drawing up the accounts of the gang. The fact that (II.vi) she specifies *three* men, further strengthens the sense that these are items to be reckoned and literally set down to her account. Earlier Mrs Peachum regrets Macheath's lack of discretion 'Upon Polly's Account', a phrase which so baffles her husband that he repeats it:

'Upon Polly's account! What a plague does the woman mean? Upon Polly's account!' (I.iv). Primarily, the reason for Peachum's bewilderment is his ignorance of Polly's attachment to Macheath. Yet the vehemence of his remonstrance is partly triggered by his wife's use of the word 'account'. Polly's name not being set down in his book of accounts, he has some intitial difficulty knowing how to account for his wife's meaning. 'Upon Polly's account' refers ostensibly to Polly's emotional sensitivities, but the word immediately reinforces the satiric tone of the opera in which all abstracts—whether moral social or emotional can only be understood in cash terms. Towards the end of the opera, Polly herself uses the term, disingenuously professing to Lucy Lockit that 'I suffer too upon your account'. Here again, though the word has *prima facie* an abstract meaning, we detect an ironic inflexion, as though Polly's suffering could be reckoned up and set down as a credit in her account with Lucy. The full financial implications of this interpenetration of commercial and emotional terms is presented in a dialogue between Lucy and Macheath. 'You see, Lucy', declares Macheath, 'in the account of love you are in my debt' (II.xv), to which she replies, some lines later, 'Come then, my dear husband—owe thy life to me'. These characters have no other vocabulary for their emotions than that of the balance-sheet.

The word 'credit' operates in just the same way. In Act 1 Peachum describes Harry Padington as 'a poor petty-larceny rascal' who 'will never come to the gallows with any credit' (I.iii). Much later, Macheath tells Lucy that Polly 'would fain the credit of being thought my widow'. (II.xiii) In both cases we might substitute the word reputation for the abstract meaning of credit. But the word that Gay uses maintains this concentrated sense that all reputations depend on cash. 'Money', as Peachum observes, 'is the true Fuller's Earth for reputations'. (I.ix).

The opposite of a creditable reputation for a tradesman is bankruptcy and ruin. And the word 'ruin', which also occurs frequently throughout the opera, is full of the same ironic implications. 'Tis your duty, my dear, to warn the girl against her ruin', remarks Peachum to his wife (I.iv) when he hears the rumour that Polly may have married Macheath. A few scenes later he demands of his daughter directly, 'Tell me, hussy, are you ruin'd or not?' (I.viii). Of course there is a more obvious joke here, for the Peachums neatly reverse the word's usual ironic implications. Ordinarily a euphemism for seduction, the word 'ruin', while conveying a sense of moral disgrace, more pertinently acknowledges the damage that the loss of virginity can do to a woman's prospects in the marriage-market. The Peachums, however, regard marriage itself as a form of ruin for the embargo it places upon free sexual trade. Unless, of course, it is contracted in a spirit of speculative investment.

> Peachum: And had not you the common views of a gentlewoman in your marriage, Polly?
> Polly: I don't know what you mean, sir.
> Peachum: Of a jointure, and of being a widow. (I.x)

Thus Gay takes a word already shop-soiled into a euphemism and gives it a new ironic twist by returning it straight to its origins in the marketplace. To the Peachums, ruin is simply a matter of money. Hence, when the word is used again, as when Macheath complains that his confinement is made worse by 'the reproaches of a wench who lays her ruin to my door' (II.viii), or when he tells Lucy that Polly claims to be married to him 'only to vex thee, and to ruin me in thy good opinion', we constantly feel that the F.T. Index rather than the Ten Commandments offers the truer guide to the nature of the ruin involved.

Lucy blames her plight on her ale-house education, 'for 'twas to that I owe my ruin', whereas her father, Lockit, blames his misfortunes on her hasty affections: 'So I am to be ruined, because, forsooth, you must be in love!' (III.ii). In fact, we see them both as victims of more skilled accountants in the commercial warfare who use love, honour, duty and so on as negotiable assets. Some other interesting usages may briefly be noted. The word 'Bilk'd' is used twice; once in a purely literal, that is financial, sense, of 'cheated'. Diana Trapes complains that 'those hussies make nothing of bilking of me'(III.vi); the other time, it is used metaphorically by Lucy who declares, 'Am I then bilk'd of my virtue'—again treating virtue as a material commodity.

'*Redeem*' is another word with both a moral and even religious meaning, and a financial meaning. Mrs Trapes hopes that Mrs Coaxer, 'for her own sake and mine . . . will persuade the captain to redeem her'. The meaning here suggests far less the saving of a soul than the reclaiming of a pledge from the pawn shop—but the satire of course resides in precisely the ambiguity between the two. We have already noted one use of *debt* when Macheath envisages not only love but also death in financial terms. 'For Death is a Debt. A Debt on demand. So take what I owe', he sings in the final Act— though, as we know, his own debt is cancelled and his pledge redeemed.

The other words which help to reinforce this atmosphere of book-keeping and trade are almost too numerous to list. 'Deal' is one. 'Depend upon it—we will deal like men of honour', says Lockit in Act 3 Scene 6 and this suggestion of a possible antithesis between 'dealers' and 'men of honour' is something to which I wish to return. 'Bargain', 'expenses', 'customers' are also all words used in an ironic double sense, both moral and financial. One particularly felicitous usage is the phrase, used by Peachum, 'The comfortable estate of widow-hood is the only hope that keeps up a wife's spirits', where the word 'estate' naturally has the primary meaning of state or condition, as in the phrase the 'honourable estate of matrimony'. But only too clearly he also has in mind the comforts of real estate, a few rolling acres to solace a grieving widow's loneliness.

Only one word in the opera is used with any frequency in apparent opposition to these pervasive commercial terms—that word is 'honour'. Honour is mentioned in the play at least thirteen times, often in the phrase 'man' [or men] of honour. But the antithesis between money and honour is more apparent than real, as we shall see. Superficially, one might expect 'honour' to be the watchword of the gentleman Macheath in opposition to the financial values of Peachum. And it is true that Macheath does use the term most often—a total of five times. But it is also a term bandied about by all sorts and conditions of other characters: Mrs Peachum, Filch, Polly, Matt of the Mint and Jenny Diver use it once each, and Lockit uses it three times.

What quickly emerges from these usages is that honour is less a moral absolute than a convenient code of self-interest. Macheath declares his confidence in his gang ('as men of honour, and as such I value and respect you' (II.ii). Lockit is also very much on his dignity as a man of honour. 'This is the first time my honour was ever called in question', he protests to Peachum in a key scene (II.x), and later promises him that 'we will deal like men of honour' (III.vi). But the context in which these protestations are made clearly indicates the circumscribed and materialistic nature of the 'honour' involved. Macheath talks much of his honour in a central scene with Lucy (II. ix) just as Lockit does in the following scene with Peachum. 'From a Man of honour, his word is as good as his bond', Macheath declares loftily to Lucy, where that cliché simile is given additional ironic force from the pervasive financial atmosphere. A few lines later he repeats. 'I am ready, my dear Lucy, to give you satisfaction—if you think there is any

in marriage—What can a Man of Honour say more?' Yet in his
soliloquy, immediately before this dialogue with Lucy, he tells us
explicitly what this declaration of honour amounts to: 'I promised
the wench marriage—What signifies a promise to a woman? Does not
a man in marriage itself promise a hundred things that he never means
to perform:' (II.viii). In the same way, Peachum and Lockit bandy the
term back and forth, but always with a clear view of its commercial
value.

Lockit:	Mr Peachum—This is the first time my honour was ever call'd in question.
Peachum:	Business is at an end—if once we act dishonourably.
Lockit:	Who accuses me?
Peachum:	You are warm, brother.
Lockit:	He that attacks my honour, attacks my livelihood.

(II.x)

Yet they quickly agree to drop this inflated vocabulary between
themselves and recognise that the only honour among thieves is a
form of mutual dependency.

Peachum:	'Tis our mutual interest; 'tis for the interest of the world we should agree.

Honour then is a concept of a strictly limited liability. It is like a
used-car dealer's guarantee, a form of warranty which is not the
antithesis to self-interest but a euphemism for it. In this there is no
difference between Peachum and Macheath; both of them interpret
'honour' as jargon for their own code of mutual assistance, the public
face of a protection racket. 'Men of honour' is a phrase rather like
'reputable dealer' that means exactly the opposite of what it says. No
character is immune from this corrupt and devalued meaning of the
word. Not even Polly. When she protests in Act 1 that she did not
marry Macheath '(as 'tis the fashion) coolly and deliberately for
honour and money', the conjunction of the two terms 'honour' and
'money', shows that she too recognises 'honour' as merely
euphemistic jargon for the commercial self-interest of the united
company of wives. Thus there is less of a contrast in the play between
the aristocratic cavalier Macheath—the 'laird of the open ground . . .
king of the Waste Land', as Empson glosses him—and the bourgeois
money-fetishist Peachum, than is sometimes suggested. They, and the

other characters, are held together by the pervasive commercial association of the language they use.

There is another important link between their modes of behaviour which has important implications for the opera's satiric meaning. They operate through gangs, that is, through organisations founded on principles of mutual assistance. In their frequent references to employments and professions, it is made evident that Peachum, Lockit and Macheath all use their organisations as the underworld parallel of various flourishing professional bodies preying upon society. Peachum makes this clear in his opening song:

> Through all the employments of life,
> Each neighbour abuses his brother;
> Whore and rogue they call husband and wife:
> All professions be-rogue one another.
> The priest calls the lawyer a cheat,
> The lawyer be-knaves the divine;
> And the statesman, because he's so great,
> Thinks his trade as honest as mine.
>
> (I.i)

Lawyers are a familiar target as a well-organised gang, with their own private jargon and rules designed for the exploitation of clients. They are mentioned again when Peachum complains. 'Lawyers are bitter enemies to those in our way. They don't care that anybody should get a clandestine livelihood but themselves' (I.ix). Surgeons are twice cited as another gang of 'fleaing rascals'. Even beggars are spoken of by the Beggar in his introduction as a corporate body. 'I own myself of the company of beggars; and I make one at their weekly festivals at St Giles.' But the most successful protection racket of all is that operated by the politicians, whose system of patronage and legalised corruption Peachum and Lockit can only imitate with envy.

The banks and joint-stock companies offered further models of successful capitalist enterprise, and it seems probable that the real inspiration for the business activities of Peachum and Lockit derived from the sudden rash of joint-stock companies associated with the South Sea Bubble. As Professsor Rogers has noted, the word 'bubbled'—meaning cheated or deceived—occurs twice in *The Beggar's Opera*. Gay uses these joint-stock swindles as his models for all other 'professional' organisations, whether of ostensibly high status—such as lawyers, surgeons and ministers—or low, such as pick-pockets, prostitutes and thieves. It has even been suggested that Peachum's business methods in the opera may be intended to parody the precepts contained in Defoe's *Complete English Tradesman,* first published in 1725.[36] Defoe's purpose in this work was an entirely serious attempt to describe both the theory and practice of business efficiency. But Charles Lamb was so disgusted by Defoe's 'studied analysis of every little mean art, every sneaking address, every trick and subterfuge (short of larceny) that is necessary to the tradesman's occupation', that he enquired ironically whether the book was actually intended as a satire. In particular, Defoe counselled the importance of keeping strict and regular accounts; 'Upon his regular keeping, and fully acquainting himself with his books, depends at least the comfort of his trade, if not the very trade itself.' In this, as in much else, Peachum shows himself a graduate of the Defoe school of business.

However, if I were to suggest a single literary source for the commercial ethics which Gay satirises in the opera, it would not be Defoe's business handbook but Bernard Mandeville's notorious and provocative poem *The Fable of the Bees.* First published in 1705, this poem was reprinted in an expanded form, together with some prose essays, in 1723 and 1724. It was in this expanded version that the works became notorious. 'Vice and luxury have found a champion and a defender, which they never did before', declared John Dennis.[37] The book was presented as a public nuisance by the Grand Jury of Middlesex, and in the five years following 1724 no less than ten books attacking the *Fable of the Bees* were published, by such eminent philosophers and churchmen as William Law, John Dennis, Francis Hutcheson, Archibald Campbell and Isaac Watts. In addition, the work was continually subject to attacks from sermons, letters to the press, and in 1728 was again presented by the Grand Jury of Middlesex. Finally, in 1729, Mandeville published a substantial second volume of the *Fable* in which he attempted to answer some of the critics. Certainly, at the time when Gay was writing *The Beggar's Opera*, Mandeville's book was frequently depicted as one of the most scandalous modern works in print.

As often happens, much of this scandal and fuss was due to a fundamental misreading of Mandeville's irony in this witty and satirical work. The poem, which bears the motto 'Private Vices, Public Benefits', ironically recommends the advantages that accrue from the encouragement of crime and the institutionalisation of vice for the benefit of society as a whole. Mandeville's real target, though, was the kind of hypocrisy which professed to combine Christian morality and Roman virtue with a life of luxury and wealth. As he later explained, the work was written

> to expose the unreasonableness and folly of those that desirous of being an opulent and flourishing people, and wonderfully greedy after all the benefits they can receive as such, are yet always murmuring at and exclaiming against those vices and inconveniences, that from the beginning of the world to this present day, have been inseparable from all kingdoms and states that ever were famed for strength, riches and politeness at the same time.[38]

Or, as he explains in the 'Moral' to his poem:

> Bare virtue can't make nations live
> In splendour; they, that would revive
> A Golden Age, must be as free
> For acorns as for honesty.

Commercial growth and expansion, Mandeville argues, depend upon vanity, vice, avarice and exploitations. A nation composed of Parson Adamses or Men of Ross would not have a very flourishing business sector. His poem depicts Britain as a 'grumbling hive' in which various groups, professions and classes of bees have banded together to promote forms of beneficial vice. The first groups that he mentions correspond with those in *The Beggar's Opera.* There are the lawyers, who

> kept off hearing wilfully,
> To finger the refreshing fee;
> And to defend a wicked cause,
> Examin'd and survey'd the laws;
> As burglars shops and houses do,
> To find out where they'd best break through.

Then the physicians, who

> valued fame and wealth
> Above the drooping patient's health.

Then the priests, hot and ignorant:

> Yet all past muster, that could hide
> Their sloth, lust, avarice and pride.

Mandeville ironically lists all those who gain an honest living out of crime, including the legal and criminal services; gaolers, turnkeys, sergeants, tip-staffs:

> and all those officers
> That squeeze a living out of tears.

Throughout society he detects one invariable rule:

> All trades and places knew some cheat
> No calling was without deceit
> Thus every part was full of vice,
> Yet the whole mass a paradise.

In his explanatory remarks added to this last couplet, Mandeville offers some illustrative examples, including this one:

A highwayman, having met with a considerable booty, gives a poor common harlot he fancys, ten pounds to new rig her from top to toe; is there a spruce mercer so conscientious that he will refuse to sell her a thread sattin, tho' he knew who she was? She must have shoes and stockings, gloves, the stay and manto-maker, the sempstress, the linnen-draper, all must get something by her, and a hundred different tradesmen dependent on those she laid her money out with, may touch part of it before a month is at an end.[39]

Matt of the Mint clearly has this philosophy if not these words in mind when he declares, 'We retrench the superfluities of mankind'. He distinguishes the free-spending ways of the highwaymen, which promote enjoyment and activity, with the avarice of misers:

The world is avaricious, and I hate avarice. A covetous fellow, like a jack-daw, steals what he was never made to enjoy, for the sake of hiding it. These are the robbers of mankind, for money was made for the freehearted and generous, and where is the injury of taking from another, what he hath not the heart to make use of.   (II.i)

The irony of having a thief condemn avarice is of a peculiarly

Mandevillian nature, and Matt here endorses precisely the kind of commercial incentives that Mandeville celebrates. Vice and crime are the most important stimulants for employment. Luxury

> employed a million of the poor
> And odious pride, a million more.

Interestingly, both Gay and Mandeville note the paradoxical form of mutual dependency—code word 'honour'—by which those whose very natures are to cheat and plunder, are forced to trust and assist each other. Thus Peachum observes, 'Lions, wolves and vultures don't live together in herds, droves and flocks. Of all animals of prey, man is the only sociable one. Every one of us preys upon his neighbour, and yet we herd together.' In the *Fable of the Bees*, Mandeville describes this harmony of contrasts which makes 'jarrings in the main agree'.

> Parties directly opposite
> Assist each other, as 'twere for spite.

Such a description might almost be regarded as a parody of the theory of *discordia concors* developed in Pope's *Windsor Forest*: 'Where order in variety we see,/And where, tho' all things differ, all agree.' But whereas Pope regards this harmonious confusion of contrasts as evidence of the designs of a benign providence, Mandeville presents it as the product of a trade cycle, generated by the dynamo of vice, which makes nonsense of all moral distinctions.

At times it seems as if Macheath is resisting the business-like professionalism of outlaws into subsidiaries of Crime Incorporated, and is clinging on to the life of a highwayman as one of individual heroism and aristocratic panache. But his language instinctively betrays him; his use of the word 'honour' shows his acknowledgement of the strictly limited liability of the group known as 'gentlemen of the road' rather than the moral absolutes of a free human being. His language has already been squeezed into the pre-formed models of an institutionalised role, however much he may seem to struggle against it.

The opera's final irony, its happy ending, can now be seen to be fully integrated into the satirical structure of the work as a whole. 'All this we must do', says the Player, referring to the reprieve for Macheath, 'to comply with the taste of the town.' This is, of course, the perfect businessman's conclusion, giving the public what they want and sending them home with a song on their lips. And the joke is that it worked, far beyond Gay's expectations. The opera was a triumphant business success, and in the phrase of the time, 'made Gay rich, and Rich gay'. For both parties, not to mention the star, Lavinia Fenton, their mutual assistance proved highly beneficial. Gay's success, and the pleasure it gave to massive audiences, was thus yet another example of the social benefits to be derived from crime, in this case from the depiction of criminal activities. And all of us, down to and including literary critics of fictionalised versions of the exploits of Jonathan Wild, may be said to be enjoying some devolved benefits from criminal acts in the distant past. We are all in the business.

CHAPTER FIVE
Fielding

The Violence of Virtue

It is not often remarked how violent Fielding's novels are. Yet it is rare for characters to proceed for more than twenty pages at a time without coming to blows over some matter of principle or interest. Miraculously, for all the roaring and bellowing, the rushing of blood and flailing of cudgels, no one actually gets hurt in these fights. As in cartoon strips, or Laurel and Hardy films, we are offered a comic spectacle of violence which has no unpleasant or lasting after-effects. Either the mock-Homerican style, as in the battle in the churchyard (*Tom Jones,* IV.8), or the slapstick situation farce, as when Parson Adams is covered with a pan full of hog's blood (*Joseph Andrews,* II.5), keeps it all at a safe level of comic hyperbole. Often the lurid exaggeration of the language has the effect of diminishing rather than strengthening its impact. Blood 'gushes' or 'spurts', people are 'drubbed' or 'thrashed'. This is the '*splat*!', '*pow*!' language of cartoon which allows the characters to bounce back in the next chapter without a scratch on them. Yet 'violent' is one of Fielding's favourite adjectives. In *Tom Jones* alone characters have violent passions, violent rages, violent agonies, violent aversions, violent perturbations, violent emotions, violent desires, violent attachments, violent fondnesses, violent dispositions and violent fits of joy. They utter violent oaths and violent screams. They experience violent headaches, violent tremblings, violent raptures, violent suspicions, violent afflictions, violent shocks, violent uproar, violent injunctions, violent measures, violent thoughts, violent impulses, violent flutters and violent despair. Bells are rung violently; doors are knocked on violently. People lay violent hands on each other. There is violent love and violent death, violent blushing and violent falls. There are violent floods of tears, violent drinking, violent swellings, violent kisses, violent shakings of the head and even violent snoring.

Nowadays violence has become an issue in its own right. Violence is something that modern democratic states cannot tolerate. Whether it is soccer violence, terrorist violence, political violence or mindless violence—the headlines all agree that it is indefensible. 'We must defeat the men of violence' is a familiar politician's cry, and always guaranteed a roar of approval. We may think, believe and say what we like, but we may not use violence to support or propagate our beliefs. If violence should enter a political dispute, that violence itself quickly becomes the major political issue, supplanting the original cause of grievance.

What is interesting is that Fielding does not share this instinctive repudiation of violence. For him it is not a taboo but rather something robust, positive and honest. There is nothing incongruous, to his way of thinking, about a clergyman, Parson Adams, who is forever becoming embroiled in fights, using either his fists or his trusty cudgel. This kind of violence is to be applauded not deplored. It is a form of muscular Christianity which literally fights the good fight and leaves behind a trail of broken heads, bruised ribs and bloody noses. Paradoxically, Fielding presents violence almost as a form of gentleness, whereas politeness may often disguise an underlying cruelty. In some ways violence may be seen as the polar antithesis of another key concept in Fielding's novels—prudence. Where prudence is a rational concept of delay, calculation and circumspection, violence is a spontaneous and impulsive exposure of the ruling passion.

For several years there has been a general critical consensus that 'prudence' plays a central part in *Tom Jones.* 'Prudence and circumspection are necessary to the best of men', observes the narrator (*Tom Jones,* III.7): 'It is not enough that your designs, nay that your actions, are intrinsically good, you must take care they shall appear so.' When assessing Tom's character, it is his lack of prudence that Allworthy most regrets:

> I am convinced, my child, that you have much goodness, generosity and honour in your temper; if you will add prudence and religion to these, you must be happy: for the three former qualities, I admit, make you worthy of happiness, but they are the latter only which will put you in possession of it.   (V.7)

At the end of the book Allworthy draws this salutory moral from

Tom's experiences, apparently for our edification as readers; 'You now see, Tom, to what dangers imprudence alone may subject virtue (for virtue, I am convinced, you love in a great degree). Prudence is indeed the duty which we owe to ourselves' (XVIII.10). And in case we still haven't got the message, we are informed on the very last page that Tom 'hath also, by reflexion on his past follies, acquired a discretion and prudence very uncommon in one of his lively parts' (XVIII.13).

Yet while critics are united in acknowledging the importance of this concept in the novel, they are far from unanimous in their interpretation of Fielding's attitude to it. For some, Tom's acquisition of prudence is the underlying moral theme of the novel, uniting its various episodes into a clear didactic structure. His quest for Sophia, whose name is the Greek for wisdom, symbolises a moral need to unite the instinctive virtues of good nature with the reflective virtues of good judgement.

Other critics, however, see Fielding's use of the term very differently. Eleanor Hitchens points out that 'the words "prudence", "prudent" and "prudential" are used unfavourably three times, as often as they are used favourably. Nearly every unadmirable character in the novel is described as prudent or is shown advocating prudence'.[1] This is undoubtedly true. The words 'prudence' and 'prudent' are quickly assimilated by the reader as part of the novel's ironic scaffolding. A few examples will suffice. The prudence of old maids (Bk I,Chs 2-3), which 'like the trained bands, is always readiest to go on duty where there is least danger', is really a form of pathetic vanity, seeking to create a virtue out of harsh necessity. Most commonly, prudence is a euphemism for meanness. Blifil is described as 'a very prudent lad, and so careful of his money, that he had laid up almost every penny which he had received from Mr Allworthy' (III.9). In an ironic aside, Fielding's narrator fears that some readers, witnessing Tom's early lack of interest in Sophia, may 'blame his prudence in neglecting an opportunity to possess himself of Mr Western's fortune' (IV.6).

The lectures on prudence which Mrs Western is forever inflicting upon Sophia are direct appeals to snobbery and self-interest. In Book VI (Ch.13) we are told that Sophia

> had been entertained by her aunt with lectures of prudence, recommending to her the example of the polite world, where love, (so the good lady said) is at present entirely laughed at, and where

women consider matrimony, as men do offices of public trust, only as the means of making their fortunes, and of advancing themselves in the world.

Again in Book VII Mrs Western reiterates her view that marriage is 'a fund in which prudent women deposit their fortunes to the best advantage, in order to receive a larger interest for them than they could have elsewhere' (VII.3). The prudence of Partridge is timidity and shallow self-interest. Indeed, prudence can often be claimed as a justification for the meanest and most uncharitable actions. Thus when a poor lame beggar retrieves Sophia's pocket-book, unaware of the bank-bill inside, we are told that 'a prudent person would, however, have taken proper advantage of the ignorance of this fellow, and would not have offered more than a shilling, or perhaps sixpence for it; nay, some perhaps would have given nothing' (XII.4). Or it can be a form of marketing, as when Nightingale remarks of Lady Bellaston that 'her favours are so prudently bestowed, that they should rather raise a man's vanity, than his gratitude' (XV.9).

In all these examples—and there are many more that could be cited—prudence is merely a euphemism for hypocrisy, the acceptable face of meanness and self-interest. As Miss Hitchens points out, 'Blifil is the most "prudent" character in the novel'.[2] A.E. Dyson writes that 'the ridicule in *Tom Jones* is used in support of a particular moral theory . . . which prefers "a good nature" to a prudential calculation'. Ethel Thornbury argues that 'prudential morality, a narrow, unhealthy performing of what is conventional just because it is prudent, is made to seem thoroughly absurd and thoroughly bad'.[3]

So what are we to think? Why should Fielding labour so mightily to have his hero acquire that very quality which so conspicuously identifies all the villains in the work? In fact, as Glenn Hatfield argues, Fielding's repetitive emphasis on the term 'prudence' represents an interrogation of the term, and an ironic analysis of its moral status. There are in fact two competing forms of prudence at work in the novel, yet both concealed within the same word. There is true prudence, in its original sense, which like charity was one of the cardinal virtues. And there is a false or sham prudence, which is concerned only for social appearances, not moral absolutes.[4] True prudence, as embodied by Sophia, represents the ideal of a 'union of a good heart with a good head'.[5] It is a moral quality which is not the opposite, but the complement of innocence, 'for simplicity, when set on its guard is often a match for cunning'.[6]

Throughout *Tom Jones* we find an ironic oscillation between these two versions of the same term, and on one page, for example, we find characteristic examples of both. The narrator relates: 'Thus did the affection of Allworthy for his nephew, betray the superior understanding to be triumphed over by the inferior; and thus is the prudence of the best of heads often defeated by the tenderness of the best of hearts' (XVI.6). While he begins the following chapter, just two paragraphs later, by telling us, 'Mrs Western was reading a lecture on prudence, and matrimonial politics to her niece'. Yet even here the contrast between the two versions of prudence is less clear-cut than might at first appear. Since, in the first quotation, the antithesis between the 'prudence of the best of heads' and the 'tenderness of the best of hearts' is made ironic by misattribution. It is Blifil, the most prudent of characters, whose vehement protestations of love for Sophia are represented by that tenderness; and Allworthy, whose naive benevolence is too easily imposed upon by Thwackum, Square, Blifil and others is supremely ineligible for the description, 'the prudence of the best of heads'.

In Hatfield's terms, Fielding takes a term which 'already had a kind of built-in ironic potential, and playing this ironigenic corrupt sense against the "proper and original" meaning of the word that is developed in the definition by action, seeks to restore the word to its original dignity of meaning.'[7] Charles Churchill, writing in 1762, notes the devaluation of the word:

> Prudence, of old a sacred term, implied
> Virtue, with godlike wisdom for her guide,
> But now in general use is known to mean
> The stalking-horse of vice, and folly's screen.
> The sense perverted we retain the name;
> Hypocrisy and Prudence are the same.[8]

In other words, Fielding's satire on prudence, like his satire on 'virtue' and 'honour' is directed at the linguistic corruption and devaluation of words from moral absolutes to social accessories. Virtue, the 'vartue' of *Shamela,* is no more than the market-value of virginity— or of the pretence of virginity. 'Honour' is defined in the Modern Glossary as 'duelling'; or, as the Scriblerian authors of *The Art of Sinking in Poetry* indicate, is a title for sale for political favours: 'Every man is honourable, who is so by law, custom or title.'[9]

The antithetical ironies that we find in Fielding's analysis of the term 'prudence' we also find, in a less deliberate but equally revealing way, in the treatment of violence. In part the pervasive use of violent reactions may be seen as part of Fielding's narrative technique for keeping his characters under strict authorial control. When characters like Mrs Western (twice), the landlady at Upton, Mrs Honour and Squire Western are described as flying, falling or, in Mrs Honour's case, bursting into a violent rage, it is a form of easy comic stereotyping which reduces their reactions to those of automata. A great deal of the action in *Joseph Andrews* takes place at the double, like a piece of speeded-up film, and the result is not only a comic exaggeration but also a number of accidents and collisions which produce further comedy.

When Molly Seagrim's sisters 'fall violently upon her' (IV.9) for her supposed vanity; or when we are told Tom was 'under the most violent perturbation' (V.6) in his feelings for Sophia we discern a note of comic exaggeration in the words which, paradoxically, has the effect of diminishing rather than strengthening the nouns. When we read that Jones 'fell into the most violent agonies, tearing his hair from his head, (VI.12) the word once again has a reductive comic effect, turning our attention away from the emotion itself, and onto the physical effects of grimaces and so on. A violent dispute (VII.11) is one in which, though blows may be exchanged, no lasting damage will be done. Real calamities are the result of prudent conspiracies, not violent disputes. Occasionally, however, violence does have an enforcing quality, as, for example, when combined with a tender or gentle noun. Thus we are told Squire Western has a 'violent fit of fondness' (VI.7) and Mrs Miller a 'violent fit of joy' (XVIII.5). When Jones expresses a 'violent flutter' of apprehension (XV.11) or blushes 'to a violent degree' (VIII.2), the violence of these tender emotions indicates their naturalness and spontaneity. In *Joseph Andrews,* Parson Adams reacts in a physical manner to all indications of good and evil, frequently starting up and snapping his fingers in irritation or exultation. At the word 'debauchery' 'Adams started up, fetch'd three strides across the room' (III.3). He capers, and more especially dances at the prospect of goodness or happiness. If any prudes are offended by the lusciousness of the description of Joseph's encounter with Fanny (II.12) the narrator advises them 'to take their eyes off from it, and survey Parson Adams dancing about the room in a rapture of joy'. When a poor pedlar offers to lend him six shillings and sixpence Adams 'gives a caper' with pleasure (II.15). This is a completely natural and spontaneous kind of dancing. It is dancing for

the joy of life, and has nothing at all in common with the superficial
fashionable accomplishments in mechanical movements taught by
dancing masters. Violence and joy are combined in a physical
spontaneity that is the instinctive expression of good nature. Even
Allworthy's violent snoring (V.9), though comic, has the effect of
reassuring us with a sense of physical normality, a natural and
spontaneous reaction.

What is the impact of all this violence? Firstly I think, it reinforces
the sense of sudden, hectic, thoughtless, activity. Violence has a direct
line to the ruling passions, and in this way may be seen as the
antithesis to hypocrisy. Hypocrisy, after all, relies upon cunning and
deception, whereas these violent rages and passions represent the
true instincts. The violence of a character's reactions betrays their
true feelings. Thus Lady Booby's emotions are revealed by the violent
agitation of her moods: 'the lady had scarce taken two turns before
she fell to knocking and ringing with great violence' and again, 'she
applied herself to the bell and rung it with infinite more violence than
was necessary (I.78). In the nearest thing to a soliloquy that she can
achieve, she asks grandly, 'whither doth this violent passion hurry
us?' (I.8). And if violence is demonstrated by the callous Trulliber and
the 'roasting' squire, it is also demonstrated by the impetuous Adams
and the instinctive Joseph. In fact, as we have already seen, Adams has
a physical reaction to most situations, dancing at goodness and
starting at vice. Morality operates not through introspection and
analysis, but through natural instincts. Innocence, which is
constantly ambushed by experience, reacts instinctively and
violently; whereas worldliness relies on cunning and guile. Bruises
are a badge of courage.

Violence also has the effect of adding muscle to morality, and
giving a certain adjectival virility to those vulnerable abstractions,
virtue, chastity, charity and prudence. The fact that Fanny feels a
violent passion for Joseph tells us that she is no pious hypocrite, but a
woman with healthy, normal impulses. The combination of violence
and virtue makes chastity *tough*: 'She loved [him] with inexpressible
violence, though with the purest and most delicate passion' (II.10).
This combination of toughness and tenderness, passion and chastity,
violence and virtue, is precisely represented in the variable pressure
of Fanny's embrace:

Tho' her modesty would only suffer her to admit his eager kisses,
her violent love made her more than passive in his embraces; and

she often pulled him to her breast with a soft pressure, which, tho'
perhaps it would not have squeezed an insect to death, caused
more emotion in the heart of Joseph than the closest Cornish hug
could have done.

(I.11)

Yet just a slight adjustment of the balance turns a positive alliance
into a satiric antithesis. One of Fielding's favourite ironic effects is to
combine a violent adjective with a timid abstract noun. Examples are
when Lady Booby attributes Joseph's bashfulness at first to the
'violent respect he preserved for her' (I.5) and even much later, to his
'too violent an awe and respect for herself' (IV.1). Or when the
narrator defers to the 'violent modesty' and 'rampant chastity' of his
female readers (I.8). There is an obvious incongruity in these
juxtapositions, but the satire comes perilously close to ridiculing the
moral stance of the book's main characters. For surely Adams is a
violent defender of virtue; Joseph and Fanny are passionate
champions of chastity; Tom Jones is an impetuous advocate of
prudence.

Violence in Fielding's works is characteristically a positive
quality—natural, honest and spontaneous. Nothing illustrates this
better than the attitude shown to 'violent' love. The violence of a
person's love is not regarded as low, vicious, bestial or degrading, but
rather as a guarantee of sincerity. In his long homily to Jenny Jones
(I.7) Allworthy declares, 'Love, however barbarously we may corrupt
and pervert its meaning, as it is a laudable, is a rational passion and can
never be violent, but when reciprocal.' He here performs quite a
syllogistic feat, making violence compatible with rationality, and
treating the true violence of love as a test of its reciprocal nature. Lest
we suspect an irony in this juxtaposition which might invite us to
smile at Allworthy's implausible benignity, we should compare this
with the narrator's own comment in Book IX (Ch.7): 'Women, to
their glory be it spoken, are more generally capable of that violent and
apparently disinterested passion of love, which seeks only the good
of its object, than men.' Here the narrator performs the no less daring
rhetorical feat of making violence synonymous with altruism. In
both cases a violent love is a way of expressing a true or generous love,
and violence thus becomes a guarantee of virtue. As a final
confirmation of this, when in the last book (XVIII.9) Allworthy
praises Tom's love for Sophia, he does so in these terms: 'If ever man
was capable of a sincere, violent and noble passion, such, I am

convinced, is my unhappy nephew's for Miss Western.'

However, just as prudence has a dual aspect, so there is another form of violence, and another use of the term in Fielding's writings. This is when violence signifies a kind of exaggeration, and when 'violent' reactions represent a false not an instinctive reaction. There are several examples of this in *Joseph Andrews*. At one point (I.8) lady readers are ironically requested by the narrator to 'bridle their rampant passion for chastity, and be at least as mild as their violent modesty and virtue will permit them'. Lady Booby imputes Joseph's coldness towards her 'to the violent respect he preserved for her' (I.5). And in *Tom Jones*, when we are told that 'the violent affection which the good waiting-woman [Mrs Honour] had formerly borne to Sophia was entirely obliterated by that great attachment which she had to her new mistress [Lady Bellaston]', the comic suddenness and apparent totality of the transition, turns 'violent' into a kind of hyperbole. Yet one might also detect a tell-tale note in the adjectives here. 'Great', as we know, is never used without an ironic suggestion of corruption and the replacement of 'violent love' by a 'great attachment' may represent, in miniature, a move from country to town values.

In all these cases the incongruous coupling of an active or masculine adjective, with a weak or feminine noun, *violent* modesty, *rampant* chastity, is meant to indicate a kind of comic affectation. This violence is a kind of ham acting—an exaggeration of gesture, a comic excess of assertion and language. This is not the violence of spontaneous instinct but a kind of violence done to those instincts, which betrays itself in incongruity. In a sense, all affectation is a kind of violence to nature, and in the Preface to *Joseph Andrews,* where Fielding discusses the two main forms of affectation, vanity and hypocrisy, which are the main subjects of his satire, hypocrisy is described as a 'violent repugnancy of nature'. As with prudence, so with violence, we are offered a series of exemplary situations demonstrating that there is a right and wrong way to apply these qualities. Prudence proceeds from the head, and violence from the instincts, and thus, given the ostensible moral polarities of these novels, prudence is generally seen in a bad light, and violence in a good one. Yet this in itself can be a trap. There is, right at the end of *Tom Jones,* a strong emphasis on the immoral and indefensible uses of violence. Twice in the final book Allworthy denounces the 'cruel violence' of Squire Western in his attempts to force Sophia into a loveless marriage with Blifil. And then, in a final gesture of compassion he declares, 'There will be no need of any violence' in punishing Blifil (XVIII.11). What is clearly offered is a distinction between violence as a spontaneous natural instinct and violence as a deliberate policy inflicted on others.

By concentrating on the uses of violence in Fielding's satiric fiction, I am not attempting to suggest any dark or disturbing sub-text beneath the sunny optimism of the surface. On the contrary, the effect of all this violence in vocabulary and actions is quite the opposite. It suggests that these things pose no threat—they are contained. They are part of a hearty, natural mode of life which is actually far healthier than vicious self-discipline or hypocritical self-restraint. Violence does not threaten the social fabric because, as a natural instinct, it is part of the same harmony of nature that forms the artistic and providential order of the novels.

Receipt to Make a Satire

In the early pages of *A Room of One's Own* Virginia Woolf draws a memorable contrast between lunch at a Men's College and dinner at a Women's College at Oxbridge. The lunch is a sensuous and aesthetic delight: soles 'sunk in a deep dish, over which the college cook had spread a counterpane of the whitest cream'; partridges 'with all their retinue of sauces and salads, the sharp and the sweet, each in its order . . . potatoes, thin as coins but not so hard, sprouts, foliated as rosebuds, but more succulent'. Dinner, by contrast is homely, humble, utilitarian: 'Here was the soup. It was a plain gravy soup. There was nothing to stir the fancy in that. . . . Next came beef with its attendant greens and potatoes—a homely trinity, suggesting the rumps of cattle in a muddy market, and sprouts curled and yellowed at the edges, and bargaining and cheapening, and women with string bags on Monday morning.'[10]

The pleasures of such a lunch, she argues, ignite that 'subtle, subterranean glow which is the rich yellow flame of rational intercourse'. Discussions of Van Dyck, Tennyson, Rossetti flow naturally from the consumption of sprouts 'foliated as rosebuds' but not from those 'curled and yellowed at the edges'. 'One cannot think well, love well, sleep well, if one has not dined well', she declares: 'The lamp in the spine does not light on beef and prunes.'

Woolf is concerned with the aesthetic, the inspirational qualities of food and cookery. The Augustan satirists, however, had different

culinary priorities. For them cookery was partly a social, partly a
cultural, partly even a political concern. But above all, food was a moral
issue. For Fielding that humble beef and two veg, which failed to light
a lamp in Woolf's spine, was a symbol of honesty and integrity. The
homely but hearty meals consumed by Tom Jones and Parson Adams,
consisting of such simple traditional fare as bread and cheese, beef and
ale and pudding are as indicative of their essential good nature as their
instinctive attitude to charity. A roast sirloin of beef, symbol of the old
English hospitality, is appropriately served to celebrate the nuptials of
Joseph and Fanny at the end of *Joseph Andrews*. Adams declares that he
enjoys his 'homely commons' of bread and cheese and ale better than
any amount of splendid dinners. 'For hunger', Fielding comments, 'is
better than a French cook' (III.8). When Tom and Partridge sit down to
a meal with the gypsies (XII.12) they enjoy a simple but hearty meal of
'bacon, fowls and mutton, to which everyone present provided better
sauce himself than the best and dearest cook can prepare'. A little later
the narrator, declining to reproduce the sallies and ripostes of a piece
of 'polite conversation' in detail, explains his reticence in these terms:

> I have known some very fine polite conversation grow extremely
> dull, when transcribed into books or repeated on the stage. Indeed,
> this mental repast is a dainty, of which those who are excluded from
> polite assemblies must be contented to remain as ignorant as they
> must be of the several dainties of French cookery, which are only
> served at the tables of the great.   (XIII.4)

Probably he has in mind Swift's ironic collection of *Polite
Conversation,* which converts a catalogue of clichés into a little
comedy of manners.[11] All such dainty titbits of small talk are like
French cooking: all decorations but no beef, sauce without meat, style
without substance. In all these examples, *haute cuisine* is seen not, as
Woolf argues, as a stimulus, but rather as a substitute for genuine
conviviality and geniality. True good nature, fellowship and warmth
require no such artificial stimulants but only a wholesome natural
appetite. A stout heart will prefer a stout piece of beef, and only a
mincing fop like Beau Didapper wants his food tricked up in a fricassee
or his sprouts foliated like rosebuds. One of the most interesting satires
on the 'New Cookery' of the early eighteenth century is William King's
Art of Cookery, an affectionate parody of Horace's *Ars Poetica*.[12] At
one point King transforms Horace's tribute to Homer into a comment
on the diet of the Homeric heroes:

> Homer more modest, if we search his books
> Will shew us that his Heroes all were Cooks:
> How lov'd Patroclus with Achilles joins,
> To quarter out the Ox and spit the Loins.
>
> (ll.200-3)

The heroes are carnivores whose tastes in food show no trace of foppishness. Indeed, King inserts an ironic comment on their lack of gastronomic refinement in one of the prefatory letters to the poem: 'Homer makes his Heroes feed so grossly, that they seem to have had more occasion for scewers than goosequills.' A similar manly appetite for roast beef was widely held to account for the triumphs of Marlborough's heroes, and the French lack of martial vigour was easily explained by their puny diet: 'Their stinking cheese and fricasy of frogs!' Yet, as John Fuller observes in his Chatterton lecture *Carving Trifles,* King ironically suggests that French cookery may yet triumph where French arms have been defeated. As the British generals celebrate their victories, they may succumb to the enemy's culinary blandishments.

> Quails, Beccofio's, Ortelans were sent
> To grace the levee of a general's tent.
> In their gilt plate all delicates were seen,
> And what was Earth before became Terrene.
>
> (ll.294-7)

As Fuller notes, that 'Earth' is both the common camp cooking-pot and the world which remains to be conquered by the British. 'Terrene' is glossed by King as 'a silver vessel fill'd with the mostly costly dainties', and the pun, which substitutes the French Terrene for the English Earth, in effects hands over our conquests to the enemy. What has been won on the battlefield is lost again at the table: 'What is the point of fighting the French if we become French ourselves?'[13]

This contrast between the roast beef of old England and the French fricassee of frogs quickly became an emblem for all those other differences between freeborn Englishmen and their priest-ridden neighbours across the channel. Hogarth perpetuated the imagery in his engraving of *The Calais Gate,* popularly known as *The Roast Beef of Old England.* The Beefsteak Club, of which Hogarth was a founder member, institutionalised the link between beef-eating and political freedom. And in his contrasting images of *Beer Street* and *Gin Lane*

Hogarth illustrated another piece of dietary politics. *Beer Street* depicts the virtues that flow from a wholesome, natural English brew while *Gin Lane* reveals the evils of addiction to a noxious liquor, originating in Holland, but whose name, Geneva, hinted at other pernicious foreign influences.

There was of course a long and extensive tradition of satires on the subject of food in both classical and Christian literature. Gluttony was one of the seven deadly sins. Like fornication, it was a kind of carnal self-indulgence, a form of sensual excess which preferred the pleasures of the body to the perfection of the soul. Trimalchio's feast, from the *Satyricon* of Petronius, was a prime example. With *hors d'oeuvres* including dormice seasoned with poppyseed and honey, and a main dish arranged as a culinary conceit based on the signs of the zodiac, this orgy of extravagance and licentiousness provided a rich source for later satirists to imitate.

The Augustans, with their characteristic emphasis upon moderation in all things, might naturally be expected to endorse such attacks on gastronomic hedonism. But there is a subtle shift in many of their more interesting satires on this subject. It's not so much the amount but rather the kind of food which concerns them. Some foods are more virtuous than others. A hearty appetite for plain English food is one of the ways in which Fielding establishes the vitality of his characters. Joseph Andrews' capacity to put away beef and ale together with his fondness for fisticuffs and hunting are demonstrations of his natural virility, and normal healthy carnal appetites, despite his virtuous and somewhat comic attachment to his own chastity. The language of eating—particularly of meat-eating— is frequently used by Fielding as a metaphor, or disguise for sex. Ned Ward, in his *Secret History of Clubs* (1709) made much of the theory that beef-eating increased sexual appetite,[14] and it is notable that in the mock-Homeric eating scene which precedes Tom's bedding of Mrs Waters at Upton, we are told that Tom consumed 'Three pounds at least of that flesh which formerly contributed to the composition of an ox'(IX.5). This is truly heroic eating. Elsewhere the language of table and bed are deliberately, and ironically, mingled. Jonathan Wild views Mrs Heartfree as a 'charming dish' and conceives for her the same kind of affection which 'a lusty divine is apt to conceive for the well-drest sir-loin or handsome buttock which the well-edified squire in gratitude sets before him'(II.8). The narrator pursues this parallel, informing us that Wild first 'projected a design of conveying [this dish] to one of those eating-houses in Covent Garden where female flesh is deliciously drest and served up to the greedy appetites of young gentlemen'. Undoubtedly there is something gross about this imagery, but the grossness lies less in the parallel than in Wild's particular attitude and taste. Unlike Tom Jones, whose appetite for both beef and sex is natural and spontaneous, Wild first 'projects a design', his appetite requires the additional stimulus of fantasy and brothel decoration; he desires his female flesh 'deliciously drest and served up', trussed and plucked. And of course the real irony is that, unlike Tom, Jonathan Wild never does achieve physical gratification; his projects and designs are constantly frustrated, and remain at the level of adolescent fantasies.

Parallels between sexual and alimentary appetites are by no means unusual, but it is worth noting the difference in tone between the uses of this figure in Fielding and Richardson. Richardson tends to concentrate on the cruelty involved in preparing dishes to satisfy the tastes of epicures and voluptuaries. Lovelace at one point remarks:

> Nor had I another time any mercy upon the daughter of an old Epicure, who had taught the girl, without the least remorse, to roast Lobsters alive; to cause a poor Pig to be whipt to death; to scrape Carp the contrary way of the scales, making them leap in the stew-pan, and dressing them in their own blood for sauce.[15]

As Carol Flynn notes, Lovelace's language faithfully represents the tortures recommended in eighteenth-century recipe books:

> 'turkeys were bled to death by hanging them upside down with a small incision in the vein of the mouth; geese were nailed to the floor; salmon and carp were hacked into collops while living to make their flesh firmer; eels were skinned alive, coiled round skewers and fixed through the eyes so they could not move . . . Calves and pigs were whipped to death with knotted ropes to make the meat more tender. . . . 'Take a red cock that is not too old and beat him to death' begins one of Dr William Kitchiner's recipes.[16]

It is worth remarking that among the many outcries against the so-called New Cookery few criticisms were levelled at these kitchen tortures. Only Pope protested at the cruelty involved in satisfying the refined tastes of cultivated epicures. 'I know nothing more shocking or horrid', he wrote, 'than the prospect of one of their kitchens cover'd with blood, and filled with cries of creatures expiring in tortures.'[17] William King artfully transforms Horace's advice that acts of violence

are better reported than represented on stage into a recommendation
for a distinct separation between the kitchen and the dining-room:

> Far from the parlour have your kitchen plac'd,
> Dainties may in their working be disgrac'd.
> In private draw your poultry, clean your tripe,
> And from your eels the slimy substance wipe.
> Let cruel offices be done by night,
> For they who like the thing, abhor the sight.
>
> (ll.244-9)

Yet even this, one notes, is a matter of etiquette rather than morality:
the priority is that one's guests should not be disturbed, rather than
that the animals should not suffer.

The eighteenth century, as several commentators have observed,
saw the beginnings of the commercialisation of leisure; and the
literature of the period reflects the growing interest in various new
recreations. Then as now, books on cookery, full of exotic recipes,
mingled with books on gardening and travels, fashion and art, to cater
for this new luxury market. According to one authority, the
restoration of Charles II ushered in 'an epidemic of recipes and new
dishes'[18] designed to replace the roast beef of England with more
daring continental fare. In 1663 the French commentator Sorbière
complained that the English 'are not very dainty, and the greatest
lords' tables, who do not keep French cooks, are covered only with
large dishes of meat.'[19] Sixteen years later Evelyn registered his
displeasure at a feast held in the Portuguese embassy: 'besides a good
olio the dishes were trifling, hash'd and condited after their way, not
at all fit for an English stomach which is for solid meat'.[20] Yet during
those intervening years a gradual revolution was taking place in
English stomachs. Works like Robert May's *The Accomplisht Cook, or
The Art and Mystery of Cookery* (1660), William Rabisha's *The Whole
Body of Cookery Dissected* (1661), Hannah Wolley's *The Cook's
Guide* (1664) and Denis Papin's *New Digester* (1681) were
transforming the tastes of the upper classes.

Thus alongside the New Science, which seemed to be questioning
the old certainties of Genesis, there was something called the New
Cookery, which threatened to dislodge some no less cherished
beliefs. The language of the attacks on the New Cookery, which was
always associated with France, frogs and fricassees, has much in
common with the attacks on Italian opera with its castrati, pampered

prima donnas and ludicrous plots. Both were represented as dangerous foreign confections designed to undermine the health of sturdy and traditional English culture. Yet, despite the protests of moralists, both French cuisine and Italian opera enjoyed a considerable vogue in the early decades of the century. Among the most outspoken critics of the New Cookery was not a satirist but a scientist. Dr John Woodward is now best remembered as a favourite target of Scriblerian satire, and the model for Dr Fossile in the collaborative play by Pope, Gay and Arbuthnot, *Three Hours After Marriage.* Woodward's attack on the New Cookery in his book *The State of Physick and Diseases* demonstrates his usual style of dogmatic hyperbole. 'The error in our diet' he wrote, 'consists partly in the nature and sort of it: in high seasoning, strong sauces, pickles, new dishes, new modes of cookery, brought amongst us by the foreigners that have come over, in so great numbers, for about 30 years past.'[21] This revolution in tastes, he asserted, had had catastrophic moral and social consequences: 'the consequences of this great increase of the arts of luxury and intemperance are vice and immorality: Irreligion, impiety: Passion, animosity, contention, faction: Neglect of thought, studies and business: Mispending of time: Ignorance; stupidity; poverty; discontent; sickness; diseases.' He offered his own pseudo-scientific account of the harmful effects of highly seasoned dishes on the bilious salts, and described the chain of alimentary causality which brought forth, 'notions and principles the most immoral; as well as irrational in the highest degree; even atheism itself. This assuredly never begins in the head, or in real reasoning: but proceeds from below, and is the result of sensuality'. As a direct result of this disturbance to the bilious salts, he concluded, 'Pride and ambition [are] incited; and a disposition to discontent, resentment, strife and faction brought on. . . . Such an ordination of things has, in all ages, led to the subversion of government; or to the dissolution of the best and wisest constitutions in church and state.'[22]

Fielding was among those who satirised Woodward's hysterical attempts to trace back all the evils of civilisation to rich pastries and highly seasoned meats. In the prefatory letter to *Shamela,* Conny Keyber lists prominently among Miss Fanny's many virtues, her 'forbearing to over-eat yourself, and this in spite of all the luscious temptings of puddings and custards, exciting the brute (as Dr Woodward calls it) to rebel'.

The character Cornelius Scriblerus, in the *Memoirs of Martin Scriblerus,* is also partly modelled on Woodward, and accordingly has his own dogmatic theories of diet. He forbids the wet-nurse who is suckling the infant Martin Scriblerus to eat beef; 'Beef, it is true, may confer a robustness on the limbs of my son', he says, 'but will hebetate and clogg his intellectuals'.[23] According to Cornelius, the different characters of the various nations can be directly attributed to difference in diet: 'What makes the English phlegmatick and melancholy but Beef? What renders the Welsh so hot and cholerick, but cheese and leeks? The French derive their levity from their Soups, Frogs and mushrooms', and so on. The Scriblerians have great fun with all this and with the absurd dogmatism of Cornelius which eventually leads him to forbid the nurse to touch 'not only beef, but likewise, whatsoever any of those Nations eat'. But, in a less extreme form, the notion that diet might have some influence on character was a kind of alimentary determinism which all, in different ways and to different degrees, accepted.

Arbuthnot, who was not only a satirist but also a scientist and physician, published in 1731 *An Essay on Aliments,* reprinted four years later with *Practical Rules of Diet.* In this he sought to offer a sober scientific critique of the various wild rumours and alarmist suggestions that were circulating among Augustan foodies. Apart from rich pastries and highly seasoned meats, Woodward had also added his voice to the many anxious attacks on the terrible trio of new beverages—coffee, tea and chocolate. These liquors, he argued swilled the 'vicious contents of the stomach into the blood, casting them upon the habit, and organs of the body. Hence the great increase of the stone, gout, rheumatism, nervine and other affections'. Arbuthnot took a less alarmist view; the 'green leaves of tea contain a narcotick juice', he wrote, but their astringent qualities, when moderated by the relaxing effect of warm water, 'refresheth the brain and animal spirits.'[24] Used in moderation, its effects were generally beneficial, though he did warn 'that the immoderate strength and quantity of this liquor may be hurtful in many cases, and to most people'. He had more serious doubts about coffee, which he noted had 'been accused of causing palsies, leanness, watchfulness, and destroying masculine vigour.'[25] One wonders whether Swift was aware of this last effect when he spent so much of his time with Vanessa drinking coffee? Was this yet another of his complex strategies for keeping his libido under control? 'When drank in too great a degree of strength or quantity', Arbuthnot concluded, coffee was 'hurtful to everybody', which contrasts sharply with Swift's observation to Vanessa, 'Remember that riches are nine parts in ten of all that is good in life, and health is the tenth; drinking coffee comes long after, and yet it is the eleventh, but without the two former you cannot drink it right.'[26]

Another more traditional basis for the satire on New Cookery was the view of it as another form of vanity, with fashion invading the domain of nature and ostentation supplanting nutrition as a dietary priority. Cookery was annexed to fashion as a new area for showing off, and status-conscious hosts would vie with each other in offering exotic beverages, far-fetched vegetables and esoteric fruits. The whole world would now be ransacked to provide dainties for the epicure's table. Gulliver informs his Houyhnhnm master that 'this whole globe of earth must be at least three times gone round, before one of our better female yahoos could get her breakfast.'[27]

This at least was something on which Woodward and the Scriblerians could agree. Among Woodward's many objections to tea was the consequent neglect 'of the much better and more wholesome products of our own country, the mispending our treasure, and carrying it even to the most distant and remote parts of the world . . . not only for trifles and things of no real use, but for such as are detrimental and injurious'.[28] Swift in his writings frequently attacks those aristocratic ladies in both England and Ireland who would no more consume their native beef and ale than they would wear clothes made from native wool or linen. And, in what is perhaps the most famous of eighteenth-century recipes, Swift's *Modest Proposal,* the narrator is anxious to stress the benefits of baby-flesh as a dish to suit all tastes and pockets. To the thrifty he observes that 'seasoned with a little pepper and salt' a fore or hind quarter will be very good 'boiled, on the fourth day, especially in winter', while for those of a more elegant and refined taste, he assures them that a year-old child will be equally delicious 'in a fricasee, or a ragout'.

William King's objections to foreign foods, expressed in his *Art of Cookery,* concentrates on the fact that olios, soups and ragouts offer nothing solid to be carved. He comments on the differences between Roman and British dishes: 'the first delighting in hodge-podge, gallimaufreys, forc'd meats, jussels, and salmagundies; the latter in spear-ribs, surloins, chines and barons'. As a possible explanation for such differences, he offers the observation that the Romans, 'lying upon a sort of couch' to eat their meals, rather than sitting up straight at the table, could only manage such slops. This was a danger which not only French cookery but also the increasing use of cushions threatened to reintroduce. If a joint is stuffed with too many other ingredients it becomes, he suggests, a kind of imposter:

> Meat forc'd too much, untouch'd at table lies
> Few care for carving trifles in disguise.
>
> (ll.418-9)

This specious, dishonest forced meat, so stuffed and moulded that it
becomes a 'trifle in disguise' is, in John Fuller's terms, 'the ancestor of
the nut cutlet and soya steak.'[29] Indeed, this kind of false meat is a
violation, or reversal of nature akin to the surreal transformations
created by Pope's Dunces who give 'to Zembla fruits, to Barca
flowers'. The chef whose sprouts are foliated as rosebuds has
something in common with the poet whose heavy harvests nod
beneath the snow, just as the culinary fantasies of Trimalchio's feast
recall the bizarre literary hybrids described by Horace at the opening
of the *Ars Poetica*. In the *Tatler* for 21 March 1710 Addison described
a meal at the house of a friend who was 'a great admirer of the French
cookery'. Every dish was so disguised that it appeared to be
something else; one dish, that appeared to be 'a roasted porcupine'
turned out to be 'a larded turkey'; an apparent pheasant was in reality
a rabbit. The table thus becomes not a place of conviviality and
hospitality but a laboratory for some virtuoso's experiments, or a little
theatre of the absurd. Both King and Addison stress the moral virtues
of 'the old British hospitality'. 'The tables of the ancient gentry of this
nation', writes Addison, 'were covered thrice a-day with hot roast
beef. . . . This was the diet which bred that hardy race of mortals who
won the fields of Cressy and Agincourt.'

Using the Horatian *'beatus ille'* formula, King celebrates the moral
values associated with a simple diet:

> Happy the man that has each Fortune try'd,
> To whom she much has giv'n, and much deny'd:
> With abstinence all delicates he sees,
> And can regale himself with toast and cheese.
>
> (ll.149-162)

A well-established literary tradition linked philosophical high-
mindedness with a plain, if not quite ascetic, diet. In the sixth satire of
his second book Horace recommended the simple fare of Pythagoras,
translated by Pope as 'beans and bacon'. Elsewhere in Horace we find
praise of homely dishes, leeks, peas and fritters for a healthy life and

untroubled sleep. The more austere and stoical philosophers were reputed to eat turnips. 'The noblest foundations of honour, justice and integrity', wrote King, 'were found to lie in turnips.' This association of high-thinking and low-eating was something to which most eighteenth-century satirists subscribed, at least in part. Swift confessed that he had 'a sad, vulgar appetite. . . . I cannot endure above one dish, nor ever could since I was a boy and loved stuffing.'[30] Addison, expressing his desire to see Swift in Dublin in 1710, wrote in these terms: 'I heartily long to eat a dish of bacon and beans in the best company in the world.'[31] Pope, in his imitation of Horace's *Second Satire of the Second Book,* ridiculed the laborious hedonism of the gourmet:

> When the tir'd glutton labours thro' a treat
> He finds no relish in the sweetest meat.
>
> (ll.31-2)

Instead, Pope finds pleasure in 'plain bread and milk':

> Content with little, I can piddle here
> On broccoli and mutton through the year.
>
> (ll.137-8)

However, as noted in Chapter 2 above, the word 'satire' itself was believed to have culinary and dietary associations. The word derived from *satura,* as used in the phrase *satura lanx,* a full dish, a platter of various foods. Dryden explained the term thus: 'the very word *satura* signifies a dish plentifully stored with all the variety of fruits and grains', and he concluded his discussion with a reference to 'that *olla,* or hotch-potch, which is properly a satire'.[32] Variety, then, was believed to be an essential element in the form of a satire, making it a literary genre whose culinary model was the miscellaneous ragout rather than the heroic baron of beef. A satire should not be uniformly solid, but should mingle the sweet with the sour, disguising its solid precepts in a piquant sauce in the civilised style of *haute cuisine.* Whereas tragedy and epic derived from the Greeks whose diet, as described by King, was heroically carnivorous, satire was mainly based on Roman models, and reflected the style of a civilisation which fed in a recumbent position. A satirist then should be neither a malicious butcher, not a puritan ascetic serving an unrelieved diet of heroic beef or philosophical turnips; rather he should be a genial and convivial host, providing a pleasing variety of titbits, some sharp and tart, others sweet and delicate.

Fielding presents himself as just such a host at the start of *Tom Jones*, comparing himself to 'one who keeps a public ordinary' and who must endeavour to gratify the palates of his guests, 'however nice and even whimsical' they may prove. His subject, he tells us, is 'HUMAN NATURE', a theme of such 'prodigious variety, that a cook will have sooner gone through all the several species of animal and vegetable food in the world, than an author will be able to exhaust so extensive a subject'. Nevertheless, he fears lest some of a delicate palate may regard this diet as too common and vulgar:

> Many exquisite viands might be rejected by the epicure if it was a sufficient cause for his contemning of them as common or vulgar, that something was to be found in the most paultry alleys under the same name. In reality, true nature is as difficult to be met with in authors as the Bayonne ham or Bologna sausage is to be found in the shops.

Continuing with the same metaphor, he assures us that 'the whole . . . consists in the cooking of the author'.

> The same animal which hath the honour to have some part of his flesh eaten at the table of a duke, may perhaps be degraded in another part, and some of his limbs gibbeted, as it were, in the vilest stall in the town. Where then lies the difference between the food of the nobleman and the porter, if both are at dinner on the same ox or calf, but in the seasoning, the dressing, the garnishing and the setting forth.

(I.i)

The ironies here offer an interesting sidelight on the relations between the art and nature, and town and country values throughout the novel. On the face of it, Fielding celebrates the qualities of art and wit—the cookery of the author—to present the enduring truths of human nature in a cultivated manner. He quotes Pope: 'True wit is nature to advantage drest, What oft was thought, but ne'er so well exprest', and the emphasis clearly falls on the word 'drest', which applies equally to clothes and to cookery. The antithesis between nature and art, the beef of human nature and the sauce of wit, runs all through the novel. The narrator goes on to boast that he will adhere to 'one of the highest principles of the best cook which the present age, or perhaps that of Heliogabalus, hath produced:

> This great man, as is well known to all polite lovers of eating, begins
> at first by setting plain things before his hungry guests, rising
> afterwards by degrees, as their stomachs may be supposed to
> decrease, to the very quintessence of sauce and spices. In like
> manner we shall represent Human Nature at first to the keen
> appetite of our reader, in that more plain and simple manner in
> which it is found in the country, and shall hereafter hash and ragoo
> it with all the high French and Italian seasoning of affectation and
> vice which courts and cities afford.
>
> (I.i)

The ironic signals here are plain enough. The description of the chef
as a 'great man' and of his customers as 'polite lovers of eating'
introduce two of Fielding's favourite terms of ironic praise. The
culinary ascent from the plain and simple fare of the country to the
French ragoos and Italian seasoning of the town clearly suggests a
corresponding downward moral progress. Molly Seagrim and Lady
Bellaston may represent much the same kind of meat, but Molly's
appeal is to the natural appetite, while Lady Bellaston relies upon all
the artifice and dressing of the accomplished coquette.

Yet Fielding begins this metaphorical section with a rather
different emphasis. By equating 'true nature' as represented in
literature with the 'true Bayonne ham or Bologna sausage', he
recommends his own literary integrity to the taste of the civilised
reader, the connoisseur who can detect a tawdry imitation or cheap
substitute. When he affects to despise the cheap cuts and offal of
human nature that are offered for sale in the paultry alleys and on the
vilest stalls of the town, it is by no means clear which way the irony
leans. In part Fielding may be taken to be attacking the vulgar
voyeurism and illiteracy at the Grub Street end of the market, where
authors like Ned Ward, Defoe or even Richardson plied their trade.
What they had to offer were, in his terms, crude, raw, unsavoury
works, unseasoned with classical learning, not dressed in the true
Homeric, Virgilian or Horation manner. Yet, on the other hand, as we
have already seen, Fielding, like the other Augustan satirists,
condemned the gastronomic refinement of high society with its
quintessences of sauces and spices, as a decadence which reduced
hospitality to a form of ostentation, and turned a meal into a sequence
of culinary conceits.

The paradox is, of course, that Fielding is a literary *cordon bleu,* a master of literary cookery, whipping up mock-heroic soufflés, serving his characters with a spice of satire, garnished with irony and glazed with wit. In his roles as both host and chef he mixes his ingredient with the confidence of a master, deliberately drawing attention to the sophistication which he affects to despise. This paradoxical blending of simplicity and sophistication is at the heart of all Fielding's writing. The innocent, unworldly good nature of Parson Adams can only triumph by courtesy of the urbane ironies and artful manipulations of the narrator. The recommendations of a plain honest homely diet of beer and ale, bread and cheese is conveyed in the highly seasoned style of a connoisseur of human nature. Look at that passage again:

> The same animal which hath the honour to have some part of his flesh eaten at the table of a duke, may perhaps be degraded in another part, and some of his limbs gibbeted, as it were, in the vilest stall in the town. Where then lies the difference between the food of the nobleman and the porter, if both are at dinner on the same ox and calf, but in the seasoning, the dressing, the garnishing and the setting forth.

Part of the phrasing here seems to echo the more cynical ironies of *Hamlet:* 'Your worm is your only emperor for diet . . . your fat king and your lean beggar is but variable service,—two dishes, but to one table' (IV.iii). A more recent parallel might be found in the mock-democratism of the Preface to John Gay's tragi-comi-pastoral-farce *The What D'Ye Call It,* where he asserts, 'the sentiments of Princes and clowns have not in reality that difference which they seem to have', being distinguished only by the relative 'pomp or meanness of diction' with which they are expressed—the dressing forth. Food and hunger are great levellers, representing one of the undeniable constants in human nature. But of course hunger also reduces man to the level of a beast, and the great divide between the cooked and the raw is one of the ways in which anthropologists have indicated the beginnings of human civilisation. The cook, like the educator or the dancing-master, seeks to apply the rules of art and experience to enhance and soften the crudities of nature. Claude Rawson has studied the ambiguous status of the dancing-master in Fielding's fiction.[33] On the one hand, the ability to move with ease and grace, rather than with an awkward, clumsy gait, like the ability to converse or write with fluency and skill, are among the arts of civilisation. Yet, at the same time, most of the dancing-masters one encounters in Augustan satire are fops and foreigners, the epitomes of vanity and affectation, seeking to inculcate a ludicrous primping, mincing step which deforms rather than enhances the natural movements of the body. Cookery is much the same. The chef who can use his skills to encourage good fellowship, conviviality and benevolence is to be cherished: but the chef who merely wishes to show off his talents by transforming natural dishes into surreal works of art, is condemned.

Thus in *Tom Jones* Blifil's lack of true natural feelings is indicated when the narrator informs us that 'he had . . . that distinguishing taste, which serves to direct men in their choice of the objects, or food of their several appetites; and this taught him to consider Sophia as a most delicious morsel, indeed to regard her with the same desires which an ortolan inspires into the soul of an epicure' (VII.6)—desires, that is, that are based on vanity and ostentation rather than enjoyment; this is the description of an appetite based on affectation rather than affection. Yet, on the other hand, those whose notion of love can never rise above the material level of prime roast beef, are also criticised. At the start of Book VI the narrator requires the reader to examine his heart and consider what exactly the word 'love' means to him. If by this word the reader understands no more than 'the desire of satisfying a voracious appetite with a certain quantity of delicate white human flesh', then the narrator advises him to cease reading directly, for 'you have, I assure you, already read more than you have understood. . . . To treat of the effects of love to you, must be as absurd as to discourse on colours to a man born blind . . . and love probably may, in your opinion very greatly resemble a dish of soup or a sir-loin of roast-beef.' So there is, after all, more to life than good roast beef. We are to cultivate more refined and noble attitudes than the natural instincts of simple carnivores. The roast beef of old England is not an adequate test for all our values and aspirations. Indeed, when later Sophia's cold hand is described as bearing 'an exact resemblance, in cold and colour, to a piece of frozen beef' (X.3) this is a distinctly unflattering usage for the meat which signifies the freedom of Englishmen.

One obvious effect of all this gastronomic imagery which I have hitherto neglected is the sensuous enjoyment, the Rabelaisian or epicurean delight in the pleasures of the table that it generates. Fielding has something of this, though usually allied with a social sense of hospitality and good nature rather than a pleasure in

gourmandising for its own sake. The cumulative effect of his
alimentary language is to create a sense of feasting and celebration. By
contrast, this is another area which seems to justify Coleridge's pithy
description of Swift as 'the soul of Rabelais dwelling in a dry place'.
Swift was not without a love of food. His memories of childhood
include the recollection of 'charming custards' in a blind alley on
Saturday afternoons; in his Market Hill poems he presents an ironic
picture of himself eating his friends the Achesons out of house and
home; letters to and from Sheridan are filled with pieces of culinary
advice, as when Sheridan reminded him to bring a cheese-toaster
with him on a forthcoming visit 'to do a mutton-chop now and
then'.[34] But for the most part, the emphasis of Swift's dietary
observations falls on the question of thrift. Trying to persuade Pope to
visit him in Dublin, he assured him that an eighteen-penny chicken
could be had there for only seven pence. He calculated to the penny
the amount he would have had to spend on food had Pope and
Parnell, when paying him a surprise visit, come for a meal.[35] He
exulted when his extensive acquaintanceships in London allowed
him to dine free, but large feasts depressed him, both by their
extravagance and their cost.

As with other indulgences, Swift kept his appetite under a firm
control, and practised certain strict forms of abstinence from motives
both of thrift and health care. He was firmly convinced that his attacks
of giddiness and deafness had been caused by 'Eating a hundred
golden pippins at a time' and afterwards always denied himself the
pleasure of eating summer fruits, though he loved them very much.[36]
An indication of Swift's no-nonsense approach to cookery is given in
a letter to him from Pulteney, with an invitation to stay as a guest.
Pulteney promises, 'you shall not have one dish of meat at my table so
disguised, but you shall easily know what it is.'[37]

Similarly, Pope, though sometimes accused of gluttony, for the
most part endorsed an ascetic and modest dietary ideal. In his kitchen
garden he grew a variety of vegetables and herbs, including broccoli,
fennel, asparagus, cabbage, spinach, endive, lettuce, beans and beets.
A poem written by a friend towards the end of his life, called 'Mr
Pope's Supper', stresses the Horatian simplicity of his diet, consisting
mainly of spinach, eggs, butter, bread, some cold fish and 'Indian
root', a kind of endive.[38] In his *Epistle to Bathurst* Pope attacked Old
Cotta's vegetarianism as a form of miserliness:

What tho' (the use of barb'rous spits forgot)

His kitchen vy'd in coolness with his grot
If Cotta liv'd on pulse, it was no more
Than Bramins, saints, and sages did before.
                                                    (ll.181-6)

However, the indications are that in fact Pope saw as much virtue in
the ascetic diet of the Brahmins and sages as in the roast beef of old
England. Considerations of health, as much as philosophical
idealism, led to his being 'content with little'. Swift commiserated
with him that the least culinary extravagance, 'if it be only two bits
and one sup more than your stint',[39] was liable to have severe
repercussions on his health. At one point in *Joseph Andrews,* Peter
Pounce demands rhetorically, 'How can any man complain of hunger
. . . in a country where such excellent salads are to be gathered in
almost every field? or of thirst, where every river and stream
produces such delicious potations?' (III.13). This is not meant,
however, as a high-minded recommendation of frugality and
asceticism, but rather is another of Fielding's devices for revealing
Pounce's uncharitable and hypocritical miserliness. If Fielding's
attack on such vegetarian parsimony here seems to carry more weight
than Pope's similar strictures on Old Cotta, that is no doubt because it
is contained in a work which elsewhere strongly celebrates the manly
virtues of meat eating. Similarly, when in *Tom Jones* we are told that
the Man on the Hill 'feeds chiefly upon herbs, which is fitter food for
a horse than a Christian' this is not a beneficial indication of the
virtues of a high-fibre diet, but a symbol of misanthropy. Meat eating is
one of the denominators of the social, and Christian, family of man.
   In his *Essay on the Nature of Aliments,* Arbuthnot came down in
favour of a varied diet:

   A constant adherence to one sort of diet may have bad effects on
   many constitutions. Nature has provided a great variety of
   nourishment for human creatures, and furnish'd us with appetites
   to desire and organs to digest them . . . a healthy man under his
   own government ought not to tie himself up to strict rules, nor to
   abstain from any sort of food in common use.[40]

This is good illustration of Arbuthnot's instinctive liberalism. Both as
a scientist and a satirist he detects complementary patterns in art and
nature. Just as nature has ordained for our health an abundant variety
of foods, so the arts of satire, which aim at the health of society,

should offer a varied dish, a *satura lanx,* of sweet and savoury dishes. Woodward, on the other hand, was all for abstinence and tying oneself to strict rules in order to extinguish the fires of vice and disease. 'By abstinence and witholding of the fuel', he wrote, 'the flame ceases, and is extinguished, an awe, modesty and correct deportment is secured, and the supply of a vicious disposition cut off.'[41]

The attitudes adopted by various satirists to questions of cookery and diet offer interesting insights into their assumptions about human nature. Less obviously overladen with moral taboos and social codes than sexual behaviour, food offers a good guide to a person's instinctive reactions to questions of physical gratification and sensual pleasure. Food can become a metaphor for need, for kindness and charity, for conviviality and good fellowship, for meanness, for selfishness and self-indulgence, for ostentation and gross display. As John Fuller observes, Augustan poets often wrote on such apparently homely or prosaic matters as money or horticulture, tea or palm oil; but beneath the mock-heroic badinage about which kinds of apples make the best cider, they instinctively see such concerns as part of an analysis of what constitutes the good life in moral and social terms.[42] In matters of food people are less likely to feel constrained to fall in behind certain prevailing moral conventions than in matters of sex; and hence vegetables may offer a better guide to a writer's instinctive attitude to sensuality, than virginity.

Among the Augustan satirists the corpulent John Gay is the only truly Rabelaisian gourmandising writer. He begins his career with a celebration of wine (*Wine,* 1708). His *Shepherd's Week* gluts us with a feast of roast beef and puddings, capons, potatoes, butter, turnips, leeks, oatmeal, white-pot, hare, pottage, cheese, beer, broth, barley-loaf, pears, mulled-cider, new-laid eggs, ale, clotted cream. *To a Young Lady with some Lampreys* runs through a whole seafood cocktail (with its supposed aphrodisiac effects) from lobsters, prawns, shrimps, lampreys to sago-cream and craw-fish soup. Gay's is a muse which expands and glows at the table.

Pope, on the other hand, customarily uses images of food to suggest either culpable excess or the new-fangled nonsense of the New Cookery. There is Helluo glutting himself to death on a salmon's belly; Timon gorging his guests with a hecatomb of a feast; the priestly chef in Book IV of *The Dunciad* whose culinary miracles combine hedonism with heresy:

> On some, a priest succinct in amice white
> Attends; all flesh is nothing in his sight!
> Beeves, at his touch, at once to jelly turn,
> And the huge Boar is shrunk into an urn:
> The board with specious miracles he loads,
> Turns Hares to Larks, and Pigeons into Toads.
>
> (ll. 549-54)

The description of the priest/chef 'succinct in amice white' not only presents him as a fashionable master-of-ceremonies, but also suggests one of his own charming confections. At once cook, conjuror and celebrant, the mysteries of divinity and diet are alike to him no more than theatrical opportunities for some feats of prestidigitation. The culinary metaphors here reverse the mysteries of transubstantiation into a triumph of the new cuisine. 'Beeves, at his touch, at once to jelly turn', links sacrilege with self-indulgence. The departure from solids which King deplored in his fantasy of 'carving trifles' corresponds here to a debasement of sacred ritual into sybaritic display. A typically mock-apologetic footnote to these lines remarks: 'Scriblerus seems at a loss in this place . . . I have searched in Apicius, Pliny, and the Feast of Trimalchio, in vain: I can only resolve it into some mysterious superstitious rite, as it is said to be done by a Priest, and soon after called a sacrifice.' To this, the more urbane commentator 'P.W.' replies, 'This good Scholiast, not being acquainted with modern luxury, was ignorant that these were only the miracles of French cookery, and that particularly Pigeons en crapeau were a common dish.'

Not only has fashion taken the place of religion; it also usurps its language and rituals:

> Knight lifts the head, for what are crowds undone
> To three essential Partridges in one?
>
> (ll. 561-2)

Robert Knight, former cashier of the South Sea Company and hence responsible for undoing crowds of investors, fled to Paris where he lived in considerable luxury. Indeed, we are told that 'persons of the first quality in England, and even Princes of the Blood of France' were happy to overlook his career of fraud and embezzlement in order to enjoy the pleasures of his table. Pope explains the parodic trinity of partridges thus: 'three essential Partridges in one: i.e. two dissolved into quintessence to make sauce for the third.' When, as in the *Art of*

Sinking in Poetry, the warlike imagery of Homer's *Iliad* is adapted to form culinary metaphors, we sense a festive mock-heroic celebration. But when, as here, the miracles of Christian doctrine are transformed into gastronomic titbits, we sense a powerful feeling of sacrilege, and see a society which has lost all capacity for moral discrimination.

Partly for health reasons, and partly from certain instinctive inhibitions concerning the physical appetite, the writings of Pope and Swift demonstrate a greater asceticism in matters of food than those of Gay and Fielding. Swift's satires are, notoriously, more concerned with what comes out of the body than what goes into it. And in one respect, too, Swift disregarded the advice of his friend Arbuthnot. Instead of enjoying the rich variety of foods and trusting to nature's own balance to keep him healthy, he showed some sympathy with the 'abstinence' theories of Woodward by denying himself the soft fruits that he loved. However, he could never give up wine. 'Good wine is 90% in living in Ireland', he declared.[43]

Interestingly, Swift's second most famous satire, *A Modest Proposal,* is devoted to a matter of diet. In it he hints at one dangerous possibility associated with the New Cookery, but one which—having been so outrageously exaggerated by Woodward—it was difficult to pose seriously. This was that *haute cuisine,* like bad writing, might not simply be a temporary affectation or bad joke; but that it might actually corrupt tastes, destroy the natural appetite, poisoning both the body and the moral sense. Cookery was a form of fashion which did not remain on the surface, but entered right into the body. In *A Modest Proposal* the taste for fricassees and ragouts is identified with violence and meanness. High fashion and sophisticated tastes are combined with thrift, as the proposer recommends the flaying of the carcass, 'the skin of which artificially dressed, will make admirable gloves for ladies, and summer boots for fine gentlemen'. These are tastes which are both gross and refined at the same time; aesthetically refined but morally gross. Tastes in food and fashion are thus presented by Swift as part of that brutality which is inseparable from the process of civilisation, the moral and social exploitation which goes with sophisticated taste and high fashion. Baby-flesh might well become the next culinary craze after ortolans, appealing to much the same kind of unnatural appetite that made Blifil favour that dish.

CHAPTER SIX
Swift

Swift and the Fictions of Satire

Recently I published a biography of Swift, and even as I write, reviews of that book continue to appear.[1] On the whole the reception has been gratifying, though among a few reviewers a consensus emerged that I had emphasised, or even exaggerated, the less pleasant aspects of Swift's personality. One reviewer wrote that I am 'almost too ready to suspect or attribute dubious motives' to the Dean; another argued that my view of the quality of Swift's satires is limited by my evident 'distaste for the man'. Yet another reviewer (and, if I may say so, one of the most perceptive) declared that the achievement of my supposedly iconoclastic enterprise was 'to have made Swift uncomfortable again . . . the Dean is really dead only when readers are at ease with his works'.[2]

Such reactions as these were not unexpected and in fact partly confirm some of my intentions in writing the biography. For my title I took some words of Bolingbroke, as recorded by Thomas Sheridan:

> He had, early in life, imbibed such a strong hatred to hypocrisy, that he fell into the opposite extreme; and no mortal ever took more pains to display his good qualities, and appear in the best light to the world, than he did to conceal his, or even to put on the semblance of their contraries. . . . Lord Bolingbroke, who knew him well, in two words summed up his character in this respect, by saying that Swift was a hypocrite reversed.[3]

Swift's adoption of the role of the 'hypocrite reversed' was no mere play-acting gesture of provocation. It is true that he would often play the misanthrope and loved to shock and tease his more sentimental friends with cynical observations in the manner of his 'favourite' La Rochefoucauld. But more seriously his attitude represented a commitment to honesty, however unpleasant, and a recognition that honesty may often involve unpleasantness because of the deeply flawed nature of the human character. Those who have taken exception to my exposure of the less attractive elements in Swift's character, seem to assume that the identification of faults implies some fundamental hostility to the man and his works. Not only is this untrue, but it seriously misses much of the point of Swift's deliberate and instinctive cultivation of a series of distorted images of himself, both in his public behaviour and throughout his writings. Pope acknowledged that 'Dr Swift has an odd blunt way that is mistaken by strangers for ill-nature.'[4] Just how mistaken it would be to confuse Swift's bluntness of manner with ill-nature is demonstrated by a remarkable letter of friendship sent to him by Dr John Arbuthnot in 1714. Arbuthnot had just heard of Swift's secret plan to return immediately to Ireland. His letter concludes thus: 'I shall want often a faithful monitor, one that would vindicate me behind my back & tell me my faults to my face. God knows, I write this with tears in my eyes'.[5]

Identifying faults and telling truths may often seem blunt or hurtful processes, not only in biography but also in life. Yet there can be no honesty or morality without them. The achievement and challenge of Swift's satires consist precisely in his unsettling recognition of the inevitable intermingling of vice and virtue, self-interest and moral principle in all human actions. That a moral of political conviction should coincide with self-interest does not, in Swift's view invalidate or undermine it. On the contrary, it is an acknowledgement of the rootedness of moral principles in common experience, and an expression that no moral values can be divorced from the taint of human fallibility. The *Drapier's Letters* may have resulted from just such a coalition of interests, being motivated partly by political principle, and partly by personal grievance and a desire to strike back at those in England who were responsible for keeping Swift in virtual exile in Dublin. This does not mean, as some have accused me of implying, that Swift was himself guilty of any hypocrisy here, by disguising private ambitions under the cloak of a national crusade. On the contrary, it acknowledges that ironic interdependence to which all Swift's satires return, between self-love and social.

There is an instinctive materialism in Swift's view of the world which reveals itself in all his most familiar metaphors and rhetorical techniques. In his private correspondence one finds him drawing up teasingly precise equations between the consolations of philosophy and friendship and the expenses of domestic hospitality which seems irresistibly to echo the satiric formulas of *The Mechanical Operation of the Spirit*. Following the death of John Gay, Swift observed to Pope in a letter, 'I endeavour to comfort myself upon the loss of friends as I do upon the loss of money, by turning to my account-book, and seeing whether I have enough left for my support.'[6] Pope was shocked by this comparison, and the Duchess of Queensberry wrote to protest that friends could never be equated with money. She herself, she asserted, could live penniless but happy as long as she had good friends. In response to her courteous reproof, Swift allowed himself to be teased into a more conventional pose. 'Sure I was never capable of comparing the loss of friend with the loss of money',[7] he lied in his best courtly manner. But in fact this equation accurately reveals his instinctive ploy of quantifying abstractions. In his satires this technique of modest computation is used to devastating effect. In *Examiner* No. 16 he presents contrasting bills of 'Roman gratitude' and 'British ingratitude', meticulously itemising every detail, down to twopence for a laurel crown, to emphasise the gross discrepancy between an austere Roman ideal and its vulgar British imitation.[8] In the fourth of his *Drapier's Letters* he playfully takes Wood at his word when he declared he would force the Irish to swallow his halfpence. Swift calculates that this will amount to 'seventeen balls of wild-fire a-piece, to be swallowed by every person in the kingdom', an operation which will require the services of some fifty thousand operators, 'which, considering the squeamishness of some stomachs, and the peevishness of young children, is but reasonable.'[9] In the *Modest Proposal* the detailed calculations concerning the costs of maintaining an adequate stock of marketable babies draws ironic attention to the ways in which economics have supplanted morality in political affairs.[10]

Yet it is when we find precisely the same method of mock computation adopted by Swift to quantify the benefits of his own social life that we become puzzled. For what had appeared as a technique of satiric attack is revealed instead as an instinctive psychological defence. Pope gives one famous illustration of Swift's behaviour in this respect. He relates how he and Gay paid a visit on Swift one evening, having already supped. Swift, however, found it strange that they should have dined before visiting him, and proceeded to calculate in the following manner:

'But if you had not supped I must have got something for you. Let me see, what should I have had? A couple of lobsters? Aye, that would have done very well—two shillings. Tarts—a shilling. But you will drink a glass of wine with me, though you supped so much before your usual time, only to spare my pocket?

'No, we had rather talk with you than drink with you. But if you had supped with me as in all reason you ought to have done, you must then have drank with me; a bottle of wine—two shillings. Two and two is four, and one is five: just two and sixpence a piece. Pope, there's half a crown for you, and there's another for you, Sir, for I won't save anything by you. I am determined.'

This was all said and done with his usual seriousness on such occasions, and in spite of everything we could say to the contrary, he actually obliged us to take the money.[11]

Swift approaches abstract values in the manner of a lawyer reckoning damages. Personal friendship, like political independence is not for sale; but it does bring its inevitable costs, which must be taken into account. It is thus entirely consistent and appropriate that the *Drapier's Letters* should be seen both as a contribution to the development of a theory and consciousness of Irish independence, and as a form of personal plea-bargaining. In Swift's view it is precisely those ideals which deny any admixture of, or accommodation with, material benefits, which are to be distrusted, since they must inevitably proceed either from hypocritical cant, or from utopian self-delusion. For him the acknowledgement of the cost of an ideal is an important element in establishing its value.

All attempts to separate the writer from the works in Swift's case are doomed to founder. As a satirist, Swift's 'own' views, which are not necessarily identical with those of his narrator or persona, are nevertheless part of the ironic texture which gives such a fine and complex orchestration to his writings. As a poet he is his own main character, creating a series of ironic, self-deprecating images as ways of simultaneously absorbing and deflecting the views of the world upon him. As a campaigner and propagandist his curious forms of detached passion and partisan independence give energy and force to what might otherwise be dreary or routine polemics. For 'Swift' both as subject of biography and as a satirical voice is always a fictional creation. Swift's own brief fragment of autobiography is full of inaccuracies which are evidently as much the results of prejudice as of forgetfulness.[12] Like the mendacious narrator of *Verses on the Death of Dr Swift,* the evasive 'Cad' of *Cadenus and Vanessa* and the disingenuous *Examiner,* Swift instinctively turns the role of autobiographer into an ironic confrontation between the subjective and objective views of experience. Whatever label we attach to any perceived discrepancy between the 'real' Swift and his authorial persona, mask, or voice, is thus not simply a matter of biographical sincerity, literary psychology or critical taxonomy. Rather it is a function of satire. For Swift's real power is precisely that unease that his works continue to create as their shifting tones glide effortlessly from platitude to paradox or from axiom to absurdity without a syntactical tremor. Whose voice? Whose authority? Whose truth? we ask, not expecting (if we know what we are about) any definite answer. By these constant oscillations between moralist and materialist, preacher and jester, Swift refashions the enduring questions of human morality in ways which prohibit us from taking refuge in conventional formulas of belief. For in every one of those conventional refuges we find yet another Swift persona, greeting us with a complacent smile.

I would like to look briefly at some of these apparent contradictions between the 'real' and the 'satirical' Swift as a means of examining the fictional complexities of Swift's satiric personas. When in *A Modest Proposal* we are invited to consider the expedient of cannibalism 'for preventing the children of poor people in Ireland from being a burden to their parents or country, and for making them beneficial to the public', we naturally recognise this as a satiric irony. Swift, we realise, has chosen this horrifying image of eating babies as a savage analogy for the callousness, inhumanity and moral apathy of the English authorities, whose policies have resulted in mass starvation in Ireland. When we read that 'a young healthy child, well nursed, is at a year old a most delicious, nourishing and wholesome food, whether stewed, roasted, baked, or boiled, and I make no doubt that it will equally serve in a fricassee, or a ragout'; or when we are advised that 'those who are more thrifty (as I must confess the times require) may flay the carcass; the skin of which artificially dressed, will make admirable gloves for ladies, and summer boots for fine gentlemen', we detect a real tone of anger at the fashionable tastes of the well-to-do which depend upon the starvation and deaths of the poor. What in particular these phrases catch is a mean tone of middle-class parsimony which wants to have high fashion at low prices. 'Fricassee' and 'ragout' are posh terms from the new French cookery, yet are used to disguise and dignify a plate of leftovers and cold-cuts.

As a satire, we rightly read this pamphlet as a denunciation of an unjust political system. But, turning to Swift's sermons, quite possibly composed at much the same time and devoted to the same subject, we find a very different attitude to the concept of thrift. Addressing himself here to his Anglican congregation of landowners and office-holders, Swift shares their perception of most charity as merely a subsidy for fecklessness and an encouragement for vice. 'Among the number of those who beg in our streets', he wrote:

> there is hardly one in a hundred who doth not owe his misfortune to his own laziness or drunkenness, or worse vices. . . . Such wretches are deservedly unhappy; they can only blame themselves; and when we are commanded to have pity on the poor, these are not understood to be of their number.[13]

For further confirmation of the 'real' Swift's views on charity we might consider his *Proposal for giving Badges to the Beggars of Dublin* (1737)[14]. This pamphlet was, most unusually, signed with Swift's own name, for which reason I shall refer to the authorial voice as 'Swift' rather than 'the narrator'. In the opening paragraph Swift observes, 'It hath been a general complaint, that the poorhouse, especially since the new constitution by Act of Parliament, hath been of no benefit to this city, for the ease of which it was wholly intended.' The emphasis here is highly revealing. An uninformed reader might, not unnaturally, have assumed that the poorhouse was 'wholly intended' for the relief and benefit of the *poor*, not the city, and for the easing of their poverty. Yet Swift instinctively sees this problem from the position of the hard-pressed ratepayer rather than from that of the starving beggar. Interestingly, one might compare his use of the word *ease* here with the Modest Proposer's use of the same word: 'I have been desired to employ my thoughts what course may be taken to ease the nation of so grievous an incumbrance.' Modern readers, schooled to detect ironies, might infer a satiric hint from the fact that it is the nation, rather than the suffering, which is to be eased. But Swift's usage in the other pamphlet puts a question-mark against such a reading. Throughout his *Proposal for Giving Badges* Swift mentions the poor in terms which range only between irritation and contempt. He refers to a starving family as 'he and his trull and litter of brats' and gives this description of those country beggars who congregate in the outer parishes of the city: 'a most insufferable nuisance, being nothing else but a profligate clan of thieves, drunkards, heathens, and whore-mongers, fitter to be rooted out off the face of the earth, than suffered to levy a vast annual tax upon the city'. He repeats his assertion that, 'among the meaner people, nineteen in twenty of those who are reduced to a starving condition, did not become so by what lawyers call the work of God, either upon their bodies or goods; but merely from their own idleness, attended with all manner of vices, particularly drunkenness, thievery and cheating.' The particular intention of his proposal is to exclude 'foreign' beggars, that is those from outside Dublin, from eligibility for charity within the city, or from what he calls, with no irony at all, 'the privileges of a Dublin beggar'. He disowns these 'foreigners' with a complete absence of either compassion or guilt, referring to them as these 'perpetual swarms of foreign beggars' which afflict the city like an infestation.

How can we square this punitive, authoritarian voice with the man who chose for his epitaph the claim 'He served human liberty?' (*Strenuum pro virili libertatis vindicatorem*). What kind of liberty is it that extends no further than to one beggar in twenty, and even then, only to those born within the pale of Dublin? Similar contradictions can be found in the poem in which Swift proclaimed that 'Fair Liberty was all his cry'. As is well known, the *Verses on the Death of Dr Swift* abound with many glaring and deliberate examples of 'the thing which is not'. There is the claim that he 'lashed the vice but spar'd the name' included in a poem which itself lashes some dozen named individuals. Or the assertion:

> To steal a hint was never known,
> But what he writ was all his own
> (ll. 317-18)

which is a direct self-contradiction, being stolen from Denham's *Elegy* on Cowley. Pope was so embarrassed by the gross exaggerations and falsifications of the poem that he edited out several of the more contentious or self-glorifying couplets before forwarding it to the press. He wrote to Swift, via a friend, expressing the hope that he would not 'dislike the liberties'[15] he had taken with the text. Swift *did* dislike these liberties very much, and quickly published his own unexpurgated Dublin edition of the poem. But it must have made him smile to read his friend's well-intentioned objections which so completely missed the irony of the poem. For what Pope's objections ignored were the fictional dynamics of the poem which give the irony its disconcerting force. We are dealing with no less that three Swifts here: the 'real' Swift who is unknowable, probably even to himself; Swift the authorial persona of the poem, and Swift the supposedly dead subject of the elegy. These last two versions of Swift are kept in balance by the alternative 'voice' of the poem, the 'impartial' eulogist at the Rose tavern whose stance of detached intimacy, combining an insider's knowledge with an outsider's objectivity, makes him a kind of Swiftian alter-ego. The confidential tone with which he mingles truth and lies in a seamless rhetoric has the hoaxster's panache of Swift from the Bickerstaff papers to *A Tale of a Tub*.

In fact the poem presents us with the conventional formulas of praise and blame which accompany the death of a public figure. *De mortuis nil nisi bonum* is a familiar admonition to obituarists, and the Rose tavern commentator deftly only accuses Swift of those 'faults' which actually redound to his credit, while deflecting the explosion of more serious charges. But an equally characteristic response to the deaths of famous men is the release of gossipy memoirs and scandalous anecdotes. Versions of the deceased quickly appear and circulate like Partridge's ghost, which serve and reflect only the self-interests, vanities and ruling passions of those who survive, and have no pretence of objectivity. Thus none of the opinions cited in the poem—whether the instinctive reaction of the ladies (the Dean is dead—and what is trumps?); or the measured praises of the obituarist—give us the 'real' man. They are public statements designed rather as satires on speaker and audience than as insights into Swift. By introducing so many untruths into his obituarist's portrait Swift gives himself two chances of enhancing his reputation. Either the sentences would be swallowed down whole by the majority of a gullible readership. Or the more discerning readers might identify the ironies and contradictions in the account, and recognise the design of provoking our suspicions of those panegyrical truths neatly packaged into bargain couplets.

Several critics have sought to distinguish between the degrees of satiric detachment in Swift's personae, treating Gulliver, for example, as an almost fully fictionalised character, whereas M.B. Drapier is a simple mouthpiece. Yet, while such analyses are useful in teaching us to approach each of Swift's various personae with a wary ear for ironic nuances, they are misguided if they attempt to assign these personae to separate and distinct categories. For, in fact, one of the most disconcerting features of Swift's personae is the apparent lack of consistency with which they are created. There are internal contradictions of tone and statement in all of them which cut across the main lines of their 'characters'. M.B. Drapier is presented as a humble linen-draper of modest education who speaks in terms, and addresses concerns, which would recommend themselves to his fellow shopkeepers and small traders. Yet at times his *Letters* sound an authoritarian tone which clearly indicates the Dean of St Patrick's, rather than the draper of Francis Street; 'What I intend to say to you now is, next to your duty to God, and the care of your salvation, of the greatest concern to yourselves and your children; your bread and clothing, and every common necessary of life entirely depend upon it'.[16]

Swift deliberately violates the carefully established character of his Modest Proposer when, in the paragraph starting 'Therefore let no man talk to me of other expedients', he runs through a catalogue of the schemes he had been proposing for the past decade. The hack 'author' of *A Tale of a Tub* glides effortlessly from one contradictory position to another with all the engaging vanity and unconcern for consistency of a chat-show host. Whether or not all such contradictions are 'intentional' is a question for the biographer rather than the literary critic. Whether Swift genuinely believed that he 'served human liberty' or whether he left that as a last provocative bluff, a paradox to puzzle later generations, need not affect the way that we read the satires themselves. Or rather, the deliberately paradoxical manner in which Swift presents his own intentions and beliefs should remind us that the most fundamental and enduring quality of his satires is their challenge to our own reasoning powers. The liberty which he served is a liberty of the mind to pierce through false images, the stereotypes of propaganda, utopian dreams and political clichés. His satire sets out to mislead and deceive us, appealing to our lust for self-deception, offering us any number of conventional resting places where we can retire from the struggles of verbal and moral analysis. 'Happiness', the Hack tells us in *A Tale of a Tub,* 'is the perpetual possession of being well deceived';[17] a 'truth' happily seized upon by those intimidated by the rhetorical roller-coaster of the 'Digression of Madness' and content to identify this sentiment as 'Swift's'. They thus ironically confirm the statement itself. As so often in Swift's satires, verbal reasoning becomes both a metaphor and an analogy for moral awareness.

Those who pose the greatest threats to human society—the politicians, projectors, fanatic preachers and utopian scientists—use a heady and deceptive rhetoric, a propaganda of half-truths to enslave their audiences. In opposition to this false rhetoric, Swift analyses language itself to release the contradictory impulses rooted in human nature. We who live in an era of global advertising and propaganda should value more highly than ever this quality of Swift's satire. It is hardly surprising that Swift was Orwell's favourite author, as the nightmare world of *1984* obviously owes much to the bleak denatured dystopia of Houyhnhnm-land. Totalitarianism brooks no contradictions. And those teasing contradictions in Swift's writings which pose such problems for his later commentators, are themselves the symbols of freedom, dissent and liberty of thought.

At the end of his *Modest Proposal,* the proposer avers:

> I profess in the sincerity of my heart that I have not the least personal interest in endeavouring to promote this necessary work, having no other motive than the public good of my country, by advancing our trade, providing for infants, relieving the poor and giving some pleasure to the rich. I have no children by which I can propose to get a single penny; the youngest being nine years old, and my wife past child-bearing.

This, if nothing else did, should convince us to shun this man as a hypocrite or a fool. The man who denies his own self-interest in the values he espouses, is the most dangerous prophet of all.

Their Master's Voice

To illustrate further some of these conflicting tendencies in Swift's satire, I should like to examine one of his lesser known prose works. Although incomplete, his volume of *Directions to Servants* has been undeservedly neglected by critics; it is often dismissed as an indulgence of his declining years, and its repeated concern with chamber-pots and their contents cited as evidence of senile decay.[18] In fact, it perfectly illustrates the conflicting impulses between authoritarian and libertarian instincts that oscillate back and forth throughout his works.

Ostensibly, the 'author' of the *Directions to Servants* is a former footman who misguidedly demeaned himself by quitting his lucrative position in service for 'an employment in the custom-house'. The treatise is thus written with all the practical and confident insight of an insider; it is full of expressions of sympathy and solidarity with servants in general and with footmen in particular.

However, the *voice* of the *Directions* is far less easy to specify. For beneath all the assertions of solidarity is a strong undertone of contempt. As the details of recommended depradations, perquisites, excuses, alibis and sharp practices are enumerated with a fastidious and meticulous precision, the tone hovers between comic indulgence and horrified fascination at the revelation of such minutely calculated anarchy, such precisely graded levels of chaos. There are notes of frustration and despair mingled with the knowing wit, and one can detect the acid voice of the master behind the confidential tones of the footman. The *Directions to Servants,* like the *Art of Sinking in Poetry,* paradoxically dignifies anarchy with its own Aristotelian system of rules. Carefully divided between rules for servants in general and rules for the several separate orders of servants, namely butlers, cooks, footmen, maids, grooms and so on, its matter-of-fact mingling of practical tips with an overall philosophy of advancement through unity of purpose suggests a parody of such conduct books as Castiglione's *The Courtier* and Machiavelli's *The Prince.* Whereas the overriding principle which must govern all the activities of Machiavelli's Prince is the interest of the state, servants too are urged to recognise their own brand of *realpolitik* and collective security. 'You may quarrel with each other as much as you please', the footman observes, 'only bear in mind that you have a common enemy, which is your master and lady, and you have a common cause to defend.'[19] He refers more than once to the need for a 'general confederacy of all the servants in every family, for the public good', where that notion of the 'public good' is a thoroughly Machiavellian euphemism for self-interest.

No union rule-book could improve upon this elaborate system of demarcations, perquisites and restrictive practices. Servants in general are cautioned, 'When your master or lady call a servant by name, if that servant be not in the way, none of you are to answer, for then there will be no end of your drudgery: And masters themselves allow, that if a servant comes when he is called, it is sufficient.'[20] All the gradations of a hierarchical system are exploited to subvert the order which they themselves parody. But the ambiguous tone of the work comes from the verbal delight which Swift displays in subverting his own order with this parodic hierarchy of chaos. *Directions to Servants,* as I have observed elsewhere, is an anarchist's handbook compiled by the chief of police;[21] and often, in its obsessive, fastidious details one can detect an unmistakable tone of distaste and horror.

Indeed, in his comic dissection of the gradations and ranks of servants' hall, carefully distinguishing the duties and perquisites of the chambermaid from those of the waiting-maid, or those of the groom from those of the coachman, Swift turns the below-stairs world into a domestic Lilliput, a miniaturised parody of the rivalries, jealousies, schemes and policies of the Court. Servants, too, are jealous of their traditional rights, privileges and precedents, and ape the gentry in their snobbish obsession with etiquette as a disguise for greed. Footmen, like courtiers, are at the mercy of Fortune's wheel. 'Be not proud in prosperity', they are counselled. 'You have heard that Fortune turns on a wheel; if you have a good place, you are at the top of the wheel.' And, as with courtiers, a handsome appearance and complaisant manner may lead on to higher things:

> I was an intimate friend to one of our brethren, who was footman to a court-lady: She had an honourable employment, was sister to an Earl, and the widow of a man of quality. She observed something so polite in my friend, the gracefulness with which he tript before her chair, and put his hair under his hat, that she made him many advances; and one day taking the air in her coach with Tom behind it, the coachman mistook the way, and stopt at a privileged chapel, where the couple were married, and Tom came home in the chariot by his lady's side. [22]

Note how that extended line of contacts (a friend . . . footman to . . . sister to . . . widow of . . .) catches the desperation of the hanger-on at the fringes of the Court, with his friend of a friend. This was a world Swift knew only too well, as he wrote in anger to Chetwode: 'I hate your account of one man, who saw another man, who saw a letter . . . .' [23]

The cook affects all the airs and privileges of a Court dame, the first lady of Servants' Hall. In deference to her affectations, the author mimics her fashionable slang, her version of the polite patois of society ladies, which Swift parodied in his collection of *Polite Conversation;* 'You can junket together at nights upon your own prog, when the rest of the house are abed; . . . and take your pleasure among your cronies, till nine or ten at night'. [24] Both 'prog' (meat) and 'crony' (friend) are to be found in the *New Canting Dictionary* (1725), a useful handbook of Hanoverian slang. But if the cook and butler preside as first lord and lady of this below-stairs world, it is the footmen whose situation most clearly imitates the uncertain life of the courtier. Indeed, if fortunate enough to be dressed in a handsome livery, he may easily pass for a gentleman. 'With a borrowed sword, a borrowed air, your master's linen, and a natural and improved confidence' a bold footman may assume 'what title you please, where you are not known.' Rather than 'grow old in the office of a footman', which the author considers 'the highest of all indignities', he counsels footmen to turn to the only career suitable for gentlemen down on their luck, or for aristocrats manqué. 'I directly advise you to go upon the road, which is the only post of honour left you: There you will meet many of your old comrades, and live a short life and a merry one, and make a figure at your exit, wherein I will give you some instructions.'[25] The footman/courtier parallel here links up with the highwayman/statesman parallel of *The Beggar's Opera;* it may be pleasant to imagine Macheath himself as a superannuated footman, devoting his remaining years to cutting a dash and making a figure at his exit.

The reference to a 'post of honour' also reminds us that honour is Macheath's watchword, though, as already noted, the word is devalued throughout *The Beggar's Opera* to become a kind of tawdry commercial guarantee. 'Honour' is also a term much used in *Directions to Servants,* occuring at least seventeen times in this short treatise. Servants are repeatedly advised to consult, preserve and enhance their master's honour in all things. On closer examination, the similarities with Gay's satire in *The Beggar's Opera,* where 'honour' is a convenient up-market euphemism for financial sharp-practice, appear even closer. The *Directions to Servants* is a handbook of the new commercial values, dressed up in the vocabulary of traditional forms. When the butler is instructed to remember 'the honour of your master; to which in all your actions you must have a special regard', the phrase has acquired an ironic gloss. We recognise 'your master's honour' as the high-sounding code which sustains and justifies a system of enlightened self-interest. The section of 'Directions to the Groom' constitutes what is almost a self-contained ironic essay on the market possibilities released by a strict attention to one's master's honour.[26] When travelling, grooms are advised to recommend their masters to stay at inns 'where you are well acquainted with the ostler and tapster'. This 'may probably be a pot and dram or two more in your way, and to your master's honour'. When visiting neighbouring gentry the groom should always insist that a servant of the house should 'hold the horse when your master mounts. . . . For brother-servants must always befriend one another, and this also concerns your master's honour, because he cannot do less than give a piece of money to him who holds the horse.' When exercising the horses, grooms may sometimes entertain themselves by running races, 'for the honour of your horses, and of your master'. A master, we are told, 'ought always to love his groom, to put him into a handsome livery; and to allow him a silver laced hat', for when dressed in this finery 'all the honours he receives on the road' will redound to his master's credit. If a groom should happen to get drunk in a gentleman's house, his master has no right to complain 'because it cost him nothing, and so you ought to tell him as well as you can in your present condition, and let him know it is both for his and the gentleman's honour to make a friend's servant welcome'. Finally, a groom ought to ensure that his master's honour is enhanced by his generosity in tipping:

> When your master is leaving a gentleman's house in the country, where he hath lain a night; then consider his honour: Let him know how many servants there are of both sexes, who expect vails; and give them their cue to attend in two lines as he leaves the house; but, desire him not to trust the money with the butler, for fear he should cheat the rest: This will force your master to be more generous; and then you may take occasion to tell your master, that squire such a one, whom you lived with last, always gave so much apiece to the common servants, and so much to the house-keeper, and the rest, naming at least double what he intended to give; but, be sure to tell the servants what a good office you did them: This will gain you love, and your master honour.

In all these instances—and in the several more which abound throughout the volume—'your master's honour' works like a charm for extracting money; a social code transformed into a system of market opportunities.

However, when one compares the ironic maxims contained in *Directions to Servants* with the stern system of 'Laws for the Dean's Servants', which Swift promulgated for his own domestic staff in December 1733, one finds another glaring contradiction between a 'liberal' satiric fantasy and an authoritarian domestic reality. The Laws for Swift's own servants have the inflexible rigour of a penal institution:[27]

> When the Dean is at home, no servant shall presume to be absent, without giving notice to the Dean, and asking leave, upon the

forfeiture of sixpence for every half-hour that he is absent, to be stopt out of his or her board-wages.

Whatever servant shall be taken in a manifest lie, shall forfeit one shilling out of his or her board-wages.

By contrast, in *Directions to Servants* we find a very different attitude expressed towards both absences and lies:

It often happens that servants sent on messages, are apt to stay out somewhat longer than the message requires, perhaps two, four, six, or eight hours, or some such trifle; for the temptation to be sure was great, and flesh and blood cannot always resist: When you return, the master storms, the lady scolds, stripping, cudgelling, and turning off, is the word. But here you ought to be provided with a set of excuses, enough to serve on all occasions: For instance, your uncle came fourscore miles to town this morning, on purpose to see you, and goes back by break of day to-morrow: A brother-servant, that borrowed money of you when he was out of place, was running away to Ireland: You were taking leave of an old fellow-servant, who was shipping for Barbados: Your father sent a cow for you to sell, and you could not find a chapman till nine at night: You were taking leave of a dear cousin who is to be hanged next Saturday: You wrencht your foot against a stone, and were forced to stay three hours in a shop, before you could stir a step: Some nastiness was thrown on you out of a garret window, and you were ashamed to come home before you were cleaned, and the smell went off: You were pressed for the sea-service, and carried before a justice of the peace, who kept you three hours before he examined you, and you got off with much a-do: A bailiff by mistake seized you for a debtor, and kept you the whole evening in a spunging-house: You were told your master had gone to a tavern, and come to some mischance, and your grief was so great that you inquired for his honour in a hundred taverns between Pall-mall and Temple-bar.[28]

It is noticeable that Swift's imagination takes flight in this passage to produce a minor but exuberant rake's progress of excuses, a teeming below-stairs world of comic misadventures. He takes the simple idea of an excuse, embellishes it and develops it into a surreal dystopia, a crowded mock-Odyssey of urban diversions. The impish, anarchic exaggeration gives poetic animation to insolence and ineptitude, raising them to the level of mock-heroic fantasy. No real-life servant would ever dream up half of these implausible alibis which range from the press-gang to the cattlemarket, from a sprained ankle to the scaffold. The clash of tenses in the narrative, and the idiomatic mimicry of the spoken voice, part wheedling, part triumphant, turns this former servant into a master of misrule, a connoisseur of chaos. These proliferating lies, which skilfully combine touches of realistic detail with grotesque exaggeration, suggest a spirit of burlesque epic. This riot of irreverence vividly recalls the idioms of the modern 'hack' of *A Tale of a Tub,* written almost forty years earlier. In both, the energy of Swift's imagination is fired by a comedy of excess as he ironically champions the irrepressible anarchic forces of wit to subvert the most categorical of rules.

In fact, Swift recognised, shared and revelled in the absurdity of seeking to confine human nature within a strait-jacket of maxims, or to circumscribe the imagination with rules. I strongly suspect that even those formidable rules for his own servants, with their officious title as 'Laws' and their meticulous system of precise penalties and fines, are at least in part self-parodic joke. Almost forty years earlier Swift had composed a similarly austere set of rules for himself. 'Resolutions when I come to be Old' include such chilling sentences of self-denial as these:

> Not to marry a young woman.
> Not to keep young company unless they really desire it.
> Not to be fond of children, or let them come near me hardly.
> Not to boast of my former beauty, or strength, or favour
>   with ladies, etc.[29]

Yet this long list of self-denying ordinances concludes with a little ironic note: 'Not to set up for observing all these rules, for fear I should observe none.' All the evidence suggests that the 'bark' of Swift's Laws may have been worse than their 'bite'. One early biographer, Tom Sheridan, tells of a servant called Blakely who was in tears when he thought he would have to leave Swift's service; and Swift caused a handsome memorial tablet to be erected in St Patrick's Cathedral to record the qualities of Saunders, another servant.

In *Directions to Servants* we can find an ironic parallel with the precise computation of fines and penalties in Swift's Laws, when the author advises waiting-maids on the market values of their personal assets:

If you are in a great family, and my lady's woman, my lord may probably like you, although you are not half so handsome as his own lady. In this case, take care to get as much out of him as you can; and never allow him the smallest liberty, not the squeezing of your hand, unless he puts a guinea into it; so, by degrees, make him pay accordingly for every new attempt, doubling upon him in proportion to the concessions you allow, and always struggling, and threatening to cry out, or tell your lady, although you receive his money: Five guineas for handling your breast is a cheap pennyworth, although you seem to resist with all your might; but never allow him the last favour under a hundred guineas, or a settlement of twenty pounds a year for life.

This might remind us not only of the economic language of the *Modest Proposal,* but also of the actuarial calculations in one of Defoe's pamphlets on marine insurance, as he reckons the value of various disabilities: 'For the loss of an eye, £25; both eyes, £100; one leg, £50; both legs, £80 . . . .'[30]

Swift, who uses mock-computation as a favourite satiric device, constantly exposes the unspoken financial assumptions upon which so many abstract moral values depend. Friendship and honour, loyalty and love are all, as noted above, exposed to his actuarial scrutiny. We should not conclude from this, however, that Swift himself believed that moral values could be reduced to financial equivalents. But he distrusted the hypocrisy or smugness of those who refused to recognise or acknowledge the social assumptions conveniently disguised by their polite moral vocabulary. 'There is not, through all nature', observes the Hack author of the *Tale,* 'another so callous and insensible a member as the world's posteriors, whether you apply to it the toe or the birch.' The world's pockets, however, are more vulnerable. Swift frequently pretends to hurt us through our pockets, using monetary terms to shock and provoke us—as though pounds, shillings and pence comprise the only universal language of morality. *The Argument against Abolishing Christianity* concludes with the clinching suggestion that abolition might cause Bank and East-India stock to fall 'at least one per cent'. 'And since that is fifty times more than ever the wisdom of our age thought fit to venture for the preservation of Christianity, there is no reason we should be at so great a loss merely for the sake of destroying it.'[31] Similarly, the final sentence of the *Modest Proposal* contains the proposer's earnest assurance of disinterestedness: 'I have no children by which I can propose to get a single penny.' The fines outlined in the Laws for the

Dean's servants are not exacted out of meanness, but as a kind of
moral *aide-memoire,* or sermons in coppers.

The contradictions we have examined run right through Swift's
career. One might contrast his *Project for the Advancement of
Religion* with his *Argument against the Abolishing of Christianity* in
the first decade of the century; his *Modest Proposal* with his sermons
in the 1720s; his *Directions to Servants* with his Laws for his own
servants in the 1730s. But the climatic opposition must be the
antithesis of Houyhnhnms and Yahoos in the last book of *Gulliver's
Travels.* It is part of the challenge of Swift's satire that there can be no
final resolution to the conflict between the forces of law and order
and the energies of human wit, imagination and fantasy. No scholarly
discovery or intellectual analysis will finally decide for us which 'side'
Swift was on in the conflicts between masters and servants,
Houyhnhnms and Yahoos.

We are left with a paradox, combining a love for order with a
suspicion of the oppression of conformity; a love of invention with a
fear of anarchy. This is not because Swift is deliberately teasing or
obscure; but because of his instinctive grasp of the essentially flawed
and mixed condition of each of us. Swift's satires are most famously
remembered and represented by his great set pieces; Flimnap on the
high wire in Lilliput; the King of Brobdingnag's denunciation of a
pernicious race of little odious vermin; the eloquent proposal for
eating babies. But the essential challenge of his satires lies in the grain
of his style; in the instinctive movement and construction of his
rhetoric, exploring the ambiguous moral values of all human actions.

Notes

Notes to Chapter 1

1. Joshua Poole, *The English Parnassus: or, a Helpe to English Poesie* (1657), p. 176.
2. Joseph Warton, *An Essay on the Genius and Writings of Pope* (1756), I.211; II.6 (1756).
3. Alexander Pope, *The First Satire of the Second Book of Horace Imitated,* 1.69.
4. Yasmine Gooneratne, *Alexander Pope,* Cambridge 1976, pp. 12-13.
5. Jonathan Swift, *The Correspondence of Jonathan Swift,* ed. Harold Williams, 5 vols, Oxford 1963-5, Vol. III, p. 293.
6. *Tom Thumb* (1730), II.iii.
7. *The Tragedy of Tragedies; or, the Life and Death of Tom Thumb the Great* (expanded version, 1731), II.x.
8. William Thackeray, *The English Humourists of the Eighteenth Century* (1851), London 1920, p. 35.
9. Matthew Arnold; 'The Study of Poetry', Introduction to *The English Poets,* ed. T.H. White (1880), reprinted in *The Complete Prose Works of Matthew Arnold,* Ann Arbor 1973, Vol. IX, p. 131. William Wordsworth, *'Preface to the Lyrical Ballads'* (1850), in *The Prose Works of William Wordsworth,* ed. W.J.B. Owen and Jane Worthington Smyser, Oxford 1974, Vol. I, p. 141.
10. Donald Davie, *Brides of Reason,* Oxford 1955, p. 34.
11. Tom Stoppard, *Travesties,* London 1975, p. 33.
12. *The First Epistle of the Second Book of Horace Imitated,* ll.1-4.
13. Lord John Hervey, *Some Materials towards Memoirs of the Reign of King George II,* ed. Romney Sedgwick, 3 vols, London 1931, p. 261. Quoted in Maynard Mack, *Alexander Pope: A Life,* New Haven and London 1985, p. 574.
14. Mack, p. 683.
15. Reuben Brower, *Alexander Pope: the Poetry of Allusion,* London, Oxford, New York, 1968.
16. Aubrey L. Williams, *Pope's Dunciad: A Study of Its Meaning,* London 1955; Howard Erskine-Hill, *The Social Milieu of Alexander Pope,* New Haven and London 1975; Maynard Mack, *The Garden and the City: Retirement and Politics in the Later Poetry of Pope,* Toronto 1969; Earl Wasserman, *The Subtler Language,* Baltimore, Md. 1959.

17. Irvin Ehrenpreis, *Literary Meaning and Augustan Values,* Charlottesville 1974, p. 13.
18. John Traugott, 'The Yahoo in the Doll's House', in *English Satire and the Satiric Tradition,* ed. Claude Rawson, Oxford 1984, pp. 127-51.
19. B. Karpman, 'Neurotic Traits of Jonathan Swift' in *Psychoanalytic Review,* XXIX (1942), pp. 165-84.
20. Norman O.Brown, 'The Excremental Vision', in *Life against Death,* London 1959; reissued 1968, p. 168.
21. Claude Rawson, *Gulliver and the Gentle Reader,* London 1973. p. 79.
22. *Ibid.,* p. 71.
23. Warton, *Essay on Pope* (1782) II.357.
24. Samuel Johnson, *Lives of the Poets,* ed. G. Birkbeck Hill, Vol. III, p. 61.
25. Louis I. Bredvold, 'The Gloom of the Tory Satirists', in *Eighteenth Century English Literature, Modern Essays in Criticism,* ed. J.L. Clifford, New York 1959, p. 8.
26. George Orwell, 'Politics vs Literature', in *The Collected Essays, Journalism and Letters of George Orwell,* vol. IV, p. 216.
27. See J.A. Downie, *Jonathan Swift, Political Writer,* London 1984.
28. Bredvold, p. 4.
29. Swift, *Correspondence,* III.329.
30. *Ibid.,* p. 412.
31. Johnson, *The History of Rasselas* (1759), Ch.8.
32. *English Satire and the Satiric Tradition,* p. viii.
33. *Essay on Criticism,* 1.135.
34. *The Dunciad* (1743), I.118; IV. 75-6.
35. *Daniel Defoe,* ed. J.T. Boulton, London 1965, Introduction, p. 3.
36. 'Defoe's Use of Irony', in *The Uses of Irony* by M.E.Novak and H.J.Davis, Los Angeles 1966, p. 8.
37. *The Letters of Daniel Defoe,* ed. G.H.Healey, Oxford 1955, pp. 211, 159.
38. *Ibid.,* p. 43.
39. Soren Kierkegaard, *The Concept of Irony,* trans. Lee M. Capel, London 1966, pp. 259-80.
40. P. K. Elkin, *The Augustan Defence of Satire,* Oxford 1973, p. 187.
41. See Michael Balfour, *Propaganda in War 1939-45,* London 1979, p. 431.
42. As an example one might instance the work of Ellen Pollak, a leading feminist critic. In her book *The Poetics of Sexual Myth: Gender and Ideology in the Verse of Swift and Pope* (Chicago 1985) she offers a polemical account of the 'phallocentric ideology' presented in the writings of the Augustan satirists, and concludes by reversing some customary value judgements. 'Swift is "better" because he's "worse" and "worse" is "better" when value is mediated by the poetic imperatives of an alienating ideology'. (p.183).
43. Richardson, *Pamela,* Letter xxiv.
44. M. Kinkead-Weekes, *Samuel Richardson, Dramatic Novelist,* London 1973.
45. Lilian Peake, *Passionate Involvement* (Mills & Boon Best Seller Romance), London 1977, p. 77.

Notes to Chapter 2

1. Donald Greene, review of Pat Rogers's *The Augustan Vision,* in *Eighteenth Century Studies* 9 (1975), 128-33.

2. Howard Weinbrot, *Augustus Caesar in 'Augustan' England,* Princeton 1978; M.E.Novak, 'Shaping the Augustan Myth', in *Greene Centennial Studies,* ed. P. J.Korshin and R.R.Allen, Charlottesville 1984, p. 2.

3. Howard Erskine-Hill, *The Augustan Idea in English Literature,* London 1983.

4. Novak, p. 3.

5. Johnson, *Lives of the Poets:* 'Dryden' World's Classics edition, Oxford 1906, 1952, 2 vols, I.332.

6. Pope, Preface to *The Works* (1717).

7. Swift, 'Proposals for Correcting, Improving and Ascertaining the English Tongue', *Prose Works* IV, p. 18.

8. Defoe, *Augustas Triumphans* (1728).

9. Wotton, *Reflections upon Ancient and Modern Learning* (1694), p. 348.

10. Temple, *Works,* 4 vols, London 1814, Vol. III, pp. 468-9.

11. *Ibid.,* p. 213.

12. *The Spectator,* 5 vols, ed. D.F.Bond, Oxford 1965, no. 69, Vol. I, p. 292.

13. *Ibid.,* Vol. I.

14. Boswell's *Life of Johnson,* ed. G. Birkbeck Hill, 6 vols, rev. ed. Oxford 1934, Vol. II, pp. 451-2.

15. Defoe, *The Serious Reflections of Robinson Crusoe,* Ch.3, 'Of the Immorality of Conversation, and the Vulgar Errors of Behaviour'.

16. Williams, *passim.*

17. Pat Rogers, 'Ermine, Gold and Lawn: *The Dunciad* and the Coronation of George II', in *Literature and Popular Culture in Eighteenth Century England,* Brighton and New Jersey 1985, p. 126.

18. Howard Erskine-Hill, *Pope: The Dunciad,* London 1972, p. 49.

19. *A Foreign View of England in the Reigns of George I and George II* by César de Saussure, ed. Madame Van Muyden, London 1902, p. 263. For further details of the coronation of 1727, see G.S.Rousseau, '"This Grand and Sacred Solemnity . . ." Of Coronations, Republics and Poetry', in *The British Journal of Eighteenth Century Studies* 5/1 (1982), pp. 1-20.

20. Temple, Vol. III, pp. 463-4.

21. T.R.Lounsbury, quoted in *Lewis Theobald* by R.F.Jones, Columbia 1919.

22. Madame Dacier's French versions and commentary upon Homer's *Iliad* and *Odyssey* were of considerable assistance to Pope in composing his own translations of the poems. A jordan is a chamber-pot.

23. *The English Parnassus* (1657).

24. Dryden, 'Discourse Concerning the Original and Progress of Satire', in *Essays,* ed. W.P. Ker, 2 vols, Oxford 1958, Vol. II, pp. 102-40.

25. *Ibid.,* Vol. II, p. 95.

26. Joseph Trapp (Professor of Poetry at Oxford), *Lectures on Poetry,* trans. W. Clarke and W. Bowyer (1742), from *Praelectiones Poeticae* (1711-15), pp. 227, 232.

27. William Goddard, *A Satyricall Dialogue* (1616?), Sig. D2r.

28. Pope, *Correspondence*, ed. George Sherburn, 5 vols, Oxford 1956, Vol. I, p. 211.
29. Swift, 'The Intelligencer', no. 3 in *Prose Works*, Vol. XII, pp. 32-7.
30. Pope, *Epilogue to the Satires*, Dialogue II, ll.212-5.
31. Gildon, *Miscellaneous Letters and Essays on Several Subjects* (1694), p. 4.
32. Swift, *The Battle of the Books*, 'The Preface', *Prose Works*, Vol. I, p. 140.
33. Swift, *Correspondence*, Vol. III, p. 293.
34. Pope, *Correspondence*, Vol. III, p. 255.
35. *Ibid.*, p. 419.
36. David B. Morris, *Alexander Pope: The Genius of Sense*, Cambridge, Mass., and London 1984, p. 226.
37. *Ibid*, pp. 226-7.
38. *The Spectator*, ed. D.F. Bond, Nos 23, 34, 451, Vol. I, pp. 97-100.
39. Pope, *Epilogue to the Satires*, I. 168.
40. *The First Satire of the Second Book of Horace Imitated*, ll.118-120.
41. *The First Satire of the Second Book*, l.41.
42. *Dunciad* (1729), I, 183-4; *Aeneid*, II.866-7.
43. *Jonathan Wild*, I.ii.
44. The patronising 'Parnassian sneer' is mentioned again in the *Epistle to Dr Arbuthnot*, l.96.
45. *Dunciad* (1729), II. 38-46.
46. *Examiner*, no. 16, *Prose Works*, Vol. III, I22.
47. Swift, *Correspondence*, Vol. III, p. 267.
48. See correspondence in *TLS*, 21 Oct. and 11 Nov. 1983, pp. 1151, 1247.
49. Swift, *Correspondence*, Vol. III, p. 276.
50. *Prose Works*, Vol. III, pp. 3, 78.
51. See F.P. Lock, *The Politics of Gulliver's Travels*, Oxford 1980; and *Swift's Tory Politics*, London 1983. See also J.A.Downie, *Jonathan Swift, Political Writer*, London 1984.
52. Swift, *Correspondence*, II.464-6.
53. Claude Rawson: '"Neo-classic" and "Augustan"', in *Order from Confusion Sprung*, London 1935, p. 247.
54. Swift, *Prose Works*, I. 234.
55. *The First Satire of the Second Book*, ll.67-8.
56. *The World*, no. 101, 5 Dec. 1754.
57. *The Review*, Vol. IV, no. 106, 16 Oct. 1707.
58. 'To the Whole People of Ireland', *Prose Works*, Vol. X, pp. 51-68.
59. *A Tale of a Tub*, Sect.VIII, *Prose Works*, 161. I (1939), p. 96.
60. *Rasselas*, Ch.11, Ch.24.
61. See L.Poliakov and J. Wulf, *Das Dritte Reich und die Juden*, p. 217. See also N.Cohen, *Warrant for Genocide*, Harmondsworth 1967, p. 207.
62. See L.W.Bondy; *Racketeers of Hatred, Julius Streicher and the Jew-baiters' International*, London 1946, pp. 36-7, 61.
63. *Hitler's Table Talk*, ed. H.P. Trevor-Roper, London 1953, p. 332.
64. Text in *Der Parteitag der Arbeit*, Zentralverlag der NSDAP, Munich 1938 p. 157; Trans. in Cohn, *Warrant for Genocide*, p. 225.
65. Keirkegaard, pp. 259-80.
66. Swift, *Correspondence*, Vol. III, p. 333.

67. Johnson, *Preface to Shakespeare*, in *Yale Edition of the Works of Samuel Johnson*, Vol. VII, p. 62.
68. Emrys Jones, 'Pope and Dulness', *Proceedings of the British Academy*, Vol. LIV, pp. 231-63.
69. J.H.Hexter, *More's Utopia: The Biography of an Idea*, Princeton 1952, p. 52.
70. 'The Godly Feast' from *The Colloquies, trans.* C.R.Thompson, Chicago 1965, pp. 46-78.
71. Temple, *Works* (1814), Vol. III, pp. 213-4, 206.
72. Rosalie Colie, *Paradoxia Epidemica*, Princeton 1966, p. 26.
73. Denis Donoghue, *An Introduction to Jonathan Swift*, Cambridge 1966, p. 37.
74. Joseph Spence, *Observations, Anecdotes and Characters of Books and Men*, ed. J.M.Osborn, 2 vols, Oxford 1966, Vol. I, item 135, p. 56.
75. Shadwell, *The Virtuoso*, II. ii.
76. For blood transfusions, see *This Long Disease, My Life* by Marjorie Nicolson and G.S.Rousseau, Princeton 1963.
77. *Prose Works*, Vol. I, pp. 147-50.
78. *Ibid.,* vol. XI, pp. 179-81, 175-7.
79. The main study of this subject is in *Science and Imagination* by Marjorie Nicolson and Nora Mohler, Ithaca 1951.
80. Pat Rogers, 'Gulliver and the Engineers', in *Eighteenth Century Encounters*, Brighton and New Jersey 1985, pp. 12, 18.
81. *Rasselas,* Ch.13.
82. *Prose Works,* Vol. XI, pp. 135-6.
83. R.F.Jones, *Lewis Theobald,* Columbia 1919, pp. 32, 34.
84. Richard Bentley, *A Dissertation upon the Epistles of Phalaris* (1697); *idem.* (ed), *Horatius Reformatus,* (1712); *idem* (ed.), *Milton's Paradise Lost: A New Edition* (1732).
85. Lewis Theobald, *Shakespeare Restored*, London 1726.
86. Pope, *Epistle to Dr Arbuthnot,* l.166.
87. Sidney, *A Defence of Poetry,* ed. J.A.Van Dorsten, Oxford 1966, p. 24.
88. Boswell, *Life of Johnson,* ed. G.Birkbeck Hill, Oxford 1887 (revised 1934) Vol. II, p. 49.
89. *Rasselas,* Ch.10.
90. Fielding, *Joseph Andrews,* Vol. III, Ch.1.
91. *Yale Edition of the Works of Samuel Johnson,* Vol. VII, p. 81.
92. *Ibid.,* Vol. V, pp. 125-9.
93. Fielding, *The Champion,* 17 May 1740; Collected eds. 1741, Vol. II, pp. 223-229.
94. *Prose Works,* Vol. VIII, p. 36.
95. *Epistle to Dr Arbuthnot,* ll.161-2.
96. *The Works of Shakespeare, edited by Mr Pope* (1725), Vol. VI, pp. 304, 551.
97. 'A Letter to a Young Gentleman lately Entered into Holy Orders', *Prose Works*, vol. IX, pp. 61-81.
98. *Dunciad* (1729), ll.70-2.

Notes to Chapter 3

1. Pope, *Correspondence,* Vol.III, p. 366.
2. Byron, *Letter to* * * * * (John Murray) (1821).
3. Matthew Arnold, Introduction to *The English Poets,* ed. T.H. Ward, London 1880.
4. Lytton Strachey, *Pope,* London 1925.
5. Catholics were subject to a complex system of regulations and prohibitions: these included bans on living within ten miles of London, owning a horse or firearms. They were forbidden to attend university, practise at the bar or inherit property. For a full discussion of the impact of this penal legislation on Pope's life, see Maynard Mack's biography *Alexander Pope,* New Haven and London 1985, pp. 38-40.
6. Dennis, *A True Character of Mr Pope* (1716), included in J.V. Guerinot's *Pamphlet Attacks on Alexander Pope 1711-1744,* London 1969, pp. 40-47. Guerinot offers a full descriptive bibliography of the abuse which Pope suffered.
7. *Epistle to Dr Arbuthnot,* ll.310-14.
8. *Epilogue to the Satires,* II. 197-3.
9. *Essay on Criticism,* ll. 297-8.
10. *Essay on Man,* Epistle II, ll. 1-2.
11. *Epistle to a Lady,* ll. 1-2.
12. Morris, *Alexander Pope: The Genius of Sense,* p. 79.
13. Spence, *Anecdotes,* Vol.I, p. 171.
14. Pope, *Correspondence,* Vol.III, p. 354.
15. John Locke, *Essay on Human Understanding,* ed. J. Yolton, 2 vols, London 1961, Book III, Ch. 5, p. 39.
16. H.C.Battestin: *The Providence of Wit: Aspects of Form in Augustan Literature and the Arts,* London 1974; reviewed by Claude Rawson in *Order from Confusion Sprung,* London 1985, pp. 383-9.
17. *Epistle to Bathurst,* ll. 101-12.
18. Lady Mary Wortley Montagu, *Verses Address'd to the Imitator of* Horace (1733), p. 4.
19. Warton, *Essay on Pope,* 1756.
20. Keats, *Sleep and Poetry,* (1817), ll. 196-7.
21. See, for example, David Fairer's *Pope's Imagination,* Manchester 1984.
22. *Epistle to Bathurst,* ll. 21-8.
23. *The Rape of the Lock* (1714; five-canto version), I. 121-44.
24. Byron, letter to Murray, March 1821.
25. It was a favourite analogy which Pope repeated in Book IV of *The Dunciad:* 'The mind, in metaphysics at a loss, May wander in a wilderness of moss' (11.449-50). However, his note to these lines strikes a less assured tone: 'Of which the naturalists count I can't tell how many hundred species.'
26. Hazlitt, 'On Dryden and Pope', *Lectures on the English Poets,* London 1818, lecture 4.
27. *Guardian,* No.61, 21 May 1713; ed. J.C. Stephens, Lexington, Kentucky, 1982, pp. 223-37.
28. Spence, *Anecdotes,* Vol.I, p. 118.

29. *Essay on Man.* Epistle III, p. 152.
30. See J.R.Moore, '*Windsor Forest* and William III,' MLN lxvi, pp. 451-5; reprinted in *Essential Articles for the Study of Pope*, ed. Maynard Mack, Hamden Conn., 1964.
31. *Of the Laws of Chance* (Huygens) translated and expanded by John Arbuthnot, 1692, The Preface.
32. *Epistle to Bathurst,* ll. 163-6.
33. Donoghue, p. 37.

Notes to Chapter 4

1. Pepys, *Diary,* ed. Robert Latham and William Matthews, London 1974, Vol. VIII, p. 543.
2. *Guardian,* ed. J.C. Stephens, Nos 22, 23, 28, 30, 32, pp. 105-38.
3. *Ibid.,* pp. 105-6. The word *pecunia* derives from *pecus,* a flock.
4. *Rasselas,* Ch. 19.
5. For a discussion of authorship of these papers, see *Guardian,* pp. 17-33.
6. *Ibid.,* p. 106.
7. *Ibid.*
8. For an historical account of the pastoral 'war' between Pope, Philips and Gay which gave rise to *The Shepherd's Week,* see *John Gay, Poetry and Prose,* ed. V.A.Dearing and C.E.Beckwith, Oxford 1974, 2 vols; Vol.II, pp. 513-5; also, George Sherburn, *The Early Career of Alexander Pope,* Oxford 1934, pp. 117-8; also Hoyt Trowbridge, 'Pope, Gay and *The Shepherd's Week',* Modern Language Quartely, v. (1944) pp. 79-88.
9. *Guardian,* pp. 160-5.
10. J.V.Curran, 'Peri Bathous: An Edition and Critical Commentary, unpublished PhD thesis, Newcastle upon Tyne 1955.
11. *Guardian,* pp. 163-4.
12. *Ibid.,* pp. 108-9.
13. Pope, *Correspondence,* Vol.I, p. 229.
14. *John Gay: Poetry and Prose,* ed. V.A. Dearing and C.E. Beckwith, Oxford 1974. 'The Shepherd's Week', Vol.I, p. 99.
15. *Ibid.,* p. 92.
16. *John Gay: Poetry and Prose,* ed. John Fuller, Oxford 1983. 'The What D'Ye Call It', Vol.I, p. 177.
17. *Poetry and Prose,* Vol. I, p. 94.
18. *The Scriblerian,* Vol. VIII, No.I, Autumn 1975, pp. 4-8.
19. *Poetry and Prose,* Vol.I, pp. 102-3.
20. *Ibid.,* p. 107.
21. *Ben Jonson, Works,* ed. C.H. Herford and P. Simpson, 11 vols, Oxford 1925-52, Vol. VIII, p. 305.
22. *Dunciad,* Bk I, ll. 69-70.
23. *Macbeth,* IV. iii.
24. *Guardian,* No.4, p. 50.
25. Swift, *Correspondence,* Vol.III, p. 267.
26. *Memoirs of Macklin* (1804), pp.53-7.

27. See correspondence between J.A. Downie, David Hunt and Yvonne Noble, in *TLS,* 21 Oct. and 11 Nov. 1983, pp. 1151, 1247.
28. Swift, *Correspondence,* Vol.III, p. 326.
29. *The Letters of John Gay,* ed. C.F. Burgess, Oxford 1966, p. 43.
30. All quotations from *The Beggar's Opera* are taken from John Fuller's edition in Gay's *Dramatic Works,* 2 vols, Oxford 1983.
31. Pat Rogers, 'Noise and Nonsense', in *Literature and Popular Culture in the Eighteenth-Century England,* Brighton 1985, p. 113.
32. Boswell, *Life of Johnson,* ed. G.B. Hill, 1934, Vol.III, p. 198.
33. William Empson, 'Mock-Pastoral as the Cult of Independence', *Some Versions of Pastoral,* London 1935, pp. 195-252.
34. *Ibid.,* p. 203.
35. Pat Rogers. 'Merchants and Ministers', in *Eighteenth Century Encounters,* Brighton 1985, p. 102.
36. *Ibid.,* p. 106.
37. *Vice and Luxury Public Mischiefs,* London 1724, pp. xvi-xvii, cited by Phillip Harth in his Introduction to *The Fable of the Bees,* Harmondsworth 1970, p. 15.
38. Mandeville, *The Fable of the Bees,* ed. F.B. Kaye, 2 vols, Oxford 1924, Vol.I, pp. 7, 37.
39. *Ibid.,* p. 88.

Notes to Chapter 5

1. Eleanor N. Hitchens, *Irony in Tom Jones,* Alabama 1965, pp. 101-18.
2. *Ibid.,*
3. A.E. Dyson, 'Satiric and Comic Theory in Relation to Fielding', *Modern Language Quarterly,* 18 (1957),237. Ethel Thornbury, *Henry Fielding's Theory of the Comic Prose Epic,* New York 1966, p. 162.
4. Glenn Hatfield, *Henry Fielding and the Language of Irony,* Chicago and London 1968, pp. 179-96.
5. 'An Essay on Conversation', in *Miscellanies* (1743), *Wesleyan Edition of the Works of Henry Fielding,* ed. H.K.Miller, Oxford 1972, Vol.I, pp. 119-52.
6. *Tom Jones,* in *Complete Works,* ed. W.F.Henley, New York, 16 vols, 1903, Vol.III, p. 352.
7. Hatfield, pp. 191-2.
8. Charles Churchill, *Night: An Epistle to Robert Lloyd* (1762). Modern Glossary in *The Covent Garden Journal,* 14 Jan. 1752.
9. *Peri Bathous, or the Art of Sinking in Poetry,* ed. E.L. Steeves, New York 1952, Ch. 4.
10. V.Woolf, *A Room of One's Own* (1928), Harmondsworth 1963, pp. 18-20.
11. Swift, 'Polite Conversation', *Prose Works,* Vol.IV, pp. 97-203.
12. William King, *The Art of Cookery,* London 1708.
13. John Fuller, *Carving Trifles: William King's Imitation of Horace,* Chatterton Lecture on an English poet, London 1976, p. 14.
14. Ned Ward, *The Secret History of Clubs,* (1709), pp. 373ff.

15. Richardson, *Clarissa,* ed. William King and Adrian Bolt, Oxford 1929-30, Vol.IV, pp. 15-16.
16. Carol H. Flynn, *Samuel Richardson: A Man of Letters,* Princeton 1982, p. 87.
17. *Guardian,* No.61, p. 235.
18. Philippa Pullar, *Consuming Passion: A History of English Food and Appetite,* London 1972, p. 160.
19. *Ibid.,* p. 131.
20. Evelyn's *Diary,* ed. E.S. deBeer, 6 vols, Oxford 1955, 4 Dec. 1679, Vol.IV, p. 190.
21. John Woodward, *The State of Physick and Diseases* (1718), pp. 194-5.
22. *Ibid.,* pp. 198-9.
23. *The Memoirs of Matinus Scriblerus,* ed. Charles Kerby Miller, New York 1966, pp. 105-6.
24. John Arbuthnot, *An Essay Concerning the Nature of Aliments, the Third Edition, to which are added Practical Rules of Diet* (1735) pp. 145-7.
25. *Ibid.,* p. 149.
26. Swift, *Correspondence,* Vol.II, p. 427.
27. *Prose Works,* Vol.XI, pp. 251-2.
28. Woodward, p. 194.
29. Fuller, pp. 17-18.
30. Swift, *Journal to Stella,* ed. Harold Williams, 2 vols, Oxford 1948, Vol.II, p. 637.
31. Swift, *Correspondence,* Vol.I, p. 161.
32. Dryden, *Essays,* Vol.II, pp. 102-4.
33. Claude Rawson, *Henry Fielding and the Augustan Ideal under Stress,* London 1972.
34. Swift, *Correspondence,* Vol.I, p. 109; Vol.IV, p. 403.
35. Spence, *Anecdotes,* Vol.I, p. 53.
36. Swift, *Correspondence,* Vol.III, p. 232.
37. *Ibid.,* p. 162.
38. 'Mr Pope's Supper' by 'Amica', included in a group of manuscript letters and poems cited by Maynard Mack in his biography, *Alexander Pope: A Life,* New Haven and London 1985, pp. 800, 927.
39. Swift, *Correspondence,* Vol.III, p. 149.
40. Arbuthnot, pp. 216-7.
41. Woodward, p. 196.
42. Fuller, p. 1.
43. David Nokes, *Jonathan Swift: A Hypocrite Reversed,* Oxford 1985, p. 346.

Notes to Chapter 6

1. Nokes, *Jonathan Swift: A Hypocrite Reversed,* Oxford 1985.
2. Reviews by Charles Peake, *THES,* 29 Nov. 1985; Ian Hislop, *The Listener,* 28 Nov. 1985; Nicholas Shrimpton, *Sunday Times,* 24 Nov. 1985. The majority of reviews, however, were highly favourable.
3. Thomas Sheridan, *Life of Jonathan Swift* (1784).

4. Spence, *Anecdotes,* Vol.I, p. 53.
5. Swift, *Correspondence,* Vol.II, p. 122.
6. *Ibid.,* Vol.IV, 108.
7. *Ibid.,* p. 126.
8. *Prose Works,* Vol.IV, p. 22.
9. *Ibid.,* Vol.X, p. 68.
10. *Ibid.,* Vol.XII, pp. 109-18.
11. Spence, *Anecdotes,* Vol.I, p. 53.
12. *Prose Works,* Vol.V, pp. 187-95.
13. *Ibid.,* Vol.IX, p. 191.
14. *Ibid.,* Vol.XIII, pp. 131-140.
15. Swift, *Correspondence,* Vol.V, p. 133.
16. *Prose Works,* Vol.X, p. 3.
17. *Ibid.,* Vol.I.
18. *Ibid.,* Vol.XIII, pp. 1-65.
19. *Ibid.,* p. 11.
20. *Ibid.,* p. 7.
21. Nokes, p. 403.
22. *Prose Works,* Vol.XIII, p. 42.
23. Swift, *Correspondence,* Vol.II, p. 173.
24. *Prose Works,* Vol. XIII, p. 27.
25. *Ibid.,* p. 44.
26. *Ibid.,* pp. 46-51.
27. *Ibid.,* pp. 161-2.
28. *Ibid.,* p. 8.
29. *Ibid.,* Vol.I, p. xxxvii.
30. Defoe, *An Essay upon Projects* (1697).
31. *Prose Works,* Vol.II, p. 38.

Index